INDEPENDENT SLOVENIA

INDEPENDENT SLOVENIA

ORIGINS, MOVEMENTS, PROSPECTS

EDITED BY
JILL BENDERLY AND EVAN KRAFT

St. Martin's Press
New York

First published in the United States of America 1994

Printed in the United States of America

Library of Congress Cataloging-in-Publication Data

Independent Slovenia : origins, movements, prospects / edited by
    Jill Benderly and Evan Kraft
            p. cm.
        Includes index.
        ISBN 0-312-09963-0
        1. Slovenia—History. I. Benderly, Jill. II. Kraft, Evan.
    DR1385.I53 1994
    949.7'3024—dc20   94-14550
                                                          CIP

INTERIOR DESIGN BY DIGITAL TYPE & DESIGN

To those bravely organizing
for peace, healing, and justice
where wars now wrack
the former Yugoslav lands

———————◆———————

▪Contents▪

▪ Editors' Introduction ▪

Why put together a book on independent Slovenia? Most Americans have never heard of the place. When we traveled to its capital, Ljubljana, to work with our authors, our friends in the United States warned us to "be careful in Bosnia."

Slovenia is a forgotten survivor of the Yugoslav wars, even for many academics who work on southeastern Europe. Slovenes are rarely invited to conferences on solving the Yugoslav crisis. This is ironic because many from the former Yugoslav republics say that Slovenia started the dissolution process: not only by seceding on July 25, 1991, but also by succeeding in developing its economy and its civil society in the 1980s to the point where seceding may have been the only viable choice.

Slovenia calculated that it could declare independence from Yugoslavia and survive, indeed flourish. Why was this possible for Slovenia, while Croatia, Serbia, and Bosnia-Hercegovina (BiH) burn like a fireball three years later? There are at least three contributing factors: ethnic homogeneity, economic development, and a strong civil society.

Perhaps the decisive point was ethnic homogeneity. Slovenia's population was 87.8 percent ethnically Slovene, as measured by the 1991 census (Zavod Republike Slovenija za Statistiko 1993). Ethnic homogeneity greeted the new small state with relatively few problems of minority human rights. Once it declared independence, there was no pocket of Serb or Croat population that could be inflamed into a protracted war by demagogues in those neighboring countries.

However, in the 1980s, Slovenia had a hidden minority: Bosnian "guest workers" (as well as ethnic Albanians from Kosova) who came to Slovenia to earn higher wages. Many of these workers were men who left their families behind in "the south," and sent most of their earnings back home. These Bosnian migrants were the subject of Silva Mežnarić's sociological inquiry, *Bosanci: A kuda idu Slovenci nedeljom?* (Bosnians: Or where do Slovenes go on Sundays?) Mežnarić wrote that "the focus of Bosnian adaptation to and participation in Slovene society was not based on the division 'Bosnians' and 'Slovenes' but on the division 'us, below' and 'those ones, above', most often—government administration" (Mežnarić 1986, 207).

The issue of Bosnians in Slovenia has only grown in significance with Slovene independence. While Slovenia's relative ethnic homogeneity favored its easier separation from the Yugoslav federation, that relative ease of independence and recovery has made Slovenia a landing point for those escaping the torments of war that followed in Croatia and Bosnia-Hercegovina. War refugees in Slovenia numbered 75,000 in March 1994. Most live in refugee camps. Current Slovene law does not allow them to work.

Although Slovenia accepted large numbers of refugees, resentment developed —reminiscent of Slovene annoyance in the 1980s about supporting Yugoslavia's federal fund to aid the less developed republics. In her book *Balkan Express,* Slavenka Drakulić describes her stint as a Croatian refugee in Ljubljana, and her reception by a Slovene neighbor, who commented, "'I've read in the newspapers that you refugees are getting more and more money per month than we retired people do, and I worked hard for forty years as a university professor for my pension. Aren't we Slovenes nice to you?'" (Drakulić 1993, 33). Thus, one of the prospective problems for independent Slovenia will be its ability to absorb, integrate, and protect the human rights of refugees from the wars in former Yugoslavia.

Slovenia's other major advantage over other ex-Yugoslav republics lies in its economic strength. Even though Slovenes accounted for 8.2 percent of Yugoslavia's population in 1989, Slovenia accounted for 16.6 percent of Yugoslavia's gross domestic product and 22.5 percent of its exports (Savezni Zavod za Statistiku 1991). Slovene companies successfully sold their goods to Western Europe. Their income per capita, at approximately $6,000 in 1993, provided living standards well above those of the poorest European Community countries.

Slovenia's tiny size—two million souls tucked into the southeastern tip of the Alps, in a land that can be traversed by car in three hours in any direction— raises questions about its economic viability. But far smaller states operate without overt economic difficulty in the European context. The presumption that economic prosperity requires a large state makes less and less sense in a world in which the economies of scale of traditional manufacturing are giving way to the decentralizing impulses of the Internet age, natural resources are less closely linked to economic success, and global economic integration renders borders ever less economically relevant.

In any case, economic viability will show itself more subtly. For all the postcommunist countries face difficult transitions and transformations, even without the redrawing of state boundaries. What, then, is the effect of smallness, as opposed to the effect of transition?

In this chaotic and trying economic environment, it seems—from the vantage point of 1994—that if any part of Yugoslavia will smoothly integrate its economy into the newly unified European market, it will be Slovenia.

Slovenia's other advantage for going it alone is its vibrant civil society. By the mid-1980s, Slovenia was the site of the most developed civil society in the

Yugoslav federation. New social movements flourished, taking action on behalf of peace, feminism, ecology, lesbians and gay men, human rights, and against nuclear power. They were living out what Hungarian dissident writer George Konrad called "antipolitics":

> Antipolitics is the political activity of those who don't want to be politicians and who refuse to share in power. Antipolitics is the emergence of independent forums that can be appealed to against political power; it is a counterpower that cannot take power and does not wish to. Power it already has, here and now, by reason of its moral and cultural weight. . . . (Konrad 1986, 230-31)

Slovene peace activist Marko Hren described in May 1987 the Slovene movements'

> nonoppositional character of our consciousness. We strictly deny our oppositional status. The movements are single issue. Though we sometimes cooperate, we are not acting on behalf of anyone, we do not speak for the workers, students or peasants. The movements produce energy. They are a natural evolution. It is not our goal to survive, but to have influence, to solve problems.[1]

Simultaneously, Slovene cultural alternatives spread, especially in Ljubljana and Maribor: punk rock,[2] multimedia performance art,[3] and alternative publishing.[4] The Communists, hostile at first, ultimately calculated that they did best to accommodate cultural and political alternatives, with what Gregor Tomc calls "repressive tolerance." Essays in the "Movements" section of this book analyze and describe the role of the alternatives in the transformation of Slovene society. They created the possibility of autonomous social activity for individuals and groups. Once the alternative pressured the Slovene Communists to make room for them, Slovene pluralism in the late 1980s found itself at what proved to be irreconcilable odds with other republics of Yugoslavia.

In the "Origins" section of this book, historian Peter Vodopivec chronicles how Yugoslavia had disintegrated even before Slovenia formally declared its independence. As communism crumbled, the common assumptions of Yugoslavia melted away. And the proponents of a looser confederative system, granting essential sovereignty to Yugoslavia's constituent republics, met aggressive opposition from centralists.

Among Communists, too, a common vision of reform and identity could not be found. In January 1990, the Slovenian Communist Party walked out of the Fourteenth Party Congress in Belgrade. "Only when we concluded that the federal party center would not stand on the side of the reform forces did we decide to leave the congress," Ciril Ribičič, president of the Slovenian Communist Party Central Committee, told a press conference after the party congress. The Slovenian party experiences the federal party "as a factor destabilizing Yugoslavia," he added. "We have left the CPY [Communist Party of Yugoslavia], but we haven't closed the door. . . . Yugoslavia remains our first and best choice. We have two options: radical changes in party relations, or creation of a parallel federation of democratic forces in Yugoslavia," concluded Ribičič (cited in Benderly 1990).

What came next is described in detail in this book.

However, some questions remain when considering Slovenia's prospects. Has independent Slovenia incorporated new social movements into the political process, or have the movements been pushed to the margins, as they have been in other postcommunist democracies in eastern Europe? What does the resurgence of old social institutions, especially the Catholic Church, signify? Will democratic rights such as the right to abortion, to legal recourse against marital rape, and protection of gay rights be extended or abolished?

In independent Slovenia, has nationalism eclipsed tolerance or are they intertwined? Is there such a thing as tolerant nationalism? In 1990, Marko Hren described a certain Slovene non-nationalist perspective:

> From this part of the planet it is easy to overcome the attachment to any state or devotion to any artificial formal identity. It is also extremely easy to recognize the stupidity of any armies, since the Slovene nation (two million people) lives on a very small territory surrounded by Italians, Austrians, Hungarians and Croatians. . . . The only natural policy for living peacefully is nourishing good links, understanding and cooperation.[5]

Another view came from Dimitrij Rupel in the same year: Europe is integrating and Slovenia desires to join this supranational process of integration. But, with Slovenia in Yugoslavia, Slovenia would be subject to two supranational authorities: Yugoslavia and Europe. Wouldn't it make more sense, he argued, for Slovenia to represent itself directly in Europe? Rupel's nationalism was at the same time internationalist (integrationist) (Rupel 1992, 53).

What will be the possibilities of regional understanding and cooperation? Will Slovenia's relationships reach only to western and central Europe, or will South Slav and Balkan ties be reconstructed? And what does the Slovene case—a favorable situation of ethnic homogeneity, relative economic strength, and civil society—tell us about the prospects for other new nations that have emerged from Yugoslavia and the Soviet Union?

This book is neither history nor social science. It is proudly interdisciplinary, for the editors believe in area studies: a firm grounding in the arts and humanities—language, literature, history, culture—and the social sciences are mutually necessary to understand a place, its people, and their transit through a particular time in the world; in this case, that famous East European postcommunist transition to something unknown.

We have seen too many sterile models of transition, and too many simplistic discussions of a particular nationalism (simplistically either defending that nation's right to self-determination or opposing its "stubborn self-interest"). This composite case study of Slovenia means to let the Slovenes tell their own story, especially those Slovenes who were simultaneously protagonists and analysts of the independence movement. Authors include key Slovene activists and analysts: Dimitrij Rupel, Slovenia's foreign minister at the moment of independence; Tomaž Mastnak, new social movement theorist and participant; feminist researcher Vlasta Jalušič; punk sociologist Gregor Tomc; as well as historians and economists from Slovenia and the United States.

OVERVIEW OF THE BOOK

Section I, "Origins," examines the history of the Slovenes. All four authors emphasize that, throughout their 12 centuries of existence, Slovenes never strongly desired independent statehood. Instead, Slovenes sought self-expression through their culture, above all their literature and their religion.

The authors also point out Slovenia's ambivalent relationship to Yugoslavia (in its various incarnations). As Carole Rogel documents, some Slovenes were interested in Illyrianism in the nineteenth century, some supported trialism at the turn of the century and chose to enter the Kingdom of Serbs, Croats, and Slovenes (KSCS) after World War I. Yet, as Peter Vodopivec argues, Slovenes never quite came to agreement with others, most notably the Serbs, about what a common life should mean.

At the same time, as noted by Rogel, Ervin Dolenc, and Žarko Lazarević, there were positive elements in Slovene participation in the KSCS and Yugoslavia. Dolenc shows the importance of the foundation of the University of Ljubljana, and the creation of Slovene language schools. Lazarević notes the economic advantages Slovenia gained under the KSCS and the first Yugoslavia.

The authors' account of Slovenia's history under communism shows the failure of the attempt to overcome nationalism. Both Vodopivec and Lazarević emphasize the way Slovenia was required to slow its own development in order to help the less-developed areas of the country. Later in the book, Evan Kraft, Milan Vodopivec, and Milan Cvikl present data that support this view even in the 1980s. But they also point out some of the benefits Slovenia enjoyed within the second Yugoslavia—such as a strong role in the internal market—and the high costs of leaving Yugoslavia.

Vodopivec also explores the continuation of national tensions and the failure to reach a satisfactory concept of democracy in a multiethnic state. This raises a fundamental question: Can multiethnic states succeed as democracies, or is the move toward smaller, more homogeneous states simply a necessary step toward democratic development? Later in the book (Section III), Dimitrij Rupel argues that consensus among ethnic groups is necessary for democracy in a multiethnic state, and that attempts to force "one-person, one vote"—as tried under the Serbian monarchy in the 1920s, and as proposed by supporters of Slobodan Milošević in the late 1980's—are interpreted by minorities as signs of impending domination. Rupel and Vodopivec, therefore, view Slovene independence as a result of Yugoslav disintegration, and not as a cause.

Section II, "Movements," examines how Slovenia broke out of communism and also out of Yugoslavia. Tomaž Mastnak and Gregor Tomc show how Slovene social movements, striving to deal with specific societal concerns, created an ever more independent civil society. For Mastnak, these movements possessed a very "soft" national concept, nationality as a form of identity, but were mainly motivated by democratic ideals and concerns such as feminism, ecology and opposition to militarism. Mastnak emphasizes the efforts of civil society activists to unite with others in Yugoslavia.

For Tomc, who writes about punk, activism was mainly defensive. Punks just wanted to be left alone to "do their own thing," and sometimes they had to fight to do it. It so happened that punks played an important role in the Slovene movement, but they are happier now to play their music and forget about politics.

In a sense, Vlasta Jalušič feels the same. The women's movement, she argues, had at best an uncomfortable relationship to the other movements. Women had no desire to be instrumentalized as part of a national movement, or to be subsumed under the rubric of civil society. At times, of course, cooperation was fruitful; women led important ecological protests and participated in the movement for alternatives to military service, for example. But the idea of a united alternative scene, or the commonality of women's concerns with those of other groups, should not be exaggerated.

Tonči Kuzmanić challenges the social movement's interpretation, arguing that the principal moving force of the Slovene Spring was the workers' movement of 1987–88. Their rebellion, he contends, destroyed the old system ideologically and practically. Kuzmanić contrasts his interpretation with the social movements' view, perhaps exemplified by Mastnak's essay, and nationalist views, which are found to an extent in Dimitrij Rupel's essay.

This brings us across the dividing line into our third section, "Prospects," which deals with the experience of independent Slovenia. Dimitrij Rupel views Slovene independence as a shift toward Europe. Slovene nationalism, he argues, represents a desire to be included in the larger European context. Evan Kraft, Milan Vodopivec, and Milan Cvikl agree, and conclude that a narrowly economic interpretation of Slovene independence would be wrong. Slovenes' aspirations toward Europe—not merely economic but political and cultural as well—were blocked as long as they remained part of Yugoslavia.

Andrej Rus and Evan Kraft, Milan Vodopivec, and Milan Cvikl explore Slovenia's road toward becoming a European society and a European-style market economy. Both chapters draw attention to the characteristics that Slovenia shares with other postcommunist states. Both point to political disputes over privatization and the resulting slow pace of ownership change as crucial obstacles to economic recovery.

Kraft, Vodopivec, and Cvikl also illustrate some of the economic successes of independent Slovenia, especially its conquest of inflation. They warn that the economic tasks in front of Slovenia remain formidable. But they argue that the economic prospects of Slovenia seem fairly good in the long run.

Rus questions whether the prevalent neo-liberal reform doctrines understand the social dimension of the transformation going on in Slovenia and eastern Europe, and he argues that a paradoxical result—increased state intervention—appears to be emerging.

Rus, along with Jalušič, question whether the attempts at a wholesale reversal of the state of things under communism are justified. For Rus, a central issue is the drastic curtailment and recentralization of the welfare system in the name of efficiency; for Jalušič, the issue is an attempt to repeal rights granted to women under communism. Both authors raise the question of what will be the bases of social and political legitimation of independent Slovenia.

The reader may ask how two Americans, not of Slovene or even any Yugoslav background, came to edit such a book. We began visiting Slovenia and Yugoslavia in 1984, attracted by the people and the land, and most of all by the multiculturalism and the social movements. Little did we know how significant these last two features would become for a rupture quite unlike any other in the postcommunist world.

As the years have gone on, acquaintances have become friends, and interest has become commitment. We view this book as one opportunity to repay a vast debt. We sincerely hope that this book will provide a way for Western readers to hear Slovene voices, and to understand more about this important, and too often tragic, part of the world.

There are many people who have contributed to this book and to our knowledge of Slovenia. In addition to the contributors to this book, we would like to thank, in no particular order, Marko Hren, Silva Mežnarić, Milan Vodopivec, Milan Cvikl, colleagues at the Inštitut Ekonomska Raziskovanja (Institute for Economic Research of the University of Ljubljana), especially Peter Stanovnik, Vlado Lavrač, Tine Stanovnik and Franci Kuzmin, the SOS Hotline, Lynne Jones, Ingrid Bakše, Mojca Dobnikar, Barbara Berce, the folks at Dom Trilobajt, Kristina Annerbrink, Goga Flaker, Dorie Wilsnack, Johanna Bjorken. Thanks also to many friends, colleagues, and activists in the other former Yugoslav republics and in the international community connected to ex-Yugoslavia. Special thanks to our mapmaker, Dr. Michael Folkoff of Salisbury State University, Department of Geography and Regional Planning. Warm thanks go to our editor, Simon Winder.

Evan Kraft would especially like to thank the Committee for the International Exchange of Scholars Fulbright program for its support for his work on this book in Ljubljana in summer 1993. An earlier grant from the International Research and Exchanges Board in 1990 was also invaluable.

Jill Benderly would like to give special thanks to Sallie Bingham, whose grant supporting her coverage of East European women financed her sojourn in 1990, to the Women's Studies Endowment and George Washington University Women's Studies program, which gave financial and academic support to her work, 1991–94, and to the Network of East-West Women for its web of support.

Finally, we would like to express our hope that this book will contribute a bit of help to the healing process, in Slovenia and the other former Yugoslav republics.

ENDNOTES

1. Marko Hren, interview with Jill Benderly, May 1987, Ljubljana.
2. For example, bands such as Pankrti (The Bastards) and Laibach (the German name for Ljubljana). For more on punk and politics in Slovenia, see Tomc, this volume.
3. Many grouped into what they provocatively named in German the Neue Slowenische Kunst (New Slovene Art), such as Laibach, Scipion Nasice experimental theater, and IRWIN (visual art collective).
4. *Mladina,* the youth magazine published in Ljubljana was joined by the KRT (Mole) publishing house and a variety of short-lived magazines and fanzines.
5. Marko Hren, interview with Jill Benderly, March 1990, Ljubljana.

BIBLIOGRAPHY

Benderly, Jill (1990). "Elections in Slovenia, Croatia." *Guardian* (New York) April.
Drakulić, Slavenka (1993). *Balkan Express*. New York: Norton.
Konrad, George (1986). *Antipolitics*. New York: Holt.
Mežnarić, Silva (1986). *Bosanci: A kuda idu Slovenci nedeljom?*
(Bosnians: Or where do Slovenes go on Sundays?) Belgrade: Filip Višnjić.
Rupel, Dimitrij (1992). *Slovenski pot do samostojnosti in priznanja*
(The Slovenian road to independence and recognition) Ljubljana: KRES.
Savezni Zavod Za Statistiku (1991). *Statistički godišnjak Jugoslavije 1990*
(Statistical yearbook of Yugoslavia 1990) Belgrade: Savezni Zavod Za
Statistiku.
Zavod Republike Slovenija za Statistiko (1993). *Statistični letopis republike
Slovenije 1992* (Statistical yearbook of Slovenia 1992) Ljubljana: Zavod
Republike Slovenija.

▪Basic Facts About Slovenia▪

Area[a]. . . . . 20,251 sq. km.
Population (1992) 1,965,986
Population density[b] . . . . 98.6 (Holland 365.9, USA 26.7)
Population growth[c] 1.1
Ethnic Slovenes as percentage
   of population 87.84
GDP per capita[d] 6186
Life expectancy at birth (1990) . . . . Men: 69.4 (Yugoslavia 68.9, USA 71.5)
   Women 77.3 (Yugoslavia 74.5, USA 78.3)
Infant mortality[e] . . . . 8.4 (Yugoslavia 20.2; USA: 9.1, Japan 4.5)
Live births[f] 10.7
Televisions[f] 222
Female share of total employment. . 47.2

[a] Unless otherwise stated, data is for 1991.
[b] per square km, 1990
[c] natural rate per 1000
[d] US dollars, 1992
[e] per 1000 live births
[f] per 1000 inhabitants

Source: Zavod Republike Slovenije za Statistiko (1993). *Statistični letopis republike Slovenije 1992* (Statistical yearbook of Slovenia 1992), Ljubljana: Zavod Republike Slovenije.

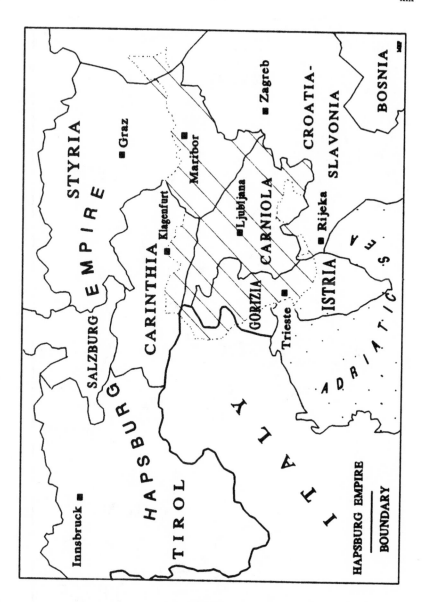

Map 1:
Slovenes in the Hapsburg Empire

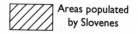

Areas populated
by Slovenes

Map 2:
Slovenia in the First Yugoslavia (1919–1941)
(Before 1929, Kingdom of Serbs, Croats, and Slovenes)

Map 3:
Slovenia in Socialist Yugoslavia 1945–1991

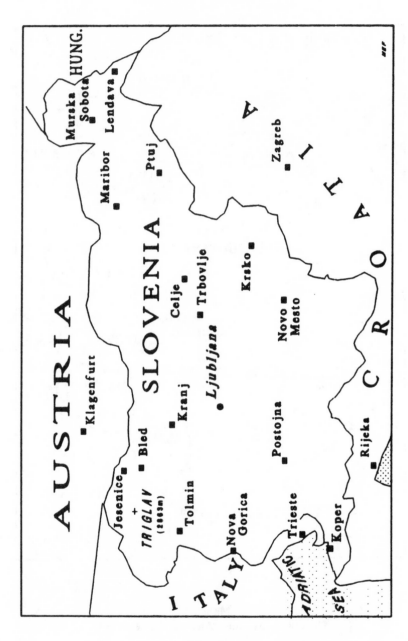

Map 4:
Independent Slovenia

SECTION I:

Origins

■ ■ ■ ■ ■ ■

1

In the Beginning: The Slovenes from the Seventh Century to 1945

Carole Rogel

Until very recently, the idea of an independent Slovenia was regarded as unrealistic. In the nineteenth century, when the notion might first have asserted itself, ethnic Slovenes were only beginning to think of themselves as belonging to a "nation." At that time, it was not considered practical for a group of about one million (mid-1800s figures) to aspire to independence. Conventional realpolitik thinking of the pre-1914 era favored the large, economically advanced, militarily powerful nations, like France and Germany. For the small so-called nations of central Europe, a multiethnic political entity such as the Habsburg Empire was deemed appropriate; protecting small national communities was even proclaimed its *raison d'état*. The Czech historian-politician František Palacký and later the socialists in the empire were leading philosophical proponents of a strong "Austria." Austro-Slavism was the term used to describe this position, which the Slovenes of various political persuasions generally supported. Similar pragmatism in the twentieth century bound Slovenes to Yugoslavia. Although empires had disappeared and the principle of national self-determination had replaced them with nation-states, numbers and size still counted in Europe in both post-world war eras. Slovenes would surely stand a better chance of facing pressures from potentially hostile neighbors—Italians, Austrian Germans, and Hungarians—if they were part of a larger state. As part of Yugoslavia, Slovenes were afforded realpolitik advantages, as well as the cultural and spiritual benefits of union with other

Southern Slavs. Being joined with Balkan lands to their south, many of which were backward territories of the former Ottoman Empire, was decidedly an economic disadvantage. Yet Slovene Yugoslavism tended to minimize the negative aspects of life in the first and second Yugoslavias.

There are many factors that contribute to the development of a national consciousness and subsequently to political nationalism. But for the Slovenes, as with most European nationalities, what was national in the modern sense of the term was simply not preponderant before the end of the eighteenth century. Slovenes lived, as they had for many centuries, as part of a medieval Europe whose institutions and world view lingered, even on the eve of the French Revolution. Slovenes first settled in their present corner of Europe (once a part of the Roman Empire) in the middle of the sixth century. Here, early in the next century, they established a political entity, Karantania, whose center was near present-day Klagenfurt (Celovec), Austria. The ruler of Karantania was elected by freemen of the duchy and participated in a unique enthronement ceremony—dressed as a peasant and presided over by an authentic peasant—which today's Slóvenes maintain inspired Enlightenment political theorists, including Thomas Jefferson, when they wrote eighteenth century political essays about contractual arrangements between the ruler and those he governed. Historically, Karantania was the only state Slovenes can claim as their own. Even then, however, the duke was vassal to the Moravian ruler. In A.D. 745 an era of sterner domination by Bavaria and the Franks, which ended in the twelfth century, began. By the ninth century the space Slovenes inhabited was more than double Slovenia's present size and included much of central Austria. War and migration of peoples gradually diminished its size (Kos 1933; *Zgodovina Slovencev* 1979, 111-72).

In the thirteenth or fourteenth centuries most Slovene lands became a part of the Habsburg feudal domain, a relationship that would end only in 1918. As subjects of the Habsburg ruler, Slovenes lived in the duchies of Carniola, Styria, Carinthia, the county of Gorica, the Margravate of Istria, and the city of Trieste. (On the western and eastern peripheries Slovene settlements were often under Venetian and Hungarian jurisdiction.) By the time Slovenes had become Habsburg subjects they had long since become a dependent people. They had no ruling class. They had been enserfed by feudal nobles, both secular and clerical, and mostly German. They had been Christianized, starting in the late eighth century by Irish missionaries sent by the Bishop of Salzburg; the Church's organization was formalized by the Franks in the wake of Charlemagne's conquest of the area. In the Middle Ages, then, Slovenes belonged to a universal community, that of Western Christendom, their lands falling within the boundaries of the Holy Roman Empire. National cultural and political distinctions were of slight importance in such times.

Even though a modern national consciousness was still centuries into the future, developments toward establishing a Slovene identity came in the sixteenth century. Humanism and Protestant reformers, stressing man and his relationship to his Creator, promoted the spread of literacy. Slovene, until then, had not been a written language. (There are extant documents from about A.D. 1000 belonging to the bishopric of Brixen in which writing in Slovene is included among Latin texts, but these fragments are significant largely because they establish, historically, that Slovene was indeed the language of prayer of Carinthia's Freising area parishioners at the time.) In the mid-1500s Primož Trubar, a Protestant reformer, produced a vernacular catechism as well as a Slovene primer (1550). His intention was to enable Slovenes to comprehend God in their own language. In this he was not unlike Luther and other religious reformers of the time. Trubar's work was carried forward by others (Rupel 1962). The crowning achievement was Jurij Dalmatin's translation of the Bible, which was completed in 1584 (*Zgodovina Slovencev* 1979, 258-300). That same year Adam Bohorič completed a Slovene grammar. The Slovenes now had a written language, in the Latin alphabet, for dealing with God and salvation. It would be another two centuries before written Slovene would be appropriated for secular use, for the Counter-Reformation came down hard on the peoples of these Habsburg lands. Those who had abandoned Rome were made to return, sometimes forcibly. Latin was declared the official language of Scripture, as it also remained the language of official secular discourse (e.g., scholarship and law). The Habsburg ruler could tolerate no other, for as Holy Roman Emperor he was the preeminent defender of Christendom and therefore of the Church at Rome. The Slovene national awakening would have to wait.

That awakening occurred in the second half of the eighteenth century. It was part of the intellectual revolution known as the Enlightenment, which had begun transforming western Europe in the previous century; it was largely an outgrowth of and also a response to comprehensive reforms that the Habsburg rulers, especially Maria Theresa (1740-80) and Joseph II (1765-90), launched to centralize authority over their far-flung feudal possessions. A powerful state required a modern defense system, and the Physiocratic thinking of the day taught that only a prosperous, tax-paying peasantry could finance that requirement. For that reason the peasant needed to be free and literate. Thus decrees were issued changing the peasants' legal status, while laws were passed making primary schooling compulsory. The reforms, however, unintentionally created conditions favorable to social change and also accelerated the secularization of life in the empire. Significantly, they also created potential for conflict with non-German speakers. As part of the all-inclusive overhaul of the empire, German replaced Latin as the language of government business

—administration, law, judiciary, and so on. In abandoning Latin for a vernacular language the Habsburgs were not espousing Germanism; they were being pragmatic. Most in the empire would agree it made sense that laws be expressed in a comprehensible, secular, "living" language. But most also felt that language should be their own, their mother tongue, which until then had been passed on mostly orally from mother to child. Obligating people to read and write made them aware of their secular or worldly identity: it begat national consciousness.[1]

Two publications of the Slovene enlightenment need to be mentioned for their role in effecting a national awakening. The first, *Kranjska gramatika* (Carniolan grammar), written by the monk Marko Pohlin, appeared in 1768. Pohlin's grammar is considered the first real expression of a national awareness among the Slovenes (Kidrič 1929, 38, 160-84). Many of the monk's contemporaries embraced that awareness, but, significantly, some expanded its scope territorially to include Slovenes in neighboring provinces who inhabited areas contiguous to Carniola. Their view was soon more influential than Pohlin's. Carniola was also central to another work; this time the subject was history. Its author was Anton Linhart, an advocate for French enlightened political philosophy, who incorporated an antifeudal, anticlerical bias into his work. Linhart's study, written in German, was entitled *Versuch einer Geschichte von Krain und der übrigen südlichen Slawen Osterreiches* (1788-91). In his search for a history of Austria's South Slavs, he sought a new approach: to tell the story of a people rather than that of its rulers and crownlands (*Zgodovina Slovencev* 1979, 387). He, too, focused on Carniola. It should be noted that at the end of the eighteenth century Carniola (Krain) was the heart of the Slovene settlement and its population was overwhelmingly Slovene, probably over 90 percent. It was therefore the logical center for the development of a modern Slovene awareness.

The quarter century from the time of the French Revolution to the Congress of Vienna, 1789 to 1815, severely disrupted the lives of all Europeans, including the Slovenes. For the intellectuals who were establishing linguistic and historical boundaries for the emerging nation, French political thought enabled a fusion of the concept of *nationhood* with that of *homeland,* a potential political entity of that, or some future, time (Zwitter 1947). More directly, ordinary Slovenes were affected by two decades of war (Austria and France were adversaries for most of the time), and between 1809 and 1813 many found themselves under French Imperial rule. In that four-year period, the lifespan of France's Illyrian provinces, its inhabitants were exposed to an enlightened French administration. Among its lasting effects was the reinforcement of an embryonic national sentiment, for the French encouraged the use of the local language, which for them was preferable to using German, the language of the defeated Austria. Slovenes used the vernacular in schools, courts, newspapers, and text books. Some Slovenes were even included in the French administration, which had its seat in Ljubljana. Significantly, large numbers—although not all—of both Slovenes and Croats were included in the Illyrian provinces. Because of that brief period of co-habitation of two Southern Slav peoples, Yugoslavism (i.e., Illyrianism or South Slavism) became an early ingredient of Slovene nationalism in the nineteenth century. But, whether the emphasis was on Slovenism or Yugoslavism, after 1815 it was impossible for Slovenes to return to a premodern, presecular, prenational world (Rogel 1977, 8-10).

Those who shaped the Slovene identity in the first half of the nineteenth century were mostly intellectuals and clergy. Accordingly they assumed unofficial leadership of this peasant people, a role the intelligentsia would continue to exercise even to the end of the twentieth century. As were their European contemporaries, these men were greatly influenced by romanticism and idealism, particularly in their thinking about nations. Believing in the uniqueness of national cultures, they sought to uncover the Slovene spirit by studying language, history, and folklore. Of special importance is the writing of Jernej Kopitar, a linguist employed by Vienna as an imperial censor, who defined Slovene as a distinct South Slavic language in his monumental work on grammar. Subsequently, Kopitar used linguistic evidence to justify support for Austro-Slavism. Also important to this formative period were Anton Slomšek, Bishop of Maribor, who was responsible for bringing the Slovene language into the schools, and Janez Bleiweis, who in 1843 began publishing a successful newspaper for farmers and craftsmen. Although not widely read at the time, Francè Prešeren, Slovenia's preeminent Romantic poet, also wrote in the 1840s. He established the basis for a contemporary secular literature, while espousing a form of political liberalism. Prešeren's poem *Zdravljica* (A toast) is now independent Slovenia's national anthem. Finally, throughout the thirties and forties, Illyrianism was also in the air. Its author was the Croat Ljudevit Gaj, who maintained there was only one South Slavic language (Illyrian), and who sought to persuade all Southern Slavs to agree to use one common idiom. But Illyrianism generated little support among the Slovenes then (Petrè 1939). Instead Slovenes concentrated on identifying the uniqueness of what they considered their own distinct language and culture.

The year 1848 (Apih 1888; Zwitter 1965) brought dramatic upheaval across continental Europe. Economic strife caused the toppling of most European governments, including Austria's, where absolutism, clericalism, censorship, repression, and vestiges of serfdom had reigned since 1815. The Slovenes' first political program was formulated in 1848; it was the work of small groups of intellectuals, mostly notables of the cultural awakening. Noted among the contributors was the Slavicist Fran Miklošič who represented Vienna's Slovenes. The objective was clear and simple: a "United Slovenia." The program called for the joining of all Slovene-inhabited lands of the empire into one administrative unit. It also demanded that Slovene, rather than German, be used in schools and administration; and, it favored the separation of Austria from the German Confederation (Holy Roman Empire until 1806), which in 1848 seemed to be emerging as a German national state. Significantly, it was the intent that a United Slovenia remain within Austria, albeit a revolutionized, federal, constitutional state. Unlike the Magyars, who declared independence in those revolutionary times, the Slovenes were not then, nor would they soon become, separatists. Nor had they become ardent Illyrians or Yugoslavs. Although there was much mutual support among Slovenes and Croats for each other's political activities in 1848-49, only individual Slovene revolutionaries, mostly from Styria, espoused a Yugoslav political program. It should be noted that 1848 was characterized by a general flurry of Pan-Slavism among Austria's Slavs, and Yugoslavism of the time might be considered one of its logical components. Ultimately, of course, Vienna stifled all political aspirations but its own, in many cases with military force. More than a decade of absolutism and repression followed the revolutions of 1848.

The intellectual and political climates of the pre- and post-1848 period differed radically. Whereas romanticism dominated the first half of the century, realism and realpolitik reigned in the second. Romanticism regarded nations as unique creations, whose cultural expression harmonized with that of others. Nations were like distinct flowers, which together formed a beautiful bouquet called Europe (nineteenth century nationalists were Eurocentric). Peace among them was considered a desirable goal. Realism, in the latter part of the century, viewed nations in a Darwinian way, in biological confrontation for power and survival. The Franco-Prussian War of 1870 is generally cited as the first example of a conflict of rival cultures supported by nationalistic sentiment. The prevailing belief was that the strongest, and therefore the best, would win; moreover, that result would benefit mankind. With such a view taking over Europe, some were bound to be losers. These would be the multinational empires, including the Habsburg, and the smaller, less developed nations, like the Slovene.

In the 1850s and 1860s, as the result of several short wars, Austria had to concede power or territory to Italy, Prussia, and Hungary, all states who were using nationalistic appeals to enlarge their domains. Vienna gave up two valuable provinces (Lombardy and Venetia) to the newly created Kingdom of Italy, forfeited to Prussia/Germany its role as the dominant power in central Europe, and agreed to the Austro-Hungarian Compromise of 1867, which created the Dual Monarchy (Austria-Hungary). The latter enabled the Hungarians to assume legal authority over the southeastern parts of the Habsburg Empire. The Slovenes, one of Europe's less-developed nations, were divided territorially by these developments. Most remained in the Austrian half of the Habsburg state, but 27,000 found themselves in Italy after 1866 and 45,000 in Hungary after the Compromise of 1867 (Zwitter 1967, 159). These numbers may not seem significant, but they were alarming to Slovenes whose population then was only about 1.1 million. Also, until at least 1871, it was expected that Prussia/Germany would absorb all former lands of the German Confederation—which included Austria and its Slovene provinces. In 1870 the future looked very bleak for the Slovenes. Prospects for the United Slovenia program were fading as Slovene territory was being dismembered, while Prussian power was threatening to finish off Austria and Germanize its inhabitants. Frantic efforts to put together a Yugoslav program in 1870 (Slovenes, Croats and Serbs—including Serbs from Serbia—held several conferences) fizzled for lack of agreement. Even if there had been a Yugoslav accord, Slovenes would probably have been left out. Some, primarily Serbs, were adamant that the Slovenes be excluded from any Yugoslav political plan, because they believed Germany would not give up Trieste and its hinterland peacefully. War with Germany was to be avoided (Zwitter 1962).

Slovene political activity resumed in the 1860s when Vienna began experimenting with new constitutions, settling in 1867 on a dual monarchy with a parliament in Vienna for the Austrian part of Austria-Hungary. Initially, the vote for parliament members was indirect and limited, but representation broadened over the decades until universal manhood suffrage was introduced in 1906. Slovene politicians from the sixties until the 1890s, when real political parties were first established, were either conservatives (old Slovenes) or liberals (young Slovenes).[2] The philosophical split had come in the late sixties over whether or not to favor a concordat with Rome, but regarding the national program there was little discernable difference between the two groups. Both were members of the same conservative (Hohenwart) parliamentary club in Vienna, because both opposed the liberal, German, centralizing agenda. The government of Prime Minister Taaffe (1879-93), which drew its support from crownland federalists, conservatives, the Church, and Slavs, was determined to keep German liberals isolated. The isolation mechanism was called Taaffe's Iron Ring, and Slovenes were a part of it. They and the Slovene language made steady headway in local administration and education in this period of decentralized rule. Advances were greatest in Carniola, where Slovenes dominated the provincial assembly after 1883 and captured the mayoral seat of its capital, Ljubljana, by 1888 (Melik 1965).

When Slovenes today express a nostalgia for old Austria, it is Taaffe's era they are reminiscing about, not the Austria that would soon become culturally and politically German. Edward Taaffe, Franz Jozef's school chum, presided over Austria when it represented, for the last time, universal principles based on a commitment to Christendom and Western civilization. That Austria was in principle "international" and united by a common culture and common values. It opposed those forces—especially nationalism—which divided nations and the universal Christian community. The preeminent enemy of the time was German nationalism.

In 1870, with Prussia's defeat of France and its creation of a Prussian-dominated German empire, many believed that Austria (including Slovene lands) would soon be part of the new Germany. This did not happen. In fact, Germany's Bismarck made his peace with Emperor Franz Josef, sealing it with the Dual Alliance. Yet, for the Slovenes, the threat of Germanism would not disappear. It would be nurtured and fortified at home, within Austria, even as—or perhaps because—Slovenes were making political and cultural gains during the Taaffe years. In the mid-nineties, German backlash challenged the advances of the smaller nationalities in the empire. That backlash resulted in a serious clash in southern Styria over plans for a Slovene language gymnasium in Celje (Cilli). It even brought down the Vienna government. As Austrian Germans became more nationalistic they conflicted more and more frequently with non-Germans—mostly Slavs. By the end of the century Germanism would even splinter the empire's multinational parties, the Christian Social and Social Democratic Parties.

At the turn of the century Slovene society was quite different from what it had been in 1848. Most Slovenes still lived in rural areas and worked the land, but legally all were free, for during the revolution the regime had abolished all remnants of serfdom. With freedom often came economic insecurity, particularly given a sizable population growth in the second half of the century. In the countryside farmers dealt with financial hardship by organizing agricultural cooperatives, some of which were very successful, but it was not enough. In search of jobs, Slovenes began to migrate to urban centers, both in Austria and abroad. Although hundreds of thousands emigrated after 1880, Austria's census of 1910 recorded 1.3 million Slovenes, nearly a quarter million increase since the last count in 1857. Austria's seaport, Trieste, had the largest number of Slovene urban dwellers, 57,000 out of a total of 230,000; while Ljubljana, still just a provincial administrative capital, had a total population of only 40,000, about half of whom were Slovene. In towns, most Slovenes became factory workers or miners; a few became entrepreneurs, bankers, and government employees. In Trieste they also found jobs in shipping and were active in workers' organizations (*Zgodovina Slovencev* 1979, 527-41). Slovene literacy, due to educational reforms which began during the eighteenth century Enlightenment, was, at 80 percent to 90 percent, exceptionally high. At the end of the nineteenth century the Slovene readers had available dozens of publications, where they might learn about events that shaped their lives. In the 1890s, three Slovene political parties, each with its own press, began rallying public support for their respective national programs.

Before World War I there were three Slovene political parties. Each was established during the 1890s and each a had distinct, clearly-articulated political philosophy. While each remained implicitly loyal to Austria, the parties were enormously troubled by Austria's growing "German-ness." As an extension of their respective Slovene national programs, all three political groups espoused some form of Yugoslavism. Making common cause with other South Slavs was their way of combating the pressures of German culture. Joining forces with Croats and possibly Serbs would also enhance their position numerically. It is important to note that from the beginning, a constant feature of Slovene national consciousness was a sense of the nation's smallness.

The Slovene *liberals* (i.e., the National Progressive Party) (Rogel 1977, 40-50) were led by town professionals and businessmen, and counted among their leading lights two long-term mayors of Ljubljana, Ivan Hribar (1896-1910) and Ivan Tavčar (1911-21). Like liberals in much of Europe, they were not democratic, in that they opposed universal suffrage, preferring to restrict the vote to dependable, sensible tax-paying males. They also tended to be anti-clerical, firmly opposing Rome's involvement in Austrian politics. The party was traditionally Pan-Slavist, idealizing Russia, urging Austro-Russian accord, yet embarrassed by Russian autocracy. As Pan-Slavists, the liberals formulated a Yugoslav program that stressed the equality of Slavic nations and their religions. If South Slavs were to live and work together, the fact that some were Catholic and others were Orthodox should not divide them. Slovene liberals collaborated with other liberal South Slavs, such as the Croat Bishop Strossmayer, whose ecumenical efforts sought to unite South Slavic Catholic and Orthodox communities. Ultimately, Slovene liberals hoped Austria would become a federal state where each nation would have its own administrative unit. In this way, the Slovene language and culture would be secure. Besides ultramontane Catholics, German liberals were seen as the greatest threat to Slovene freedom. As far as Slovene liberals were concerned, Germanism was to be resisted at all costs.

Like the liberals, Slovene *clericals* (Slovene People's Party) formally organized in the 1890s (Rogel 1977, 28-39). The party evolved from the conservative politicians' camp, and during the quarter century before the First World

War developed two distinct branches. One, led by Ivan Šušteršič, was more traditionally conservative—"for religion, home, and emperor" was its slogan—while the other, headed by the priest Janez Evangelist Krek, was strongly Christian socialist. The former worked closely with Vienna, while Krek labored among the workers organizing cooperatives. The clericals also feared Germanism, especially when it originated in Germany, bastion of Protestantism. (Bismarck's *kulturkampf,* a campaign against Catholics in his empire, loomed in their minds.) They worried especially about Germany's growing influence over Austria. Clericals therefore developed a strategy of encouraging Austria to stop thinking of herself as a German power (formerly head of the Holy Roman Empire and of the German Confederation). Austria's raison d'étre, they argued, was as defender of Christendom on the borders of Western civilization in the Balkans. Had Austria forgotten what had made her great? If so, it was time to remind Austria of her mission, clericals believed. Toward that end they promoted trialism, a plan to join the South Slav lands of the Habsburg Empire—including Bosnia and Hercegovina (annexed in 1908)—in a separate administrative unit. The Dual Monarchy would become a triple monarchy, putting the Yugoslav unit on the front lines of that noble Austrian Christianizing mission.

Clericals worked with Catholic Croats to promote their goals. In 1912 the clericals even united briefly with the Croat Party of Right, led by Ante Starčević, to promote trialism. The merger was never strong, and the Croats soon dropped out. They worried that Vienna would not allow South Slavs from Austria to join with those (largely Croats) from Hungary, because Vienna then would be separated from Trieste, its only seaport. Besides, if Vienna wished to diminish Hungarian power—as it did—giving the South Slavs of Hungary autonomy would do the trick. Uniting them with Slovene lands and Dalmatia would only create another potential power challenge to Vienna. The Croats and Slovene clericals continued to support trialism; it was said the Archduke Franz Ferdinand was in favor of it. The heir to the throne, however, was never precise about how he would govern. The priest, Anton Korošec, who would later help bring Slovenia into a Yugoslav kingdom, once asked Franz Ferdinand about trialism. His answer was wonderfully ambiguous: "I have great plans for the Yugoslavs" (Kranjec 1962, 220). Slovene clericals continued to hope he meant them as well.

Yugoslavism was also a feature of the Slovene Socialists' program (Rogel 1977, 51-62; Gantar Godina 1987). Their very name, Yugoslav Social Democratic Party, made their position immediately clear. The Socialists were strongest in Trieste, where Italians, Slovenes, and Croats constituted the emerging proletariat, and they promoted cooperation among all workers in that commercial and shipping center. Leaders of the party were often intellectuals, many of whom had studied in Vienna, Zagreb, Graz, and Prague. In the latter city they usually came into contact with the future president of Czechoslovakia, Tomáš Masaryk, who was then a professor of philosophy and a charismatic influence on the empire's Slavic intellectuals. The Masarykites a few decades earlier might have been liberals, but liberalism as a dynamic force was expiring in Austria, as in the rest of Europe, unable to come up with imaginative or effective solutions to the mounting social and economic problems which accompanied the industrial revolution. Many Masarykites therefore became Socialists. The Austrian Social Democratic Party (ASDP), a multinational organization founded in 1889, provided a home for Slovene socialists. The party was Austro-Marxist, standing unwaveringly by the Austrian state unit. Large political units, they believed, were imperative for economic expansion and ultimately were the soundest foundation for the establishment of socialism. The empire would, of course, have to be transformed into a democratic federation, based on administrative rather than national units. The Austrian party experienced some serious internal nationalistic conflicts and skirmishes, yet upheld internationalism as a guiding principle. The Slovene socialists' contribution to that internationalism was Yugoslavism, articulated most clearly in the Tivoli Resolution of 1909. Aside from political demands which were consistent with Austro-Marxism, the Tivoli document contained a comprehensive cultural program. It called for "the complete national unification of all Yugoslavs, irrespective of name, religion, alphabet and dialect or language" (*Rdeči prapor* 1909). The Slovene socialists were calling for cultural amalgamation, and although the Masarykites opposed it, the ASDP made it official policy.

In the decade before 1914, Slovenes generated a variety of both cultural and political Yugoslavisms. It was as though there was no question but that the Slovene future was to be intimately tied to that of other South Slavs. This was particularly so after 1908 when Austria's annexation of Bosnia and Hercegovina placed Yugoslav issues permanently on the front pages of the press. Debates over cultural Yugoslavism (a revived Illyrianism) monopolized the learned journals. In 1911 *Veda* even took a poll on the subject (Rogel 1977, 75-89; *Veda* 1911-13). The central issue was Illyrianism versus Slovenism. Virtually every respondent agreed that some linguistic and cultural merging was bound to occur naturally, but they disagreed about whether deliberate policies should be implemented to accelerate the process. The Illyrianists were anxious to begin immediately by adopting the Serbo-Croatian language; others advised waiting, beginning amalgamation gradually after political union took place. Slovenists, on the other hand, resisted artificial cultural merging of any kind. A strong political union was not, they felt, dependent on linguistic and cultural homogeneity.

The dialogue over cultural Yugoslavism did not affect the Slovenes' basic commitment to Austria. Neither did political events, nor the Balkan Wars (1912-13). Slovene parties, granted, grew ever more wary of Austria's foreign and domestic policies. The close alliance with Germany, Austria's growing hostility to Russia (a particular worry to Slovene Pan-Slavists), treason trials in Zagreb and Vienna involving Croats and Serbs, were some of the things that troubled Slovenes. Yet the parties continued to expect their respective Yugoslav programs to be realized within Austria. They also expected the empire to continue to expand southward, and that someday soon even Serbia (independent since 1878) would be a part of it. In their minds, secession from Austria was not a working option.

Only a few radicals, some free spirits such as the writer Ivan Cankar, and several hundred gymnasium students associated with the paper *Preporod,* advocated separation from Austria (Rogel 1977, 102-117). The Preporodovci, who organized in 1912 and had fairly wide-ranging contacts in the Balkans, favored Slovene union with Serbia. The Preporodovci were pursued by the state police and many were arrested and prosecuted for treason after the assassination of the Austrian Archduke in Sarajevo, June 28, 1914. Internal security also monitored Ivan Cankar, who was imprisoned for an inflammatory speech, delivered in Ljubljana in April 1913. Cankar, incidentally, formulated the only Yugoslav program that proved prophetic: cultural Slovenism and political Yugoslavism (outside Austria). The combination, however, only became realistic in the last stages of World War I when the empire's collapse was imminent. Until then, even if Slovenes sought to work with Croats and/or Serbs, the inclination was seldom reciprocal. Both Croats and Serbs suspected—as did R. W. Seton-Watson when he excluded Slovenes from his book *The Southern Slav Question and the Habsburg Monarchy* in 1911—that Slovenia's location was of vital geopolitical concern to Vienna, and perhaps to Berlin as well. Without a war Slovenia could not become part of an independent Yugoslavia. That understanding of Slovenia's basic relationship to central Europe may have left a lasting impression on thinking in Serbia at least, and may help explain why Belgrade let Slovenia go so easily in 1991.

The First World War began when Austria retaliated against Serbia for the archduke's assassination. The war required that Slovene Yugoslavism be significantly recast (Pleterski 1971). With Franz Ferdinand's death, the plan to achieve a South Slav state by an act from above (trialism) was essentially dead. Even more relevant to the future of Yugoslavism was the fact that Austria-Hungary and Serbia became adversaries in a conflict that would last four exhausting years. Slovenes, together with the empire's Croats and Serbs, were conscripted into the Austro-Hungarian army to fight Serbia. (They would fight also on the Russian front and, after Italy's entry into the war in 1915, there would be a western front as well.) Already at the beginning of the war, a considerable number of Slovenes volunteered to serve in the Serbian army. Others joined later, often after deserting from the Austrian army while at the Russian front (where aversion to fighting fellow Slavs was also often a factor). Slovenes fought with real self-interest only on the western front—for Austria against Italy—because they were defending their own territory. The battleground, where Italian losses in major fighting in 1917 were catastrophic compared with those of Austria, straddles the current Italian-Slovene border.

Slovene liberals and clericals, especially the Šušteršič wing of the latter group, stood behind Vienna in the initial stages of the war (Ževčević 1977; Banac 1984, 340-51). But as hostilities dragged on and the empire deteriorated within, verging in 1917 and 1918 on the kind of social revolution that was rocking Russia, Slovene national politics was radicalized. This development was symbolized by the May 1917 declaration, which called for the unification of the South Slavs of Austria-Hungary in one state under Habsburg rule. Popular support, known as the declaration movement, grew in the next year and a half, until the logical next step was taken. On October 29, 1918, the National Council, a recently formed body which spoke for the empire's Slovenes, Croats and Serbs, declared the establishment of a totally independent South Slav state. The priest Anton Korošec, a clerical who had recently come to head the Slovene People's Party, was president of that National Council; the act, which separated the South Slavs from Austria preceded the final collapse of the Habsburg state by more than two weeks. The new South Slav state, comprised of the empire's Yugoslavs, joined with Serbia and Montenegro on November 24. The establishment of the Kingdom of Serbs, Croats, and Slovenes was announced on December 1, 1918, in Belgrade, capital of Serbia.

A United Slovenia had been the goal of Slovene politicians since 1848. It had not been attained within Austria, nor would it be realized in the First Yugoslavia. Essentially, it was the Entente powers who thwarted Slovene aspirations by supporting Italian claims to territories in the northern and eastern Adriatic. By treaty ratified at Rapallo in November 1920, nearly one-third of ethnic Slovenes came under Italian rule. The separation from these western territories, especially Trieste, was regarded as a major economic setback, particularly by the Slovene socialists. That city had the largest Slovene urban population (just under 57,000 in 1910), one actively engaged in industrial and commercial life. (About the same time Ljubljana's total population, about half of which was Slovene, was only 40,000. Primarily a provincial capital, Ljubljana's character was shaped by the government administrators and bureaucrats who constituted its often stodgy elite.) The Entente powers also enabled Austria, a successor state of the Habsburg empire, to retain some ethnically Slovene lands. In a plebiscite held in southern Carinthia, October 10, 1920, and supervised by Entente monitors, the vote favored affiliation with Austria. In the aftermath of World War I, prospects for the United Slovenia program seemed dimmer than ever.

Slovenes in the Kingdom of Serbs, Croats, and Slovenes (renamed the Kingdom of Yugoslavia, October 3, 1929) (Mikuž 1965) were spared the Italianizing and Germanizing pressures exerted on Italian and Austrian Slovenes, but their experience also fell far short of expectations. This was so largely because Yugoslavia was created before there was agreement about how it would be governed. The South Slavs of the Habsburg lands generally favored a federalistic arrangement, with autonomy for each of the national components. Indeed federalism had always been fundamental to their understanding of the Yugoslav idea. However, Serbia, as a "winner" state after World War I, was able to impose centralist rule and Serbian hegemony upon the new state. The Vidovdan Constitution of 1921, which put the Serbian Karadjordjević dynasty at the head of the state, was even promulgated on a Serbian national holiday, June 28. The twenties were thus characterized by political impasse between those favoring a unitary state (centralists) and those insisting on national autonomy (federalists). With numerous ineffectual governments between 1921 and 1929, the new kingdom was extremely unstable. Political assassination—including the shooting of Stjepan Radić, the leading Croat political figure, in 1928—was not uncommon.

In the twenties Slovene political leaders found themselves struggling with Belgrade in ways they had struggled with Vienna. Slovene clericals, whose spokesman was Anton Korošec, continued to support autonomy for the Slovenes. Their program was for a kind of United Slovenia within the Kingdom of Serbs, Croats, and Slovenes. Various Slovene liberal groups for the most part tried to work with Belgrade in building a unitary state. Meanwhile the Slovene Communists, members of a newly forming party, who planned class rather than national revolution, were grappling with a number of challenges, not the least of which was trying to stay out of jail in a country where the Communist Party was outlawed. Because of their comfortable distance from Belgrade, and because some Slovene politicians were willing to work with the national government, the Slovenes, who constituted 9 percent of the country's inhabitants, fared less badly than other non-Serbs in the kingdom. That the Slovene language was only marginally comprehensible to many to the south also allowed Slovenes more autonomy than Belgrade might have intended. But life in the interwar state was certainly not what Slovene leaders had in mind when they cast their nation's lot with that of other Southern Slavs. National sovereignty, especially, seemed strangely elusive.

The political chaos of the twenties spawned the proclamation of royal dictatorship on January 6, 1929 (*Zgodovina Slovencev* 1979, 655-85). King Alexander nullified the 1921 constitution, changed the name of the country to Yugoslavia, and divided the land into nine administrative units, or *banovinas*. Slovene lands became the *Dravska banovina*. Alexander's intention was to deemphasize national units, while maintaining Serbian hegemony. (Six of the nine *banovinas* had Serb majorities.) The result was radicalization of politics in the state, particularly among the Croats. The extremist Croats collaborated with violent and revisionist elements in neighboring states to undermine Serb rule in Belgrade. Together they were responsible for the assassination of King Alexander in Marseilles in 1934.

The thirties, if anything, were worse than the preceding decade. International developments, including global economic collapse and the rise of fascism, were particularly threatening to Yugoslavia. The state had neither fully completed postwar reconstruction, nor had it firmly established an integrated economic infrastructure for the country (a patchwork of remnants from a half dozen pre-war states), before the depression began. The fascism of neighboring Italy (thriving already in the mid-twenties) and the imperialism of the German Reich (after 1933) would have direct bearing on Yugoslavia's future. Both states were revisionist with respect to the post-world war territorial settlements; both would forward claims to Yugoslav lands and encourage Yugoslavia's other neighbors to do the same. Both would also bolster revisionist elements within the South Slav kingdom, the most dangerous being the Ustaši movement in Croatia. The government, responsible no longer to parliament but rather to the monarchy (headed by a prince regent who ruled on behalf of the minor King Peter), fumbled along. It attempted to head off Croat fascism by concluding a political compromise (Sporazum of 1939) with Croat moderates, thereby enlarging Croatia and giving it greater autonomy. The Slovenes, however, were not afforded the same advantages, even though Korošec was powerful and a minister in many of the thirties' governments.

When World War II began in Yugoslavia, virtually all the rest of continental Europe had already come under German or Italian domination. On April 6, 1941, Yugoslavia was invaded because it refused to adhere to the Axis tripartite pact. It was quickly dismembered. Croatia, under the Ustaši head Ante Pavelić, became a German-Italian client state. Subduing the rest of the country took all of twelve days. Slovene lands were overrun and partitioned by her neighbors, Italy, Hungary, and Germany. (Its annexation of Austria in spring 1938 had given the German Reich a common border with Slovenia [*Zgodovina Slovencev* 1979, 734-43].) The occupying powers promptly initiated de-Slovenizing policies, which included arrests, torture, executions, and deportations to Europe's notorious concentration camps. The political and intellectual elite were its prime targets; the harshest treatment of Slovenes was experienced in the German-occupied territories. It should be noted that, unlike Croatia, Slovenia did not have a strong indigenous fascist party and therefore when the war began there was no counterpart to the Croat Ustaši that might be entrusted with managing a Slovene Nazi or fascist "puppet" state.

With the Axis invasion, the royal government, unprepared for defense of the country, fled, leaving its subjects to fend for themselves. Eventually King Peter's spokesmen would reinvolve the monarchy in affairs at home. From exile in London, for instance, they would announce support for a resistance movement led by the royalist Serb general Draža Mihailović. Until then the abandoned Yugoslavs organized their own opposition to the foreign occupation. In Slovenia the resistance movement, Liberation Front of the Slovene Nation (LF), was organized on April 27, 1941 (*Zgodovina Slovencev* 1979, 744-63). It was led by the Communist Party of Slovenia (CPS), which coordinated its efforts with the Communist Party of Yugoslavia (CPY), although the fact of Communist leadership was deliberately played down in order to allow broadest possible participation in the resistance (it was renamed the resistance/revolution after the partisan/Communist victory was secured). Besides party members, the LF attracted Christian Socialists, the Sokols (liberal nationalist members of gymnastic societies), and leftist intellectuals. It was especially strong among Slovenes who had lived under repressive regimes in Austria and Italy in the interwar years. In early 1943, when the LF seemed to be breaking into its component parts—some wanted the resistance to be reorganized as a coalition—the leadership insisted on firm unity behind the CPS. The result was the "Dolomite declaration," which affirmed Communist control. The failure to win a coalition at this point is regarded by those who supported Slovene political pluralism in the late eighties as a tragically missed opportunity. The Dolomite agreement would lock Slovenia into one-party rule for nearly half a century.

The resistance in Slovenia, as in many parts of Europe, was complicated by civil war, fought amongst the Slovenes over conflicting political ideologies. The White Guard, conservative, church-supported, and opposed to the LF's resistance to the occupation forces, was operating already in the summer of 1942. The broader-based Home Guard (*domobranci*) became engaged after Italy's capitulation in the autumn of 1943, when it appeared that the postwar political future of Slovenia was at stake. Home Guardists firmly opposed communism and sought to prevent the CPS from establishing irreversible political control in the liberated areas. By April 1944 the Home Guard, in seeking support against the hated ideology, committed itself to cooperating with Germany, which then helped organize the guard's fighting battalions. The guardist political program, announced toward the end of the war, featured a United Slovenia within a federal Yugoslav kingdom. In the last days of the war, as the LF was completing its victory in Slovenia, General Rupnik, who commanded the Home Guard, retreated with his forces into Austrian Carinthia. Once there, many guardists were apprehended and returned to Slovenia, where they were treated as collaborators and summarily executed. Others, who managed to establish new lives in exile abroad, have sustained a vocal, bitter opposition to Slovenia's postwar Communist government.

The Communist-led partisan resistance, or LF, came out the winner in the events of 1941-45. At home it had broad support from those who were eager to fight the German and Italian invaders, and among those who felt little loyalty to a Serbian dynasty that had deserted them in time of need. Significantly, the LF also received decisive backing and arms from the Allies after 1943. The LF, in its association with the larger partisan resistance in Yugoslavia, also subscribed to a postwar plan for a federal Yugoslav republic in which Slovenia (United Slovenia) would constitute a separate unit. The Communist leadership also stressed that the second Yugoslavia, unlike the first, would be a people's democracy. This feature would appeal to the Slovene Left.

When World War II ended Slovenia was substantially enlarged, at Italy's expense. A change of boundaries, one of the very few territorial adjustments coming out of the war in Europe, was approved by the Paris Peace Conference in 1946. Thousands of Slovenes, however, still remained in Italy, and the final settlement for Trieste (Novak 1970), concluded some years later, left that city to Italy as well. Also, Slovenia's claims to southern Carinthia were settled in favor of Austria. Nevertheless, it seemed, that the United Slovenia program was getting a second chance.

ENDNOTES

1 Zwitter (1990), a collection of essays, most previously published elsewhere, examines virtually every aspect of the Slovene national question.
2. The traditional periodization of Slovene cultural-political history was established in Prijatelj's five-volume work (Prijatelj 1955-61).

BIBLIOGRAPHY

Apih, Josip (1888). *Slovenci in 1848* (The Slovenes and 1848). Ljubljana.

Banac, Ivo (1984). *The National Question in Yugoslavia: Origins, History, Politics.* Ithaca: Cornell University Press.

Gantar Godina, Irena (1987). *Masaryk in Masarykovstvo pri Slovencih* (Masaryk and Masarykism among the Slovenes). Ljubljana: Slovenska matica.

Gestrin, Ferdo and Vasilij Melik (1950). *Slovenska zgodovina* (Slovene history). Ljubljana: Slovenska matica.

Kidrič, Fran (1929-38). *Zgodovina slovenskega slovstva* (History of Slovene literature). Ljubljana: Slovenska matica.

Kos, Milko (1933). *Zgodovina Slovencev od naselitve do konca petnajstega stoletja* (History of the Slovenes from first settlement to the end of the fifteenth century). Ljubljana: Slovenska matica.

Kranjec, Silvo (1962). "Koroščevo predavanje o postanku Jugoslavije" (Korošec's speech about the establishment of Yugoslavia). *Zgodovinski časopis* 16: 218-29.

Melik, Vasilij (1965). *Volitve na Slovenskem 1861-1918* (Elections in Slovenia 1861-1918). Ljubljana: Slovenska matica.

Mikuž, Metod (1965). *Oris zgodovine Slovencev v stari Jugoslaviji* (An outline of the history of the Slovenes in old Yugoslavia). Ljubljana: Mladinska knjiga.

Novak, Bogdan (1970). *Trieste 1941-54: The Ethnic, Political and Ideological Struggle.* Chicago: University of Chicago Press.

Petrè, Francè (1939). *Poizkus Ilirizma pri Slovencih* (An attempt at Illyrianism among the Slovenes). Ljubljana: Slovenska matica.

Pirjevec, Jože (1993). "Slovenes in Yugoslavia, 1918-1991." *Nationalities Papers* 21: 109-118.

Pleterski, Janko (1971). *Prva odločitev Slovencev za Jugoslavijo: Politika na domačih tleh med vojno 1914-18* (The Slovene's first decision for Yugoslavia: Politics on the home front during the war, 1914-1918). Ljubljana: Državna založba Slovenije.

Prijatelj, Ivan (1955-61). *Slovenska kulturnopolitična in slovstvena zgodovina* (Slovene cultural-political and literary history). 5 vol. Ljubljana: Državna založba Slovenije.

Prunk, Janko (1992). *Slovenski narodni vzpon: Narodna politika (1768-1992)* (The Slovene national ascent: National politics). Ljubljana: Državna založba Slovenije.

Rdeči prapor (1909). No. 128, November 25, 1909. Ljubljana.

Rogel, Carole (1977). *The Slovenes and Yugoslavism, 1890-1914.* New York: East European Monographs.

Rupel, Mirko (1962). *Primož Trubar—življenje in delo* (Primož Trubar—life and works). Ljubljana: Mladinska knjiga.

Seton-Watson, R. W. (1911). *The Southern Slav Question and the Habsburg Monarchy.* London: Constable.

Singleton, Fred (1985). *A Short History of the Yugoslav Peoples.* Cambridge: Cambridge University Press.

Veda (1911-13). Nos. 1-3, Gorica.

Vodopivec, Peter (1992). "Slovenes and Yugoslavia, 1918-1991." *East European Politics and Societies* 6 (3): 230-41.

Vodopivec, Peter (1993). "Slovenes in the Habsburg Empire or Monarchy."
    Nationalities Papers 21: 159-70.
Zgodovina Slovencev (A History of the Slovenes) (1979). Ljubljana: Cankarjeva
    založba.
Zwitter, Fran (1947). "Narodnost in politika pri Slovencih" (Nationality and politics
    among the Slovenes). *Zgodovinski časopis* 1.
Zwitter, Fran (1962). "Nekaj problemov okrog jugoslovanskega kongresa v Ljubljani
    leta 1870" (Some problems relating to the Ljubljana congress of 1870).
    Zgodovinski časopis 16.
Zwitter, Fran (1965). "Slovenski politični preporod XIX stoletja v okviru evropske
    nacionalne problematike" (The Slovene political awakening of the 19th century
    within the framework of European national problems). *Zgodovinski časopis* 18:
    75-153.
Zwitter, Fran (1967). "The Slovenes and the Habsburg Monarchy." *Austrian History
    Yearbook,* III, Part 2: 159-88.
Zwitter, Fran (1990). *O Slovenskem narodnem vprašanju* (On the Slovene national
    question). Ljubljana: Slovenska matica.
Ževčević, Momčilo (1977). *Slovenska ljudska stranka in jugoslovansko zedinjenje
    1917-21* (The Slovene people's party and Yugoslav unity, 1917-21). Maribor.

2

Seven Decades of Unconfronted Incongruities: The Slovenes and Yugoslavia

PETER VODOPIVEC

In April 1991, three months before the proclamation of Slovene independence, Slovene writer Drago Jančar wrote an essay entitled "The Broken Jug," (Jančar 1992) based on Heinrich von Kleist's 1808 comedy of the same name (Kleist 1988). "Do you see the jug?" the woman plaintiff asks the judge in Kleist's comedy. "Of course," the judge replies. "You see nothing, you see only the pieces of the jug that remain," the plaintiff retorts. But the judge and the higher councilor of the court are not interested in the jug. They do not know the jug's history or the way it was painted. They do not know who drank out of it, or what battles and fires it survived. What they have are the pieces of the jug. And therefore they do not understand why there is such a fuss about the broken jug, about broken love, about the divided community and about the heads over which it broke.

Jančar's modern-day allusion to Yugoslavia is clear; the swift disintegration of the Yugoslav state in 1991 can be explained only if we know the (hi)story and the real image of the "jug." At first glance, it might seem paradoxical that the first to leave Yugoslavia were the Slovenes. They had no tradition of an independent state. Never in modern history had they considered very vocally or decisively full independence as a national state. The great majority of Slovenes hoped right up to the end that it would be possible to reform Yugoslavia into a looser and more open multinational community.

But by 1990, when the newly founded Slovene democratic and oppositional parties formulated the Slovene Declaration of Self-Determination, Yugoslavia was no longer able to reform. The declaration pointed out the danger of civil war in Yugoslavia. Confronted with Serbian (centralist) political pressure, Slovenes demanded in the declaration a plebiscite deciding the Slovene political future. At the same time the declaration still offered the possibility of Slovene participation in a loose "Confederation of Yugoslav Nations" (*Nova revija* 1990). This idea was never seriously discussed by the Yugoslav federal government and Serbian political elites. On the contrary, these authorities decided to strengthen by force their control over an already highly disintegrated country.

Slovene independence was in this sense not a cause of Yugoslav disintegration, but rather a result of it. What ultimately happened in Yugoslavia in 1991 was anticipated as early as 1915 by farsighted and well-informed experts who knew the Balkans and the South Slav nations. The French scholar Louis Leger, who predicted the disintegration of Austria-Hungary and the rise of Yugoslavia in his 1915 book *La Liquidation de l'Autriche-Hongrie,* maintained that an "Illyrian Federation" could only be successful if it were organized as "some form of Slavic Switzerland," composed of autonomous cantons, which would be made up of "the Slovene lands, Croatia, Dalmatia, central Serbia, and Bosnia and Hercegovina; Belgrade, as the seat of the central government, should have the same role as Bern in the 'Helvetian community'"(Leger 1915). The Niš Declaration, with which Serbia proclaimed the founding of a strong Serb-Croat-Slovene state as its war aim, was in Leger's eyes a significant political act, but he cautioned the Serbs about the Swiss confederative model, warning them not to have overzealous Piedmontian or unitarist ambitions.

As a first-rate authority on the conditions in the South Slav lands, he was well aware of the great social, economic, and cultural-historical differences between the peoples who were destined to be united in a common Yugoslav state. But he was also aware that these peoples were, for the most part, already established social and national-political communities that would strive to preserve and develop further their national individuality in the new South Slavic state framework.

Of a similar mind was the most important writer of the Slovene Moderna, Ivan Cankar. In a lecture entitled "Slovenes and Yugoslavs," which he gave on April 12, 1913, in Ljubljana, he rejected critically the reflections of some Slovene intellectuals who were under the sway of advancing Germanization, the aggravated national conflicts in the Habsburg monarchy, and the awareness of Slovenia's small size. These educated Slovenes wrote and spoke of

Serbs, Croats, and Slovenes as three "tribes" of a formerly unified Yugoslav nation that had been dissolved tragically in the course of history. They also forecast their return to linguistic and cultural union. In Cankar's view those were baseless predictions, symbols of cowardliness and of a lack of national consciousness. "By blood we are brothers; by language, cousins; but by culture, which is the fruit of the separate upbringing of several centuries—there we are less familiar to one another than one of our Upper Carniolan peasants to a Tiroler," he noted in a well-known statement that has since been cited countless times in Slovenia. For Cankar the Yugoslav question was exclusively a political decision: if the Yugoslav peoples "think and desire that it would be easiest and best for them to live united, then let things happen according to their wish." But the state they would construct had to be a federal republic and had to reflect in its internal organization the varied ethnic, social, economic, and cultural landscape it encompassed. In 1913 Cankar was convinced that "such a settlement of the Yugoslav question, which would be most natural, is a utopia," but at the same time he maintained that "utopias have a peculiar way of coming true." With this statement he incurred the wrath of the Austrian authorities and earned himself a week in prison (Cankar 1977; Rogel 1971).

In the first and second Yugoslavias, Cankar's notion of utopias likely to come true was interpreted as a sign of his farsightedness. The rise and the existence of Yugoslavia was held to confirm his predictions. But today, since Yugoslavia has ceased to exist, it is necessary to examine such utopias from a different perspective. When Cankar began speaking of the "utopianism of the Yugoslav idea" almost eighty years ago, he did so in the hope of its realization.

The incredibly bloody and brutal events accompanying the breakup of Yugoslavia spur us to inquire whether the Yugoslav idea at some point simply stopped being a utopia. What happens to "utopias which stop coming true?" Of its 73 years, Yugoslavia spent more than 60 in exceptional conditions. First, there was the authoritarian, centralistic regime from the dictatorship of 1929 to the outbreak of the Second World War. After that came the war period from 1941 to 1945, which saw at once resistance to the occupiers, a Bolshevik social revolution, and a fratricidal settling of domestic accounts. Finally, there was the communist system. In the 1950s and 1960s, this system was by far the most liberal in Eastern Europe. Even with its power concentrated in the hands of a single party and its elite, there was enough balance to keep national antagonisms hidden below the surface, although with varying degrees of success at different times. It is not surprising that Yugoslavia entered a severe political crisis directly after 1980, when Tito's death was followed by a gradual diminution of the authority of the central communist institutions. The Albanian uprising in Kosova in 1981 was the first harbinger of this new national and political fragility. In the center, in Belgrade, a void developed, which the federal and Serbian communist bureaucracies tried to fill rather forcibly and ineffectively with poorly conceived centralistic initiatives. The whole later course of events showed those people to be right who, since the end of the 1960s, pessimistically maintained that the existence of Yugoslavia was not possible in a democracy (Zver 1992).

The branding of the Yugoslav idea as utopian explains nothing and can only be a rhetorical notion. On one hand, this idea was never just a single idea, but rather several, such that even political representatives of the same peoples had various notions about what kind of Yugoslavia they wanted. On the other hand, it was not ideas alone that destroyed Yugoslavia; it was also the execution of these ideas and issues of concrete policy. A merely superficial glance at the more than 70 years of Yugoslav history shows immediately that Yugoslavia fell apart in 1991 because of its incapacity to confront the contradictions attending it all the way from its inception in 1918. Its last years, from 1987 to 1990, like the years after its formation (1918-21), passed in an atmosphere of tense and ever less tolerant debates about the constitutional and political arrangements of the state. This confirmed the traditional political divisions: eastern, Serbo-Montenegrin pressure for centralism, along with insistence on the partly reformed authoritarian (Bolshevik) patterns of power, versus the Slovene-Croat concern for gradual decentralization and democratization along Western European lines.

While one may criticize the Communist regime after 1945 for not having resolved anything, it is not possible to declare it the chief culprit in promoting the ethnic antagonisms and hatred that have now been driven to such extremes. These antagonisms have their roots in the processes of national-political polarization of the latter decades of the nineteenth century. In particular, the incongruities caused by Serbian political pressure for the Yugoslav state to be organized—in contradiction to its multicultural and multiethnic reality—according to the French model of *l'état-nation* and to be changed into a centrally administered whole caused tension. Many negative stereotypes, prejudices, and reproaches that one or the other national group was secessionist, nationalist, and hegemonistic only came in the first years the Yugoslav peoples lived together in a common state. They have endured with incredible persistence until its end.

The reader of today who leafs through Serbian, Croatian, and Slovene newspapers from the beginning of the 1920s and compares them with those from the end of the 1980s will be astonished at how little the resentment, mutual accusations, and poor opinions of one another have changed. Even language proves to have modernized more quickly than the thought it is supposed to express. Yugoslavia passed its 70 years in accordance with Braudel's schema (Braudel 1977). On the political surface, turbulent events, with numerous splits and sudden changes; on the level of economic and social history, gradual but persistent modernization; and as regards the collective mentality, behavioral patterns and norms of value, a cycle of lengthy duration. A contemporary observer could therefore legitimately inquire about the measure to which the social processes of political and economic modernization actually take hold in history and reach to where Braudel searched for the lowest "historical story."

Until 1918 the great majority of Slovenes lived in the Austrian half of Austria-Hungary. According to the census of 1910, the 1,253,148 Slovenes represented 4.48 percent of the citizens of this western half of the monarchy (Zwitter 1965, 224). The Slovene national program was formulated in 1848 by a small group of educated Slovenes who demanded that their ethnic territory—hitherto split administratively—be combined into a "unified Slovenia." Slovenes did not have a medieval tradition of statehood like the Czechs or Croats and had to base their demands on principles of natural law. They conceived of unified Slovenia as an autonomous, self-governing unit within the framework of a federalized Habsburg monarchy; one of the fundamental characteristics of this autonomy was to be the free use of the Slovene language in offices, schools, and public life. Until the fall of the Dual Monarchy, the demand for a unified Slovenia remained the main goal of the Slovene national movement, which took on a mass character in the second half of the nineteenth century.

After 1848, and especially after the unification of Germany in 1870, certain individuals pointed out that Slovenes would not be able to achieve their political goals by themselves. They would have to seek allies among the other South Slavs of the monarchy, Croats and Serbs. But until the end of the nineteenth century, Slovene politicians hoped to be able to attain some specific political goals, most relating to the broadened use of the Slovene language, by relying on German conservatives and joining together with the Czechs in the Parliament at Vienna. The heightened Slovene-German national antagonisms, which came with the ever more deliberate Germanization of the Slovene lands after 1890, buried these hopes. This process cemented the conviction among the Slovene political elite that it was necessary to seek a solution to their national question through closer cooperation with the other South Slavs of the monarchy (Rogel 1971).

In the years before the First World War, all three Slovene parties (Catholic, Liberal, and Social Democrat) espoused the Yugoslav idea; thoughts on what this Yugoslav cooperation and its results would be like in practice varied greatly. Common to all was the view that the Slovenes were pressed into a corner between the hostile Germans and Italians. Slovenes were too few to achieve a unified Slovenia without allies; in addition, in the words of the writer Fran Milcinski in 1913, they were settled on a territory not much bigger than "a family burial vault." Thus they needed to combine their forces with those of "the fraternal Slavic neighbors." The idea that the result of that type of alliance could be an "association of the South Slavs of the monarchy in a separate political organism" under the Habsburg aegis found expression in Ljubljana after the annexation of Bosnia-Hercegovina in 1909 (cited in Melik 1988, 525-32). It gained broad popular support in the last two years of the First World War when the so-called May Declaration of the Yugoslav delegates to the Austrian Parliament, which had called for the union of the South Slav lands of Austria-Hungary into a Yugoslav state with the Habsburg dynasty at its head, was signed by more than 200,000 Slovenes. It is difficult to say how the great majority of the signers—who came from a population composed of Catholic peasants—conceived of such a Yugoslavia that would still be connected to the Habsburg dynasty. Undoubtedly they expected that it would repel German national pressure once and for all, secure free use of the Slovene language on all levels, and bring to reality Slovene wishes for national self-government. The prevailing conviction was that although affairs with the Germans had turned for the worse, everything would be different with the (South) Slavs' mutual support. Only isolated individuals were considering a possible union with Serbia. The sudden dissolution of Austria-Hungary at the end of October 1918 was, thus, a genuine surprise for the Slovene political parties and their leaders (Melik 1988).

News of the cessation of Habsburg authority and the proclamation of the State of Slovenes, Croats, and Serbs, which unified most of the South Slavic lands of the defunct monarchy, met with celebration in Ljubljana and Zagreb on October 29, 1918. The Slovene Catholic leader Anton Korošec was appointed to head the Narodno Vijeće (National Assembly), which had been founded in Zagreb. The appointment of Korošec seemed to the Slovene public an assurance that their interests would be honored in the negotiations regarding the internal disposition of the state. But the debate over how the state should be set up and what should be the position of the Slovenes in it had only just begun. A part of the Slovene educated strata had reflected primarily on two possibilities before the war: In the first, based on the examples of Italian and German unification, the establishment of Yugoslavia would be the first step toward the melting together of the three peoples into a new Yugoslav people. For the Slovenes this would entail their gradual linguistic and ethnic assimilation into the Serbian and Croatian majority.

The second possibility was presented by Ivan Cankar in his famous 1913 lecture (Cankar 1977). As others had advocated, Yugoslavia would have to be a federal state founded on the recognition of equal rights and national individuality of all of the nations included in the common state, whether big or small. Polarization around these two standpoints continued after the collapse of Austria-Hungary, but the events of November 1918 had already revealed that the idea of a different Yugoslavia had the indisputable support of the majority; it would be a Yugoslavia that would guarantee the Slovenes a certain degree of self-government, equality of national rights, and undisturbed future national development. So people in Ljubljana decisively took up the cause of a federative-confederative arrangement in the State of Slovenes, Croats, and Serbs (SCS). This arrangement left a fair amount of independence to the administrative organs in Ljubljana in relation to the central government in Zagreb. At the same time it vouched for Slovene cultural autonomy (Grafenauer 1988, 533-41; Vodopivec 1990, 364-71). Even before the fusion of the State of SCS with the Kingdom of Serbia, Slovene policy and the public were split. There was a minority centralist group, which later, in the 1920s and 1930s, enjoyed the reputation of being "genuinely Yugoslav," and there was a majority bloc that supported federalism and autonomy. Despite its loyalty to the first Yugoslav state until its collapse in 1941, this latter group was always subjected to charges of separatism.

The decision on the quick unification of the State of SCS with the Kingdom of Serbia on December 1, 1918, did not produce any very loud objections. The republican and Catholic opponents of the Serbian dynasty were an insignificant minority; the State of SCS, which was not internationally recognized, could not effectively protect the Slovene ethnic boundaries from Italian and Austrian territorial ambitions. The general atmosphere, too, was more reserved than at the time of the proclamation of the State of SCS, but it was not unfavorable to the changes in the state framework. After all, the Kingdom of Serbia had been an internationally recognized ally of the victors in the war. Its sacrifices and heroism in the struggle against Austria-Hungary were fresh in everyone's memory, and the Serbian political elite in Belgrade promised an agreeable arrangement on the future of a common state. Despite political decisions and measures that revealed immediately after December 1, 1918 that these negotiations would not proceed without complications, people in Ljubljana continued for some time to look optimistically to Belgrade.

The founding of a series of educational and cultural institutions, which the Slovenes had not had until that time, and the start of work on a Slovene university in Ljubljana in 1919, were interpreted by politicians and intellectuals as promising signs that a new era was beginning for the Slovenes within the

Yugoslav state. Thus, it is possible to understand how all Slovene parties in the spring of 1919 accepted the thesis that with the unification of 1918 "the first step toward the formation of a unitary Yugoslav people was made" (Ževčević 1986). The receptive parties even included the autonomy-minded Slovene People's Party, but not the Croatian Peasant Party or Party of Rights.

Placability of this type had no special future. That there would be no compromise between the supporters of centralism and federalism had already been revealed by the preparations for elections to a constituent assembly and the debates about the fundamentals of the future constitution.

In 1920 and 1921 demands for a federal system and for Slovene autonomy in the Kingdom of the Serbs, Croats, and Slovenes (KSCS) won out. Serbian centralist plans and proposals were supported only by liberals, socialists, a few of the Communists, and several smaller parties, while, especially in educated circles, a strong movement for autonomy developed. Albin Prepeluh clearly formulated the Slovene view of the constitutional question by noting in 1921 that it was by no means a juridical and political issue but above all a matter of sociology. The constitution, to be effective and avert conflicts, would have to reflect the realities of the area of governance and respect the diversity of life there. "The 'tribes' which have been united into the Yugoslav state developed for centuries severed from each other, and they took on their cultural-historical, religious, and socio-economic forms in milieux that were completely different, even mutually contradictory," stated Prepeluh (1921). He continued:

> The constitutional issues are therefore not any sort of juridical question but rather chiefly a conflict between existing social forces. . . . If there is, for instance, a difference in the everyday life of a Montenegrin shepherd and a Slovene industrial worker, I have to realize that I do not abolish that diversity in its material and spiritual aspects just because I write down on a piece of paper that there is not one. (Pp. 49-53)

Prepeluh proposed a division of the KSCS into autonomous units, through which not only the three so-called constituent peoples (Serbs, Croats, and Slovenes) would get autonomy, but also Bosnia and Hercegovina, the Vojvodina, Montenegro, and Macedonia.

In the eyes of Slovene autonomists it seemed natural and intelligible that no governmental stability or domestic unity could be achieved by force. The Ljubljana professor of law, Leonid Pitamic, maintained that affection between the South Slav peoples and also specifically between the Slovenes and the Serb-Croat population would have to originate by itself, not by dint of state efforts. He also viewed the state as the product of this affection, not its precondition (Pitamic 1921, 69; Nećak 1992, 93-108).

The centralistic Vidovdan Constitution, which was passed in Belgrade on June 28, 1918, with a majority of votes from the eastern part of the monarchy and which divided the Yugoslav state into 33 provinces with no regard for ethnic composition, thus signified a great disappointment to both Slovenes and Croats. In the following years Ljubljana became increasingly removed from Belgrade. It was then, in the first half of the 1920s, that many Serbian and Slovene negative stereotypes about each other sprang up. These stereotypes were even to outlast Yugoslavia. For instance, Serbian newspapers wrote of Slovene egoism and conceitedness, their exaggerated enthusiasm for things Austrian, and their separatism. Meanwhile, Slovene papers told of Balkanism, hegemonism, militarism, and the dissolution and authoritarianism of Serbian politics. The Slovene feeling that they were nationally threatened seemed justified in all respects: not only did they lose a large piece of ethnic territory in the delimitation of borders with Austria and Italy, but they also failed to gain the unified Slovenia and political autonomy that had been their goals since 1848. They believed their fears to be confirmed when they entered Yugoslavia and found their territory divided into two provinces subordinated to the central authorities in Belgrade. This left more than 100,000 Slovenes in Austria and over 300,000 in Italy. In the KSCS itself, the 1,023,600 Slovenes accounted for 8.5 percent of the total population, while Serbs and Montenegrins made up 39 percent and Croats 23 percent. This meant that within the centralist system the Slovenes were condemned to remain a perpetual minority.

The paradoxical economic conditions, under which the economically least developed Croatian and Slovene lands of the former Habsburg monarchy became the most developed parts of the new Yugoslav state after 1918, intensified the antagonisms still more. If the new economic connections proved to be useful for developing Croatian and Slovene industry to a certain extent, it was also harmful to agriculture, from which the majority of the population in both regions continued to live. In the 1930s the crisis in agriculture was one of the chief causes of Slovene emigration, which far exceeded the rate of emigration from the rest of Yugoslavia, relative to percentage of population. These things combined to cement the conviction among the Slovenes that Yugoslavia was exploiting them economically. In 1927 Korošec summed this up in a stereotype, which remained popular among the Slovenes until the fall of Yugoslavia: "In Yugoslavia it is thus: The Serbs rule, the Croats debate, and the Slovenes work" (Sundhausen 1982, 67).

It was in such circumstances that the autonomy- and federalism-oriented Catholic party (SPP) found itself in the 1920s and 1930s the strongest and most influential political force in Slovenia. For the most part its leaders sought political allies not in Zagreb but rather in Belgrade. They persistently and pragmatically struck compromises with the government and court there, but although they enjoyed some diplomatic success they were unable to alter Slovenia's situation in the long run. Opposed to this policy of compromise were smaller political groups, which advocated Slovene autonomy and the constitutional reform of the kingdom, including the Slovene Communists, who were still an insignificant group in the 1920s. Some of these demanded legislative autonomy for Slovenia or wrote and talked about a possible Slovene future in a loose South Slav or Balkan confederation, but none of them took on the cause of total Slovene independence. Such an idea seemed obviously and completely unrealistic (Perovšek 1984; Pleterski 1967; Ude 1928; Grdina 1989).

The Croat Peasant Republican Party, led by Stjepan Radić, did not succeed in winning the lasting sympathies of Slovenes. According to Slovene historians, this failure was because of the rivalry between Radić and Korošec on one hand and, on the other hand, Radić's overly patronizing attitude toward the Slovenes. Significant long-term cooperation between Slovene and Croat intellectuals never took place in the 1920s and 1930s, a fact loudly bemoaned in Slovene cultural journals. It was impossible to shake the impression that the majority of liberal-minded Slovene intellectuals looked more to Belgrade than to Zagreb.

In the 1930s, a sense of catastrophe came to the fore in Slovenia. The question of the Slovene national future remained the central theme of Slovene national political debates and schisms right up to the Second World War. Centralist pressure began after the introduction of the royal dictatorship in 1929 and the ideology of strengthened Yugoslav unitarism manifested itself in slogans about the spiritual unity of Serbs, Croats, and Slovenes and in the suppression of nationalist signs, symbols, and titles. This led to the impression, especially among educated Slovenes, that their national existence was direly threatened a mere decade after their entrance into Yugoslavia. At that time the supporters of centralism were limited to a narrow circle of liberals and socialists, whereas even the Communists admitted that "most of the working people of Slovenia are not fighting for communism, but rather for an independent Slovenia, for the right to determine their fate and make use of their money as they see fit" (Nedog 1973, 69).

In spite of everything, however, one should not interpret such admonishments literally. Even the most ardent Slovene autonomists supported federalism, and in their criticisms of centralism and Serbian Yugoslavism, they did not advocate Slovene withdrawal from Yugoslavia. Up to 1941 there were no political groups or parties in Slovenia openly considering the possibility of an independent Slovene state. On the contrary, the proximity of Fascist Italy and, after 1938, of the German Reich along the Karawanken strengthened the conviction that Slovenes could survive as a nation only in a broad multinational community capable of resisting the pressure of hostile neighbors. There were individuals, however, mostly from the ranks of the conservative Catholics, who were in despair over Yugoslavia and were reflecting on a Slovenian future that would ultimately be outside the Yugoslav framework. Such people occasionally came up with unrealistic ideas about the possible formation of a central or pan-European federation that would link the small nations from the Baltic to the Atlantic and would presumably include Slovenia (Mlakar 1982, 212-22; Žebot 1988).

The swift defeat of Yugoslavia in 1941 caught the Yugoslav and Slovene middle classes completely unprepared. The Slovene National Council formed by the Slovene political parties at the beginning of the war could not prevent the German and Italian military occupation of Slovene territory. The regime in the German occupation zone (the northern and western part of Slovenia) was characterized by an aggressive policy of Germanization, which completely paralyzed Slovene political activities. The Italian regime in central Slovenia (the so-called Province of Ljubljana) was less aggressive and was, at least at the beginning of the war, ready for compromise. It left the Slovene political parties a certain degree of self-government in civil administration; most Slovene cultural institutions could continue their work; and newspapers, magazines, and books in Slovene continued to come out more or less regularly (Žebot 1988, 201-28).

In such a situation, the Slovene political parties had to solve a complicated dilemma: whether to organize illegal and armed resistance against the occupiers, or to try to find a temporary *modus vivendi* and to wait until the war was over. The leading elites of the main Slovene parties, Catholic and Liberal, influenced by the situation in the Italian occupation zone, chose the second solution, with tragic consequences. Their political activities and existence became more and more dependent on the Italian authorities, and, after the Italian capitulation in 1943, on the Germans. Later in the war, the Catholic and Liberal political elites organized their own military units, which were supposed to join the Western allies after the German defeat and help them liberate Slovenia.

Thus post-1941 Slovene resistance to the German and Italian occupiers was organized primarily by the left political groups and the Communists, and was joined only by a small number of groups and individuals associated with Catholic, Liberal, and other political parties who were unsatisfied with their party leaderships' hesitant policies. At first, the liberation movement had widespread support among the population. But it became, by increments, more of an instrument of communist policy. In 1942 and 1943 the Slovenes split into two blocks: the first supported the armed resistance, and the second backed the middle-class political parties. The Liberation Front (Communist) policy of punishing "the traitors" led to the organization of anticommunist military units. The tragic consequence of this development was a civil war.

The Liberation Front, led by the Communists, combined the liberation struggle in Slovenia with struggles of the other Yugoslav peoples and was thus the only movement in Slovenia that had direct contact with the rest of Yugoslavia the entire time from 1941 to 1945. A group of middle-class politicians reestablished more or less regular contacts with the Yugoslav government in London. But direct contacts between members of Slovene, Croat, and Serbian middle-class parties who remained on Yugoslav soil after the occupation were for the most part broken off.

In spite of the break in relations with the rest of Yugoslavia, and despite the decision of the leadership of the middle-class parties—faced with the Communist leadership of the liberation struggle—to consent to military cooperation with the occupiers, from 1941 to 1945 none of the more important political groups in Slovenia made plans for the independence of Slovenia (Mlakar 1982). The leadership of the middle-class parties, the Liberals and the Catholics, counted on the victory of the Western Allies and the USSR. With the exception of a rather small number of extremists, the Slovene leaders held to their view that Yugoslavia would have to be restored and reconfigured after the war. Conceptions of what this postwar Yugoslavia would be like were divided, but the majority opinion (represented especially by the Catholic party) was that the country should remain a kingdom and should be organized into a federation of Serbs, Croats, and Slovenes. In short, even during the Second World War the Slovenes did not unite against Yugoslavia, but rather for it.

The leadership of the Slovene national liberation struggle, despite connections to Tito's leadership and to the rest of Yugoslavia, proceeded in a fairly independent manner until 1944. At that time it proclaimed as its goal the liberation of all Slovenes and their inclusion in a Slovene state inside Yugoslavia (with the permanent right of secession). On November 29, 1943, in Jajce, Bosnia, they concluded an agreement with the representatives of the partisan resistance from the rest of Yugoslavia. Here we see the beginning of new Slovene state authority on Slovene territory, supervised by partisan units while the war lasted. This authority was gradually restricted by the Yugoslav Communist-partisan leadership from the spring of 1944 on (Repe 1992, 286). The Communists took more power in their hands in 1944-45, and completely controlled the political system when the war was over. In 1945, Yugoslavia was formally organized as a federation, in which Slovenia too was to receive its own republic. But in reality, after 1945 all power was in the hands of the Communist party, which itself was organized in an expressly hierarchical and centralistic manner and as a matter of principle hewed to a supranational, "internationalist" line (Repe 1982).

In May 1945, some days before the partisan army entered the Slovene capital Ljubljana, the leaders of the Slovene middle-class parties, who were opposed to the Communists and the Liberation Front during the war, formed their government. This government proclaimed the formation of the Slovene state within the Kingdom of Yugoslavia and claimed itself to be the only representative of the Slovene nation to negotiate with the victorious Allies. It was too late, however. When the partisan army approached Ljubljana some days later, the majority of the Slovene middle-class political elite left the town and joined the refugees, who—whether because they opposed the partisan movement during the war, or because they were influenced by anticommunist propaganda—withdrew northwards to Carinthia, Austria, to surrender to British army forces. In May 1945, there were about 24,000 Slovenes in the British refugee camps in southern Austria, among them more than 10,000 soldiers of the Slovene antipartisan military units, the *domobranci*. Some 11,000-12,000 Slovene anticommunist soldiers and civilians were sent back to Slovenia by the British military authorities in late May to early June 1945; most of them were secretly massacred by the Communists in June of the same year (Vodušek-Starič 1992, 225-50). For the rest of the refugees—including the leaders of the middle class political parties—it was possible to go into exile. The majority went to the United States and Argentina.

It is well-known that the Yugoslav Communists faithfully copied the Soviet system after the war. In November 1945 the first postwar elections took place. There was only one list of candidates, that of Tito's Liberation Front. In Slovenia, it received more than 90 percent of the votes cast (Vodušek-Starič 1992, 363-69). The few middle-class politicians who remained in Yugoslavia and Slovenia after the Communist ascension—most of whom were sympathizers of the liberation movement during the war—tried to form an opposition. They were persecuted, accused of spying for Western allies, put on trial and sentenced to prison or even to death.[1]

The political pressure grew in 1947-48, when the Yugoslav and Slovene Communist leadership—faced with Moscow's criticism—feared that their Party membership could split into Stalinist and Titoist blocs. At the same time, the South Slav Communists strived to show the Soviets they were firmly adhering to the Party line and idea. This situation began to change only at the beginning of the 1950s. Yugoslavia found itself isolated from both East and West after its 1948 conflict with Stalin. The newly-formed state had to look for its own way to modernize, to open to the West, but to remain Communist. The relaxation of political oppression was gradual, though belated. After the early 1950s it was accompanied by the introduction of workers' self-management in the factories and the decentralization of the Yugoslav state-administrative system.

Under such conditions there was no far-reaching public analysis of the relations between the Yugoslav peoples until the second half of the 1950s. Political leaders and ideologues maintained that the national question was solved once and for all through social revolution and the restructuring of Yugoslavia into a federalist state; the federal system with its constitutional and political mechanisms purportedly assured each of the peoples a position of equal rights and self-determination. The political pressures and the remembrance of the Second World War's tragic consequences did actually calm national passions and disagreements for a short time. However, there was already, in the period of 1945-50, much criticism of postwar Yugoslav economic policy, even on the part of the Slovene Communist political elite. The Communist policy of industrialization insisted on active and generous support by the industrialized regions of those left behind in their social and economic development. In Slovenia, as early as the second half of the 1940s, this policy was considered a "false solidarity" and became an important cause of political tensions and misunderstandings. The first reports mentioning "the comrades" who "fear the centralization coming from Belgrade" dated from 1946. These reports were energetically refuted not only by Communist leaders in Belgrade, but also in Ljubljana. For example, Boris Kidrič, a Slovene and in 1946 a minister for industrialization in the Yugoslav federal government, openly declared that these were "future investments" to be made above all in the underdeveloped regions. Slovenia was supposed to have, in this sense, special obligations to the rest of Yugoslavia (Prinčič 1992, 29-50).

The Slovene Communist leadership prevented an open discussion on this issue. It was only in the 1950s that it again became possible to discuss in public the relations among the republics and nations. The first sign of dissatisfaction with centralism and with the status of the national question in socialist Yugoslavia quickly found public expression, and it was evident that the old national antagonisms and prewar national concepts had not been overcome. In 1957, leading Yugoslav Communist ideologist Edvard Kardelj, who was to remain in the forefront of Yugoslav constitutional policy up to his death in 1979, publicly acknowledged this breach for the first time. In the introduction to the second edition of his book *On the Development of the Slovene National Question* he attributed the tenacity of intra-Yugoslav national tensions after 1945 to "remnants of bourgeois nationalism," to the differences in development between different parts of Yugoslavia, and to bureaucratic-centralist tendencies in the top Yugoslav leadership (Repe 1992, 287). Getting rid of developmental disparities should be, according to Kardelj, primarily a matter of a balanced and effective economic policy, which would be determined by both regional and general Yugoslav appropriations and investments. Resolving the conflict between "bourgeois nationalism" and centralist Yugoslavism that negates the existence of individual nations should be a rather broad task of all socialist forces. The basis of Yugoslav political, socioeconomic, and cultural integration was this idea of socialism linking the various peoples and becoming the foundation of the new Yugoslav (patriotic) consciousness (Kardelj 1957, xlvii-lxxvii). Socialist Yugoslavia clearly acknowledged the equal rights and individuality of all its peoples and took a stand against their forcible combination.

In 1958 at the Seventh Congress of the League of Communists of Yugoslavia (LCY), Kardelj's views split the delegates into two blocs. The first bloc approved of Kardelj's critiques of centralism, and the other asserted that particularism among the republics represented the chief danger to Yugoslavia. In the leading Party and state circles this split led to stormy differences of opinion throughout the first half of the 1960s. In these years Kardelj fell into disfavor with Tito and found himself pushed out of the decision-making process. Meanwhile, the centralized economic system was bringing on the first public conflicts. In 1962, Slovene delegates first walked out of a parliamentary session in Belgrade, because they did not want to vote to approve the economic plan that had been proposed (Repe 1992, 289). The polemics of federal functionaries and those of the Slovene republic were accompanied by one more controversy that carried the debate into the circles of writers and intellectuals. This controversy, which has echoes of Kardelj's criticisms of "Belgrade centralism," was set off by Dobrica Ćosić, who was then Yugoslav- and centralist-oriented (and in 1992 was the great-Serbian president of the third Yugoslavia). Ćosić asserted many times in speeches and writings that republic borders render exchanges and cooperation between the peoples of Yugoslavia more difficult. He also assessed critically the revival of "democratic discipline vis-à-vis the federal governmental organs," and at the same time proclaimed Yugoslavism to be an "internationalist practice" and a component part of "the historically unavoidable integration of the world and the inception of socialist civilization on the planet."

In the name of Slovenes, the literary historian Dušan Pirjevec responded to Ćosić by remarking that "nationality is a constituent element of human personality, the basis of human existence, and the starting point for human communication with the world." For that reason, genuine integration must not be a course of action that restricts and encroaches upon smaller individual groups that already exist; rather, it must affirm national identity. "Over time the process will emphasize ever more the category of the nation as the elemental form of association," Pirjevec believed. This meant that even Yugoslavism will remain preserved if it maintains diversity and makes possible "the unmolested development of existing groups and organisms" (Pirjevec 1961). Ćosić later stated that he then recognized that "the Slovene intellectuals were reorganizing Yugoslavia into a federation of national states" (Repe 1992, 289). Pirjevec, however, told Ćosić quite openly an idea that had been circulating among informed Slovenes throughout various social and political conditions since the 1920s and 1930s: no Yugoslavia is possible within an abstract or coercive uniformity; it is only possible in all of its multiplicity. The president of the Slovene Academy of Sciences, Josip Vidmar, repeated this in a new argument with Ćosić in 1964. In the middle of the 1960s, the national question became one of the central themes of Slovene journalism and cultural discussion, especially after the dismissal of vice-president and chief of the secret police Aleksandar Ranković, who had been the advocate of centralism and a "firm hand." But there was no talk of what kind of Slovene national program, more or less independently of the LCY, would push for the cause of greater self-governance for Slovenia.

Various initiatives for the reform of the federation and the LCY also came down from the top with Tito's blessing in the latter half of the 1960s. For the most part they also followed Kardelj's concepts, in which overeager criticism of centralism was not exactly welcome. This manifested itself clearly at the Sixth Congress of the League of Communists of Slovenia (LCS) in 1968 in Ljubljana, when speakers criticized the postwar national policy, spoke of the republics' sovereignty and of Slovene statehood, and even engaged in polemics concerning the organization of the Yugoslav army. To this Kardelj objected strongly. The discussions about the possibility of independent and more consistent national programs in the Slovene Communist Party thus came to an end (Repe 1992, 291).

The years from 1968 to 1972 were, perhaps, those that promised the most, before the last chance for serious and effective reforms was missed. As is well known, more modern and liberal-thinking Communists made their way into leadership roles in most republics at the end of the 1960s. They were keenly aware of the difficult economic conditions and were convinced that socialism could be reformed into a relatively democratic social order. They proposed swift economic and social modernization. The government of Slovene Prime Minister Stane Kavčič, which advocated this reform, directed all of its efforts to the formulation of an economic program that did not renounce either socialism or the single-party communist system, but did foresee gradual political democratization in all areas and set itself the goal of "a market economy with a social state." A precondition for the success of the planned reforms was to be the opening of Slovenia to the world, and its more independent position within Yugoslavia. These changes would make possible a direct renewal of the Slovene government's contacts to the other republics without the mediation of Belgrade. In addition, the republics should place financial resources in the form of credits and investments directly into undeveloped regions and conclude separate contracts with them, instead of working through the federal fund for the underdeveloped areas. From Belgrade's point of view, the most difficult point to accept was undoubtedly the reform of the army, yet the Kavčič government supported the formation of Slovenian military units. The Kavčič program did not differ in essence from the demands put together by reform leaders in other Yugoslav republics, especially in Serbia and Croatia, but the reform movement in Slovenia, unlike that of Croatia, did not take on a mass character.

Views on Slovenia's future were certainly varied, but the majority of discussions took place without exaggerated emotions. The Slovene reactions to the mass movement in Croatia were in this sense mostly ambivalent, prudent, even mistrustful. The newspapers, in general supporting Kavčič and his program, gave their support in principle also to the Croatian demands. But they were becoming more restrained in their reaction to the growing Croatian mass euphoria. "The Croats just rise and fall," Stane Kavčič wrote later in his memoirs (Kavčič 1988, 29). Kavčič himself was convinced that Yugoslavia's survival could be assured by proposed new agreements to regulate the country's common life. Thus the decision from the top of the Communist ranks to suspend and alter reform policies in all republics was experienced not only as a personal but also as a Yugoslav catastrophe (Kavčič 1988, 29). Pessimism was justified. After 1972 it was no longer possible to express freely one's political views, and the republics' Communist leadership, true to Tito, tried to bring affairs back under federal control at any cost.

The constitution of 1974 and the debates surrounding it continually revealed the inconsistent nature of the Tito-Kardelj national-political concepts. On one hand the new constitution increased the autonomy of the peoples and republics, while on the other it strengthened the power and authority of the Communist Party, which, despite its external decentralization, continued to function in an explicitly hierarchical and centralist manner. The Slovene Communist leadership pushed Kavčič aside in 1972 and then dominated Slovene politics until the second half of the 1980s. It supported the 1974 constitution in its entirety, which at once guaranteed it a political monopoly and, by means of its stipulations for the autonomous jurisdiction of the republics, left some possibility of negotiations in Belgrade any time a particular Slovene interest seemed threatened. The Slovene Communists were therefore still sworn to this constitution in the late 1980s. They even rejected the idea of putting together their own national program after the schizophrenic constitutional structure began bursting at the seams after Tito's death in 1980.[2]

But the crisis was not to be prevented. After 1980 the Yugoslav Communist system showed itself to be utterly incapable of resolving the accumulated social, economic, political, and national antagonisms. The 1981 uprising of ethnic Albanians in Kosova called for an upgrade of Kosova's status from an autonomous province of Serbia to a republic of Yugoslavia. Serbia responded with repression and demanded the strengthening of the "Serbian republic," while Slovenia called for negotiations and accommodation, and the Yugoslav political elite sought to keep the status quo. At the same time the country's huge foreign debt became a source of new tensions. Economic reform plans formulated in Belgrade in 1982, and including the participation of partly Slovene Communists true to Kardelj's ideas, rejected the "market economy" and were cast in traditional Yugoslav Communist ideological and political molds. In 1983 the federal government called for everyone to help pay the debt regardless of how much of the debt each individual republic itself had incurred. This decree signified a great burden for successful, export-oriented enterprises, especially in Croatia and Slovenia and it caused loud dissatisfaction in both those republics. In any event, federal economic policy was just one of the causes of Slovenia's increasingly critical attitude toward Yugoslavia. Calls in favor of centralization in the fields of education, science, and culture and for repressive measures against opposition intellectuals did more to mobilize public opinion than did the economic problems. With these measures the federal Communist bureaucracy attempted to shore up its dwindling authority. In Slovene eyes such designs abolished traditional, autonomous national-republican jurisdiction and subordinated the republics to Belgrade in the cultural and linguistic spheres, where Slovenes were most sensitive.

In the mid-1980s, Yugoslavia was for the most part already divided into an eastern centralist bloc and a western autonomist bloc; Serbia ever more loudly accused Slovenia and Croatia of aiming at the progressive disintegration of the state (Nećak 1991, 193-94; Huttenbach and Vodopivec 1993, 177-81). Simultaneously, strained polemics about "Yugoslavism," "nationalism, unitarism, and federalism," "unity," and "the right to diversity" carried over into the ranks of writers and completely crippled the Yugoslav writers' organization. Cooperation between the Slovene, Croat, and Serb educated strata was nonetheless not interrupted. Part of the democratic opposition in Ljubljana even believed that the opposition intelligentsia in Yugoslavia, regardless of differences in their views, must cooperate even more closely in efforts to democratize society and do away with the Communist power monopoly. In 1985 the editors of *Nova revija,* which had become a focal point for a conspicuous number of Slovene opposition intellectuals, met in Ljubljana with some of the most prominent Serb intellectuals to discuss the possibility of a "Third and Democratic Yugoslavia." The meeting was a disappointment for both sides. The Slovenes participating in the discussion had the impression that their Serb colleagues were talking all the time about Serbia while only the Slovenes addressed the future prospects of a reformed Yugoslav federation. The Slovene participants in the meeting also suggested the reciprocal printing of publications, which would introduce the Serb public to Slovene positions and vice versa, and would facilitate a dialogue between the two peoples. This idea was never carried out, in part because of insufficient interest in Belgrade (Hribar 1993).

The differences in views were really quite great, a fact pointed out very clearly by the expressly centralist "Memorandum of the Serbian Academy" of 1986. In addition it became more and more obvious that the processes of democratization and of liberation from Communist ideological schemes were proceeding much faster in the western part of Yugoslavia than in the east. In Slovenia, spontaneous movements espousing a radical settling of accounts with the remaining set of Bolshevik-Communist symbols spread widely after 1985. These groups advocated freedom of ideas and opinions, civilian control of the military, and a society that would be founded on respect for internationally recognized human rights. The pathetic oaths sworn to confirm Yugoslavism would be rejected and the movements wanted to come to terms critically with Yugoslavia's multinational reality. The harsh Serb critiques of Slovene "separatism," which was supposedly expressed, *inter alia,* in the Slovene standpoint that the situation in Kosova should be dealt with by understandings with the Albanians instead of by repression, ran parallel to Belgrade's pressure on Slovene Communists to act decisively—even with force—to "settle the score" with the opponents of socialism and Yugoslavism. Slovene Communist politics found itself in the lurch, and the Slovene economy was quickly failing under the strains of the countrywide economic crisis, but among the public and educated elite there was still no firm recognition that socialism in Yugoslavia had experienced a complete collapse. Rather it was thought that the various nations needed to make multilateral arrangements and place their common state on foundations of mutual interests instead of on progressive, Bolshevik, or other ideologies.

In this atmosphere the Slovene educated strata, centered around the writers' society and *Nova revija,* formulated a national program. With it they pushed for "realization of the Slovene right to self-determination" and to an independent state (*Nova revija* 1987). Simply put, they conceived of the Slovene state as a democracy in the Western mold, with a market economy and a constitutional system that would be based on respect for human rights and citizens' liberties. The issue of Yugoslavia itself they left open: the main argument against Yugoslavia, as seen by the authors of the new constitutional concepts of 1988, was that the Slovenes, as a small people in a system operating on majority voting principles, were fated to be a perpetual minority. As such they did not have any chance of realizing their national political ideas and pursuing their interests. The developments of the past few years were cited to confirm this fact. But this argument did not mean that Slovenes had rejected out of hand the thought of some sort of association with Yugoslavia, and intended to say farewell to it forever. Right up until 1990 the assertion that "Yugoslavia is still a Slovene option" appeared in the local press, but it would have had to be a Yugoslavia in the form of a confederation of independent states, which would freely follow their own lights and ambitions and would conclude contracts based on their own criteria of national and governmental usefulness (*Nova revija* 1990).

The events after 1987, when Slobodan Milošević rose to the top of the Serbian Communist party, took place under the pressure of Serbia's violent threats against everyone who did not accept mottoes about a "strong Serbia in a strong Yugoslavia." This quickly shattered the illusion that an agreement among the various peoples would be possible at some time in the future. The Serbian media (newspapers and television) staged a propaganda war against opponents of Belgrade's positions; the army began to meddle by threatening to intervene and by arresting civilians; the Serbian use of force in Kosova was stepped up; and Serbs threatened to organize mass political meetings outside their republic's borders and thereby generated the more or less justified impression that the Milošević policy would be to try to subordinate the rest of Yugoslavia after reducing Kosova to obedience. The election of Ante Marković as president of the federal government was the last attempt to hold Yugoslavia together. But, obviously, Marković did not understand the true dimensions of the Yugoslav political crisis and was convinced that with the eradication of its socioeconomic causes there would come a political truce and an attenuation of national passions; he underestimated the destructive effects of the political conflicts. Thus, his government was quite weak and took a back seat to disintegrative forces not only in the political but also in the economic arena. Marković's ineffectiveness became quite clear when Serbia broke off economic relations with Slovenia in 1989 and then the following year made its intrusion upon the federal financial system. In the spring of 1990, after the Slovene Communists walked out of the Fourteenth Congress of the LCY, the Yugoslav Communist

Party fell apart. Of the three "supporting pillars" that had personified Yugoslav unity—Tito, the LCY, and the army—only the last remained (Nećak 1991).

Therefore, Yugoslavia had disintegrated even before Slovenia formally declared its independence. The first political organizations in Slovenia that were not communist sprang up in 1989 and later grew into political parties; multiparty elections followed in 1990. Such elections then took place in Croatia, Macedonia, and Bosnia-Hercegovina. The Slovene decision to deny the validity of several federal laws together with the Slovene plebiscite in which more than 88 percent of the population opted for governmental independence reflected the already very advanced disintegration of the Yugoslav state in 1990; they were not the causes of it. The prevailing mood in Slovenia in spring 1991 tended toward a confederative arrangement. It was only the military intervention in Slovenia on June 27, 1991, that dealt the final blow to this option.

In 1940, as the Second World War encroached upon Yugoslavia, the Slovene poet Edvard Kocbek published a brief essay entitled "Central Europe" (Kocbek 1940). He stated that the peoples of the region had developed in a substantially different way from those of western Europe, and that even in the twentieth century their aspirations had been fatefully torn between Herderian and Hegelian principles. With Herder they supported the right to have their own national characteristics and with Hegel that of their own state, something which in the very diverse, multiethnic, and multicultural surroundings of Central Europe inevitably caused bloody national conflicts and feuds. To Kocbek, the only way for Central Europe to assure its development while maintaining its diversity was to accept its variety as a positive quality. It would have to organize itself as a federation, that is, to recognize the cultural-linguistic individuality of its individual peoples but to join them into a common "economic space" for practical reasons, such as achieving the unhampered exchange of goods and ideas.

Kocbek's conception of Central Europe was, as I have tried to show, the Slovene conception of Yugoslavia all along. It was more or less the idea of the Austrian Social Democrats (the so-called Austro-Marxists), conceived in the late nineteenth and early twentieth centuries. And it is still today an idea which some well-known European specialists on central Europe are proposing "as an ideal model of interethnic coexistence" in central Europe, the Balkans and the former-Yugoslav territory (see, for example, Gellner 1993). From the Slovene point of view there is only one problem: this entire conception was never really tried in practice, and insofar as it was tried, it did not work in the long term.

Slovene willingness to live with other South Slav people in a common state was, after 1918 as well as after 1945, an indisputable fact. But it is also a fact that Yugoslavia did not fall apart because of a lack of unity; rather it happened because of intolerance and, even more, Serbian incapacity to accept Yugoslavia's ethnic and cultural diversity as a reality and a benefit. For the latter reason, one can say without exaggeration that from the Slovene perspective the Serbian's equation of Yugoslavia with Serbia contributed substantially to the Slovene shift from Herder to Hegel, a move that ultimately led to the emergence of an independent Slovene state. Serbia had tried since 1918 to turn Yugoslavia into an association of individuals, although it was in reality a community of collective personalities.

Translated by John K. Cox and Jill Benderly

ENDNOTES

Partly revised and expanded article, originally published under the title "Slovenes and Yugoslavia, 1918-1991" in *East European Politics and Society,* Volume 6, Number 3, Fall 1992.

1. One of the best-known political trials against the "bourgeois opposition" was the trial against the so-called Črtomir Nagode group in July-August 1947. The 15 mostly liberal-minded "members of the Nagode spying organization" never in reality formed a political group. Some did not even know each other. Three of the accused were sentenced to death. Črtomir Nagode was executed immediately after the trial, professor of law Boris Furlana and Ljubo Sirc had their sentences commuted to 20 years imprisonment and were released after 5 years in prison. One of the accused, Metod Kumelj, committed suicide. Most of the others were sentenced to prison for terms ranging from 1 to 18 years, but were released in the 1950s. The trial as a whole was a pure political construction.

2. In 1984, one of the oldest Slovene Communists, France Klopčič, proposed a national program to the Slovene Communist Party and called upon it to take a national stand. The leadership refused to do so. See Klopčič (1992).

BIBLIOGRAPHY

Braudel, Fernand (1977). *Capitalism and Material Life 1400-1800.* New York: Harper & Row.

Cankar, Ivan (1977). *Zbrano Delo* (Collected works). Ljubljana: Državna Založba Slovenije.

Gellner, Ernst (1993). Interview in *Oesterreichische Zeitschrift fur Geschichtswissenschaften.* 4. jg. Heft 1.

Grafenauer, Bogo (1988). "Iz starega v novi prostor" (From the old to the new space). *Zgodovinski časopis* 42.

Grdina, Igor (1989). "Kratka zgodovina Slovenske zemljoradničke in Slovenske republikanske stranke Antona Novačana" (A short history of the Slovenian Agricultural Workers' Party and Slovene Republican Party of Anton Novačan). *Zgodovinski časopis* 43: 77-96.

Hribar, Spomenka (1993). "Sestanek pri Mraku" (The Meeting at *pri Mraku* Hotel). *Delo* December 4.

Huttenbach, Henry R., and Peter Vodopivec, eds. (1993). *Voices from the Slovene Nation.* Special issue of *Nationalities Papers* (Spring).

Jančar, Drago (1992). *Razbiti vrč* (The Broken Jug). Ljubljana: Mihelač.

Kardelj, Edvard (1957). *Razvoj slovenskega narodnega vprašanja* (Development of the Slovene national question). Ljubljana: Državna Založba Slovenije.

Kavčič, Stane (1988). *Dnevnik in spomini* (Diary and memoirs). Ljubljana: Časopis za Kritiko Znanosti.

Kleist, Heinrich von (1988). *The Broken Jug.* In *Five Plays.* New Haven and London: Yale University Press.

Klopčič, France (1992). "Slovenski nacionalni program med graditvijo socializma" (The Slovene national program and the building of socialism). *Borec* 5/6: 301-80.

Kocbek, Edvard (1940). "Srednja Evropa" (Central Europe). *Dejanje* 3.

Leger, Louis (1915). *La Liquidation de l'Autriche-Hongrie.* Paris.

Melik, Vasilij (1988). "Leto 1918 v slovenski zgodovini" (The year 1918 in Slovene history). *Zgodovinski časopis* 42.

Mlakar, Boris (1982). "O političnih programih slovenske kontrarevolucije 1941-45" (On the political programs of Slovene counterrevolutionaries 1941-45). *Prispevki za zgodovino delavskega gibanja* 22.

Nećak, Dušan (1991). "A chronology of the decay of Tito's Yugoslavia 1980-1991" in *The Case of Slovenia.* Ljubljana: Nova Revija.

Nećak, Dušan (1992). "Revija Nova Evropa in Slovenci" (The review *New Europe* and the Slovenes). *Zgodovinski časopis* 46.

Nedog, Alenka (1973). "Povezovanje revolucionarnih sil v okviru ljudskofrontovskega gibanja na Slovenskem" (Alliances of revolutionary forces in the Popular Front Movement in Slovenia). In *Elementi revolucionarnosti v političnem življenju na Slovenskem* (Revolutionary elements in Slovene political life). Ljubljana.

Nova revija (1987). *Prispevki za slovenski nacionalni program* (Contributions to the Slovene National Program). No 57.

Nova revija (1990). *Samostojna Slovenija* (Independent Slovenia). Number 95.

Perovšek, Jure (1984). "Oblikovanje programskih načrtov o nacionalni samoodločbi v slovenski politiki do ustanovitve Neodvisne delavske stranke Jugoslavije" (Formation of the programmatic sketch on national-self-determination policy until the formation of the Independent Workers' Party of Yugoslavia). *Zgodovinski časopis* 38.

Pirjevec, Dušan (1961). "Slovenstvo, jugoslovanstvo, socializem" (The Slovenes, the Yugoslav idea, and socialism). *Naša Sodobnost* 9: 1099-1129.

Pitamic, Leonid (1921). "Slovenački problem" (The Slovenian Problem). *Nova Evropa* 7

Pleterski, Janko (1967). "Nacionalno vprašanje v Jugoslaviji v teoriji in politiki KPJ-KPS" (The National question in Yugoslavia in the theory and politics of the LCY-LCS). *Prispevki za zgodovino delavskega gibanja* VII.

Prepeluh, Albin (1921). "Zakaj smo avtonomisti" (Why we are autonomists). *Naši zapiski* 13.

Prinčič, Jože (1992). *Slovenska industrija v jugoslovanskem primežu 1945-1956* (Slovene industry in the Yugoslav vise 1945-1956). Novo Mesto: Dolenjska Založba.

Repe, Božo (1992). "Slovenski nacionalni programi od druge svetovne vojne do začetka osemdesetih let" (Slovenian national programs from the Second World War to the 1980s). *Borec* 5/6.

Rogel, Carole (1971). "The Slovenes and Yugoslavia 1890-1914." *East European Quarterly* 4:4.

Sundhausen, Holm (1982). *Geschichte Jugoslawiens* (History of Yugoslavia). Stuttgart.

Ude, Lojze (1928). "Značilnost zadnjega volilnega boja in današnji notranje-politični položaj v svitu borbe za samostojno in združeno Slovenijo" (The significance of the last electoral campaign for today's domestic political fight for a self-reliant and united Slovenia). *Mladina* 2; *Svobodna Mladina* 1-2.

Vodopivec, Peter (1990). "Pred ponovno odločitvijo" (Facing another decision). *Nova revija* 95.

Vodušek-Starič, Jera (1992). *Prevzem Oblasti 1944-46* (The Seizure of Power 1944-46). Ljubljana: Cankarjeva Založba.

Ževčević, Momčilo (1986). *Na zgodonski prelomnici* (On historical turning-points). Maribor: Obzorja.

Žebot, Ciril (1988). *Neminljiva Slovenija* (The Enduring Slovenia). Celovec/Klagenfurt: Mohorjeva.

Zver, Milan (1992). "Protiliberalni udar v partiji" (The anti-liberal coup in the party). *Naši razgledi—razgledi po svetu*. July 3 1992.

Zwitter, Fran (1965). *Nacionalni problemi v Habsburški monarhiji* (The national problem in the Hapsburg monarchy). Ljubljana: Slovenska Matica.

3

Economic History of Twentieth-Century Slovenia

Žarko Lazarević

I n this century Slovenes have experienced no fewer than four politically different state systems; each time the political framework changed, economic restructuring of Slovenia likewise took place.

Up to 1918, the Slovene economy developed within the large Austro-Hungarian market, where the Slovene territory was considered a less-developed rural area and a source of raw materials for the nearby industrial countries. In 1918 Slovenia found itself in the newly created market of the first Yugoslavia, from which it benefitted a great deal for about two decades. Thanks to its technology, Slovenia immediately became the most developed region in the new state. The unified Yugoslav market, hungry for consumer goods, encouraged its rapid industrialization. The process was all the faster because there already existed a developed transport infrastructure and the first supplies of electricity and educated labor. At least at the beginning, Yugoslav tariff protection was also a stimulant.

After World War II Slovenia remained within the same state, its territory enlarged through the addition of the Istrian Littoral. But the political and economic changes introduced by the Communists were much more radical than the earlier ones. Due to its economic lead in prewar Yugoslavia, Slovenia was now allotted the task of underwriting economic development in other parts of the state, which in turn slackened its own progress. It should be pointed out, however, that the mid-1960s, and especially the 1970s, saw the beginning of the Yugoslav market's disintegration, brought about by the introduction of "national economies," which gave Slovenia and other federal units more independence. The last turn of the tide occurred not long ago, in 1991, when Slovenia left the South Slav entity and declared its independence. Today Slovenia is faced with reorienting its trade and including itself in European economic flows; in one sense, we can say that Slovenia has to return to the economic milieu of the pre-1918 period.

Apart from the above-mentioned turning points there is another element that every presentation of Slovene economic history should take into consideration. Whereas in about the first 40 years of the twentieth century Slovenes lived within states with capitalist economies, it was the principles of socialist economy to which they had to conform between 1945 and 1990. Now, after independence, Slovenia is trying hard to plow its way back into the world of the market economy. There is, therefore, an obvious parallel to the situation in 1918, when Slovenia lost its accustomed markets. Then, it successfully overcame the difficulties of adapting to the new circumstances by making good use of its advantages and there followed relatively rapid economic growth. The current situation differs in that today Slovenia's interests lie in a trade zone that is not vacant as was that of the first Yugoslavia. Of course, we shall only be able to assess and comment more substantially on the present transformations, the results of which can hardly be foreseen at the moment, from the necessary historical distance.

Thus, Slovenia's twentieth century economic history could be split into two periodizations. One periodization, based on socio-economic relations, would comprise two periods, namely the capitalist market and socialist economy periods, with World War II as the dividing point. The other periodization would be based on the four different political units Slovenes have lived in.

The first periodization turns out to be more useful. It deals with political, social, and economic structures and marks off two approximately fifty-year periods. By contrast, the second periodization does not emphasize adequately the great turning-point of 1945, when the Communists assumed power.

1900-1945: AUSTRIA-HUNGARY AND THE FIRST YUGOSLAVIA
Austria-Hungary (to 1918)

The first half of the twentieth century can be further divided into two subperiods, the Austrian and Yugoslav periods, with 1918 as the dividing line. The industrialization of Slovenia began under the Habsburg Empire. It was undertaken by Austrian, rather than Slovene, capital. By the last decade of the nineteenth century industrial production had been modernized and expanded; from then to the outbreak of World War I, the Slovene economy flourished.

The following data show how fast this progress was. From 1880 to 1890 the number of industrial enterprises grew by 30 percent, in 1890-1900 by 54 percent and in the first 10 years of the 20th century by 44 percent (Grafenauer 1968). In early twentieth century Slovenia, mining and metallurgical industries employed the majority of Slovene workers. Wood and building materials industries followed, as well as building construction. Also important were chemical, food and electrical industries, but their progress was average. On the other hand, the output of paper and leather-working industries were above-average. Due to the increased cultural activities following the Slovene cultural emancipation in the second half of the nineteenth century, printing also prospered. Moreover, the foundations were laid for the development of textile, especially spinning and weaving, industries (Grafenauer 1968). The clothing industry became more powerful only later in the Yugoslav period; in the early years of this century, the demand for clothes was to a large extent still satisfied by craft production. From the mid-nineteenth century the state tobacco factory in Ljubljana likewise showed promise.

The electrification of the country began with the first power stations in towns, first supplying street lighting and then to industries. Slovenia's transport capacities improved above all with the construction of railways; to the main Vienna-Trieste line, traversing Slovene territory, a network of local lines were attached (Gestrin 1969). Beside railway and telegraph connections, a telephone network was beginning to take shape at the end of the last century. In 1897 the Ljubljana area, for example, acquired its own network and joined the interurban link between Vienna and Trieste (Lazarević 1987).

In the last ten years of the nineteenth century the rapid decline of various crafts was finally halted. The decline, caused both by industrialization and greater mobility resulting from the expansion of railways, had been characteristic of the pre-nineties decades. By about 1890, most craftspeople unable to compete with large-scale industrial enterprises had given up their businesses. Some of them, however, had managed to adapt, either by purchasing basic machinery and setting up their own firms or, in the entrepreneurial spirit, by trying to "fill in the gaps" in the market system. Instead of using their own materials and working for mass-market sales, these people applied themselves to completing custom orders for a wealthy clientele or to running repair shops (Gestrin 1969).

Another marked feature of Slovene economy at the turn of the century was the accumulation of domestic capital. Slovene capital accumulated on the one hand in the newly forming Slovene banks and, on the other, in a number of small mutual loan societies and savings banks growing briskly in the country-side and towns respectively. The cooperative movement was mostly in the hands of politicians and was used not only for charitable purposes, but also to strengthen their political positions. The two cooperative unions in that period reflected the two poles of Slovene politics: the Union of Slovene Cooperatives was backed by the National Progressive Party, that is, Slovene liberals, and the Cooperative Union was espoused by Slovene "clericals." It is noteworthy that the first Slovene insurance company, established in 1900, was founded by "Catholic" capital. All existing financial institutions invested in some degree in turn in industrial equipment or the construction of new enterprises. In the countryside a decisive step forward was taken by loan cooperatives giving credit to peasants. Despite the substantial amounts of money accumulated in this manner, foreign capital still dominated by a ratio of 10:1. It should be added here that only the Czechs associated themselves with Slovenes in cap-ital investments, whereas other foreigners preferred partnership with Austrian or German capital (Gestrin 1969).

In the early twentieth century the situation in agriculture likewise started changing for the better. Industrial growth caused a drop in the prices of agri-cultural implements and machines, which thereby became accessible to a greater number of peasants. The owners of medium-sized as well as small holdings could now work their land with iron plows and other manufactured machinery. Cultivation of land was quite intensive in Carinthia, Styria, and some parts of Carniola, especially in the Ljubljana basin and Upper Carniola. The owners of large estates and big farms used fertilizers increasingly. Productivity on the whole increased, although in Slovenia the yield per hectare was still much smaller than it was in Western Europe. That period furthermore saw a revival of wine production and fruit growing. In the Savinja valley the cultivation of hops grew in importance. Stock breeding benefited from mod-ernization and the introduction of new breeds; by 1914 the number of cattle rose by about one fifth. Pig and cattle rearing continued to prevail. Forestry was another constant source of income to those large estate or farm owners whose woods were ample enough to be worth logging.

By the outbreak of World War I prices in agriculture had gone up by about one-third from 1900 levels. Soaring prices advanced the intensification of agri-cultural methods and at the same time allowed peasants to better meet their needs. But higher income entailed higher expense, a process which led, despite all the progress, to a decline from which agriculture would not recover before the end of the era. The majority of peasants, however, were still able to make a living by farming alone. This was important because it stopped the streams of emigrants characteristic of the latter half of the nineteenth century, when the number of emigrants from the territory encompassed by today's Slovenia amounted to no less than a half of the natural increase in population.

Beside the noteworthy achievements there were some negative trends affecting, above all, the structure of landownership. Due to the ongoing breakup of farms, in 1902 most Slovene landowners were smallholders: 12.5 percent of farms covered fewer than 50 ares, 23 percent 0.5-2 hectares; a good 21.5 percent of peasants had farms of 2-5 hectares, 18 percent held 5-10 hectares and only 25 percent of landowners held more than 10 hectares (Gestrin and Melik 1966).

The First Yugoslavia (1918-1941)

After the dissolution of the Habsburg monarchy, the Slovene economy encountered entirely new challenges. Although Slovenia did not enter the first Yugoslavia "empty-handed," it was nevertheless compelled by the new political situation to seek new routes of development; besides, it now covered a mere two-thirds of the territory inhabited by Slovenes. Slovene trade, which had mainly run along the Vienna-Trieste line, had to turn toward the south, that is toward Belgrade, and Slovenia's economic role in the first Yugoslavia radically changed. Whereas in the multiethnic Austro-Hungarian Empire the Slovene region had the position of a poorly developed and mostly rural area that supplied raw materials to the nearest industrial towns like Graz and Trieste, it was now the most advanced part of a state that was as multiethnic as the empire had been. The transition to a culturally and economically very different world had good and ill effects, but the benefits the Slovene economy enjoyed outweighed the disadvantages. Commercial and industrial progress, particularly that of processing industries, was promoted first by a great demand for various consumer goods in the Yugoslav market, then by a comparatively well-organized traffic network, a good supply of electric power, educated, adaptable, and cheap labor, and protective tariffs. On the other hand, the economic policies of Yugoslavia proved to be less beneficial to Slovene agriculture.

Slovene industries made relatively rapid progress, especially in the twenties; in the thirties, industrialization was stalled by the worldwide depression. In 1918 there were 275 factories in Slovenia. By World War II their number would almost double (523). Most of the new factories (161) were erected in the twenties; only 92 were set up in the following decade. (These figures, based on the inadequate statistics of that period, do not take into account modernization or enlargement of existing plants.) On the average, the interwar period saw the opening of a new factory every month (Šorn 1959).

The reasons for the setback in Slovene industry in the thirties lie not merely in the great economic crisis of 1930-35, but also in Yugoslav economic policy, which now concentrated on the more systematic industrialization of other Yugoslav regions. Slovene development was accorded less attention. Another hypothesis, which has yet to be adequately tested, suggests that the decrease in industrial enterprises was caused by cartelization (Šorn 1959). The quantitative aspect of industrialization, and the significance of particular branches, is illustrated in table 3.1. The situation in 1918 is compared with that of 1939 by means of output indices.

TABLE 3.1. GROWTH OF SELECTED INDUSTRIES, 1918-1939		
Industries	**1918**	**1939**
Mining	100	107
Iron	100	190
Chemical	100	184
Textile	100	936
Leather	100	180
Wood	100	137
Food	100	205
Building	100	159
Paper	100	177
Glass	100	166
Total	**100**	**190**

The statistics show that by far the greatest progress in that era was made in textile industries, where most capital was invested by Czechs. In 20 years the number of plants increased almost tenfold and before World War II Slovene output represented up to 37 percent of the total Yugoslav textile production (Šorn 1959). The textile industries became the third most important industrial branch in Slovenia, after woodworking and metallurgy. The mining industry, among the better developed pre–World War I industries, grew, not surprisingly, at the slowest pace. Mining received more support in other Yugoslav regions; besides, in Slovenia the natural resources on which this industry depended were quite limited.

The development in industries determined the degree of industrial employment, as can be seen from the following data: Until 1923 the number of employees rose sharply; then it fell for two years, as a consequence of the government's anti-inflation policy. From 1925 through 1930, when it reached its peak, employment rose again, though somewhat slower. In the first two years of the economic crisis (1930-32) employment dropped at the same rate as it had been increasing prior to 1930. The year 1935 finally saw a renewed, but short-term increase: up to 1938 the number of industrial workers grew at a rate equal to that of the second half of the twenties. During the last few years before the war the employment level was again on the decline. Of course the impact of the depression was very negative; the 1930 level was not attained again until the end of 1937 (Kresal 1974). The decrease in employment, particularly after the mid-thirties, was also influenced by the modernization and intensification of industrial production.

Industrialization could not have been carried out without financing. Immediately after the birth of Yugoslavia, heated debates broke out among the newly united regions, at the center of which was the question of the new state currency. The chaotic situation was mostly due to the regions' having different exchange rates before entering the state, which hindered economic flows within the state. The attempts to retain and protect the value of the Austrian crowns—issued in large quantities after the war and now flooding the Yugoslav area of the former Empire—by stamping them soon turned out to be futile. It was clear that monetary reform was badly needed, but there arose the question of the exchange rate between the crown and the dinar, which had in the meantime become the sole Yugoslav currency. Slovenia argued for the "al pari" exchange and felt cheated when the central government in 1920 decided on the rate of 4:1. With the dinar overvalued, Slovene savings and annuities in crowns were particularly affected. In addition, inflation at the time of exchange considerably depreciated the dinar, bringing its purchasing power below that of the crown. Some estimate that Slovenes thereby incurred a loss of no less than 80 percent of the value of their savings (Kresal 1974).

Despite such an irritating start, the financial institutions dealing with Slovene capital soon recovered. At first the nationalization of foreign branch banks greatly contributed to their expansion. At that time nationalization meant that the majority of shares were to be held by Yugoslav citizens; in this way local control of Slovene finance was assured. In the first inflationary years banks and their branches multiplied at a fast rate. Owing to the restrictive monetary policy concerning credit, however, a great number of smaller banks were soon faced with liquidity problems, which they resolved by rationalizing their work. The progress in banking emerges from the following figures: in 1918 there were 9 foreign branches and 3 domestic banks in Slovenia; whereas in the latter half of the thirties there were 10 banks and 18 branches (Spominski zbornik 1939). The establishment of the Stock Exchange in the twenties was another stimulant to the money market and the expansion of Slovene banking.

Most of the banks were situated in towns. The money they invested either in the form of credits (investment credits) or of direct capital investments went into industry and commerce. On the other hand, agricultural credit cooperatives, rarely investing in nonagricultural enterprises, continued to meet the demands for loans in the countryside. The two biggest cooperative unions, dating back to the prewar period, still dominated. It is worth noting that the Catholic-backed cooperative union achieved greater success than its rival, the liberally oriented Union of Slovene Cooperatives.

The economic crisis of the thirties did not spare any financial institution in Slovenia. Banking was hurt above all by the outflow of foreign capital following the legal stabilization of the dinar in 1931. This drain was all the more damaging because foreign capital played a highly significant role both in industry and banking; as much as a third of industrial production was dependent on it. The slightest change in the economic position of the capital-exporting countries could therefore considerably affect the Yugoslav economy (Vučković 1976). May 1931, for example, saw the collapse of the Creditanstalt, a huge Viennese institution which was the owner of some powerful Yugoslav banks and of more than 30 industrial enterprises. Its downfall resulted in the outflow of large amounts of capital from Yugoslavia right when it was most needed. The thirties were marked, moreover, by crowds of depositors, upset by the bankruptcy of large renowned financial institutions, lining up at banks to withdraw their deposits. In 1932, much harm was done to peasant credit cooperatives in Slovenia, as well as to banks elsewhere in Yugoslavia, by the introduction of a moratorium on peasant debts; the moratorium paralyzed their work, leaving them without the necessary inflow of capital. The government tried to remedy their troubles by freezing deposits for five years, but the attempted cure shook depositors' confidence. Things were only made worse by the restrictive monetary policy, based on a belief that the value of the dinar mounted with the decline in prices (Tomašević 1935). Such a policy, however, could not but enhance the illiquidity of banks. More radical financial reforms in credit cooperatives, banks and savings banks were launched only after the mid-thirties. The government took over the nonperforming investments, for example, peasants' debts, and offered at the same time a substantial amount of cheap credit to the "patients" to help them improve their financial position. In attempting to lay new foundations for economic growth, the state spent a great deal of money. Local authorities in Slovenia (called *Dravska banovina*) also provided assistance, but since the authorities were mostly Catholic, only the Cooperative Union, which shared their political views, received support (Lazarević 1992).

The transportation system of that era was comparatively well developed. The basic railroad network, already constructed to a large extent before World War I, was now expanded by a mere 60 kilometers. The loss of the Trieste seaport, which was a severe blow to the Slovene economy, encouraged Slovenes to set out on a search for the most suitable access to the sea, but the project did not go beyond the planning stage. The road network was dense, but maintenance was neglected. In the second half of the thirties the first concrete road was built in Slovenia, going from Ljubljana via Kranj to Jesenice with a turning to Bled. The Slovene road system was in its infancy and could not compete with the railroad. The year 1932 saw the establishment of the Ljubljana-Belgrade air-route; a regular international route Ljubljana-Klagenfurt-Vienna-Berlin, was set up two years later.

In the twenties, Slovenes at large also became acquainted with one of the achievements in modern communication, radio broadcasting. In 1928 Ljubljana got its first radio station and within ten years the number of listeners increased about five times. Rapid development occurred as well in the field of telecommunications. Although the basic structure of the telegraph system had been set in the Austrian period, the number of telegraphic stations in that era rose by almost a half. Even greater progress was made in telephone communications. In the thirties three automatic telephone exchanges were opened and very soon the number of telephone subscribers grew nearly sixfold.

Extensive electrification of Slovenia began after World War I, and ran in two directions. One system started at Završnica in Upper Carniola and headed east, controlled by the Electrical Works of Carniola. The other set out at the Styrian Fala near Maribor and went toward the south, but the expansion of electricity in that region was much slower. The enterprise that had undertaken the north-south electrification did not show much interest in supplying the countryside, setting up electric power stations only in towns with comparatively well-developed industries, where there were a sufficient number of consumers to make the project remunerative. The countryside was supplied only wholesale and the distribution stations were constructed at the expense of the local people. Besides, its electric current was more expensive than that of the Electrical Works of Carniola. There were towns and villages which had their own electricity works and local grids, but these were gradually bought up by more powerful enterprises for the production and transfer of the electric current. At that time many a big factory likewise had its own supplies (Kresal 1974).

As we have seen above, the Slovene economy in general profited from Slovenia's becoming part of Yugoslavia. But the effects of the transition were not as beneficial for Slovene agriculture as they were for industry. For as soon as the Yugoslav frontiers had been settled, access to traditional markets was blocked by the protectionist policies of neighboring countries. In addition, Slovene peasants were confronted with the competitive prices of products coming from the other, entirely agrarian, regions of Yugoslavia. With the exception of the first few years, which were marked by inflation, Slovene agriculture was in constant crisis, signalled by a high degree of peasant indebtedness. Apart from the internal difficulties and weaknesses (i.e., disintegration of farms, outdated technology, and overpopulation) the reasons for the agricultural recession lie in the general economic conditions at home and abroad, most notably in the depression of the thirties.

Despite this gloomy introduction, Slovene agriculture in the period of the first Yugoslavia, thanks above all to the zeal of the Service for the Promotion of Slovene Agriculture, which helped peasants to adapt to market conditions, did make a step forward. The achievements in agriculture were not as noteworthy as those of some industries, but they were the more significant, since as much as two-thirds of the Slovene population earned their living by agriculture. The quantitative and qualitative rise in production was rendered possible to a large extent by standardization of products. The yield per hectare increased; that of wheat, for example, grew by one-seventh and exceeded the average national yield of wheat, although it was still very small compared to Western European yields. In stockbreeding, still the most important agricultural sector, the quality of stock was also improved by standardization and selection of breeds with regard to the area where they could be raised best. In that era the importance of fruit growing increased; in particular, there was a great demand for the export of apples. Exported wines, on the other hand, which were also of good quality, were restrained from a more rapid development by the poor state of vineyards; most of them required modernization. In the Savinja valley the production of hops, a product that was cheap and much in demand among the European breweries, was still bringing profits to the local growers.

The structure of landownership—there were an excessive number of small farms—still hindered a wider expansion of agriculture. The agrarian reform of the twenties did little to solve this problem: not much land was distributed to smallholders; only a few big landowners were dispossessed, in fact, only those who were aliens. But on the small, split-up farms neither specialization nor intensification of production on a larger scale would, of course, be feasible. Slovenia thus remained a country of small farmers with 60 percent of farms 5 hectares or less. On the other hand, a mere 1 percent of all peasants had farms exceeding 50 hectares. It would, however, be wrong to think of these as large estates, for most of them measured less than 100 hectares (Lazarević 1992).

Smallholders have always had difficulty adapting to changes in economic conditions. From the mid-1920s, when the prices of crops were falling, owing to restrictive domestic policies and foreign protective tariffs, the majority of peasants accumulated substantial debts. Peasant debts climaxed in 1932, when the effects of the great economic crisis were felt. Prices dropped by half. According to statistics from 1931, 60 percent of Slovenes still lived by farming, and during the crisis no less than 40 percent of estates were heavily encumbered with debt, affecting about one-fourth of the population (Lazarević 1992). It is interesting that the experts of that time were right in predicting that approximately 40 percent of Slovene farms would have to be incorporated into bigger estates. Only bigger estate owners would be able to take up the challenges of market economy. The government envisaged the employment of the surplus rural population in various industries. But there were not many who could buy the bankrupt farms without substantial credit; the crisis-ridden landowners of medium-sized as well as large estates had become insolvent, losing, on average, about half of their income. A considerable number of auctions of failed farms in the 1930s is eloquent proof of the plight of the Slovene peasants.

The peasants burdened with heavy debts were far too numerous to be left to their fate. Because it was easy to foresee that the social and political troubles involved in allowing massive bankruptcies would be enormous, in 1932 a four-year moratorium on peasant debts, badly hurting creditors, was declared. After four years, half of the debts were simply written off; the rest were to be defrayed in 12 years at a reduced rate of interest. The National Bank took over the peasant debts to various financial institutions and debentures that could be used as collateral securities were issued in order to help these institutions improve their liquidity.

The school system in Slovenia, within which a great effort was made to elevate Slovene culture, also played a large part in the economic progress of the country. From 1919 one could attend lectures in economics at the newly founded Slovene university in Ljubljana. At the same time the Technical High School, with a series of institutes, opened its doors; there students were trained for leading posts in industry. While the university course in economics was to provide future economists with a good theoretical knowledge, a number of trade, technical, and agricultural schools attended to demands for more practical professions. Slovene experts and foremen easily replaced the foreign ones, making a significant step forward toward the formation of a domestic intelligentsia. Special attention was devoted to the enlightenment and instruction of the rural population. During the winter, when peasants had more leisure, various courses and lectures on new, more productive methods in farming were organized. The classes also contributed to a somewhat more agreeable everyday life in the country.

In spite of the considerable achievements in industrialization, Slovene industrial enterprises were too few to absorb all the surplus rural population.

In contrast to the custom of the second half of the nineteenth century, leaving home for "the promised land" was out of the question. Industrial workers were, as opposed to those in the Austrian period, recruited largely from townsmen. On the other hand, modernization in the thirties increased the efficiency of Slovene industrial production and, thus, decreased the demand for labor.

The political, cultural, and economic emancipation of Slovenes, however, considerably strengthened their self-confidence. Slovene self-confidence was also buoyed by statistics showing that Slovenia, which covered 6 percent of the Yugoslav land area and constituted 8 percent of the population, produced as much as 25 percent of the national product; accordingly, the average Slovene income per capita exceeded the average national income by 42 percent (Šorn 1979).

The Second (Socialist) Yugoslavia (1945-1991)

At the end of the interwar period, Slovenia still could not be described as an industrial country. An industrialized society, therefore, became the chief objective set by the Communists as soon as they came to power in 1945. To accelerate the process of industrialization, however, was not the only task in the Communists' struggle for a radical transformation of the political, economic, and social structure of the country. The Slovene economy underwent some fundamental changes in the years following World War II. These were due, above all, to the suppression of private enterprises through the nationalization of the means of production, to the introduction of central economic plans and to the collectivization of agriculture.

The Communists were not wrong in regarding further industrialization of Slovenia as a must; prewar politicians had been of the same opinion. But there was a highly important question to be answered, namely, how to carry out the necessary transformations at the least possible cost. Neither before the war nor after it did the Communists trouble their heads, as had the members of other political groups prior to 1941, about the costs and other problems connected with industrialization. Furthermore, they did not care to work out their own, well-grounded strategy for the realization of their vision, but relied instead on the Soviet model. During the first postwar decade the Soviet Union remained the one and only model of a state turning economically and socially into an industrial socialist society. In their callow enthusiasm for this model, the Yugoslav (and Slovene) communists proved even "more Catholic than the Pope." The project was besides so extensive, so exaggerated and so lacking in a real financial base that even the advisors coming from the "cradle of socialism," and accustomed to such large-scale planning, expressed serious doubts, whereas Western observers could but only stand in amazement.

It is, therefore, to the "original sin" of communist utopianism that Slovenes and all the ex-Yugoslavs owe the present inconvenient economic structure. The postwar industrialization was for the most part characterized by improvisation, megalomania, ad hoc decisions, and the absence of realism on which to base a compromise between purely wishful thinking and reality. Considerable means were put into insatiable industrial enterprises, often contrary to good sense. Apart from factories in heavy and basic industries, electricity works were being erected and maintained at costs that by far exceeded the value of their output. There was a high rate of employment and economic growth was, as the Communist leaders boasted, among the fastest in the world. But by concentrating on the quantitative side of industrial progress, that is, on the construction of new plants, the state neglected the quality of products and the efficiency of labor.

After a decade of pursuing an economic policy that can be called a blind imitation of the Soviet model, the leaders became aware that the accelerated industrialization project, fostering the development of only a few sectors, had to abandoned. In 1955 they decided upon a more harmonious economic policy. More attention was to be devoted to processing industries. Planners would no longer ignore the safety of investments, and they now tried to rationalize the process of industrialization. The working people, whose salaries and standard of living remained as low as they had been before the "decade of drudgery," were to be rewarded. Furthermore, in the fifties the idea arose that improved social as well as personal welfare could be achieved by dint of foreign capital, that is by foreign loans, while the accumulated funds of mostly domestic capital would finance subsequent industrialization. Since very little capital was accumulated by the Yugoslav economy itself, the state was soon compelled to take out bigger and bigger loans; this explains the immense national debt in the eighties.

Another dimension of the post–World War II industrialization, harmful to both the economic and political position of such a multiethnic state as Yugoslavia, was a centrally planned redistribution of means of production. Slovenia, without regard to either its needs or goals, had to support the development of other Yugoslav republics. At the same time the northern republic, adhering to the orders coming from Belgrade, held back its own economic progress. The forms of Slovene help, of course, changed in the course of time: at first, Slovenia helped in kind and with skilled labor; later on, with contributions to the federal investment funds and the Fund for the Development of the Less-Developed Regions, a system that existed until the dissolution of

Yugoslavia. On the other hand, Slovenia rarely got federal budgetary support for its own investments, even though it was itself a very generous contributor (Prinčič 1992a).

After the changes in 1955 Slovenes, nevertheless, expected they would be allowed to increase the tempo of their economic growth. They wanted, above all, to modernize industrial machinery, which had to a large extent fallen into disuse through a ten-year-old "don't care" attitude. Their hopes, however, proved too optimistic, for the introduction of decentralization was but a make-believe act; political power, in socialism always correlated with economic power, remained in the hands of the elite Party bodies. From 1955 up to the early 1960s, attempts were made to promote Slovene processing industries and enhance the living standards of individuals and of the community as a whole. Relatively good results were also achieved in the industries producing consumer goods, but the expected growth of national income as well as industrial and especially agricultural productivity, did not materialize; on the contrary, there were declines. That is why in 1961 new economic reforms were launched, encouraging the agents to act in accordance with market-economy principles, but still within the framework of the socialist creed. Political leaders remained unwilling to surrender direct control of economic development and, thus, hindered private enterprise, the only force which could stimulate the expansion of the Yugoslav and Slovene economies. Even in 1967, when a great deal of political and economic power passed from the federal to republican authorities, most decisions were more political than economic. Under these conditions, economic reform efforts could not but come to a bad end.

The development of *communes,* administrative units with a structure and competence parallel to those of the state, rendered possible, despite the declared emancipation of the economy, politicians' interference in the affairs and policies (most notably cadre policy) of the firms. The newly established relation between republics and communes replaced in many ways the earlier state-republic relationship. The inevitable disintegration of the Yugoslav market started soon thereafter, the united market gradually becoming a loose association of the republic, that is "national" economies.

The great number of Yugoslav constitutions attest to the numerous attempts at economic reform. Common to all these attempts is an endeavor to adjust the progress of the economy to current political concepts. At the heart of the constitutional reforms there was one question for the Communists: how to improve economic results without losing political and economic control. In socialist countries, Yugoslavia and Slovenia being no exceptions to the rule, the common feature of all kinds of reforms was that the process of reformation, regardless of results, was allowed to go on only until the monopoly of the Party was considered endangered by the initiative of the emancipated economic actors; then some new reform had to be imposed. In Yugoslavia the seventies were in this respect exemplary, for in that decade the enterprise-level Party committees set themselves the task of fighting against the "centers of power, alienated from workers" as well as against "technocratism." In principle their reforms acknowledged private initiative, but in reality there were so many obstacles that the private sector never played a role worthy of consideration.

The Constitution of 1974 and the Law on Associated Labor in 1976 were the final blows to the Yugoslav and Slovene economies. In an attempt to ensure direct decision making of workers—self-management—concerning the essential questions in production, the well-organized and economical entities were divided into much smaller production units. The reform was not bad in itself, since smaller work units adapt more easily to the changing law of supply and demand. But the creation of the "basic organizations of associated labor" should have been a spontaneous process conforming to circumstances rather than the execution of a command from above. The newly-formed organizations immediately assumed both the role and structure of independent enterprises, and soon brought about a considerable increase in costs per product along with a fall in productivity. The introduction of self-management into all spheres of life also led to an increase in the number of state and "para-state" bodies at the republic and municipal levels. It also led to an extension of social rights entailing the growth of social welfare and public expenditure. It has to be pointed out, though, that in Slovenia the consequences of these changes were on the whole not as damaging as in the other parts of Yugoslavia. At that time the republics could, moreover, urge forward the establishment of their own national economies and strive for autarky.

In the following years, economic conditions in Yugoslavia grew worse, and more difficult to conceal. The evil effects of inappropriate economic policies had been mitigated by foreign loans; as soon as they dried up—at the same time as less-developed countries experienced a debt crisis—the Yugoslav economy slumped. Very soon, the economy fell into a stagflation that did not stop before the disintegration of the Yugoslav federation.

If we look back again on the socialist post-World War II period, we can see that the first three decades were characterized by rather rapid economic growth. Those decades were the "balmy days" of the twentieth century world economy; Yugoslavia, including Slovenia, was touched by warm breezes from booming economies. Although at that time still primarily an agrarian country, Slovenia had, for some time, enough potential for extensive industrialization. But when the policy fostering quantitative industrial expansion gave way to the promotion of quality products, the pillars of the monopolistic one-party system proved unshakable, and thus Slovene economic progress could only come to a halt. (That is also why we deem that there would be no point in quoting here the figures illustrating the growth of individual industrial or agricultural sectors in the whole postwar period.) It is significant, however, that despite the efforts the second Yugoslavia made to even up the different levels of development, the prewar disparities remained and were anything but decreasing.

The imposed industrialization altered not merely the industrial, but also the social, face of Slovenia. The percentage of rural population fell to 20 percent in 1971 (Slovenija 1975) and now amounts to 8 percent. The process of de-agrarianization was accompanied by a rapid growth in employment in the industrial as well as service sectors, where higher education was required. The school system was complex and successful in satisfying the demand for educated labor, smoothing the path to promotion for many. The most developed prewar industries (textile, wood, and leather) declined in the communist period, their growth rate being below average. The electrical industry, embryonic before the war, became the most important Slovene industry, followed by chemical, rubber, metal, paper, and food industries.

Another factor in Slovene economic development was Yugoslavia's open borders after 1965. On the one hand, there was unhindered communication with other nations, and, on the other hand, a considerable outflow of skilled labor aspiring to a higher standard of living that was difficult to attain at home. The Slovenes, had, nevertheless a comparatively good living standard and almost no unemployment in the 1970s. Liberal health, pension, and social insurance were available to everyone. Unfortunately, the economic achievements were not adequate to cover the costs of this fairly expensive system; at the end of the eighties, the state had to start limiting social rights.

The suppression of private enterprises was carried out not only in secondary and tertiary sectors, but in agriculture as well. One of the most important measures was agrarian reform, similar to the reforms of that kind in other European socialist countries in that its primary aim was to nationalize the land (and not to distribute it to the peasants). Fostering private property in agriculture was not in the interest of the state, but the Yugoslav Communists were aware that nationalizing all the land would mean losing the support they enjoyed. They therefore made a compromise, setting a maximum land area for private proprietors that was so small that the state could still dispossess and nationalize large areas. The land acquired was transformed into large state farms, and only a tiny part of it was left over to peasants and other petitioners. The next step was collectivization, that is, the formation of "peasant cultivating cooperatives" organized along the lines of Soviet *kolkhozes*. The authorities then compelled the peasants to enter these cooperatives and to farm according to principles of collective agriculture.

It was important for the Communist leaders that the agrarian reform should not be in discord with their centrally planned economy projects. Agriculture had to stay, they thought, under direct control of the state so that a harmonious development of all the economic sectors could be orchestrated. Yugoslav Communists, emulating the Soviets, mistrusted the peasants; for them the countryside was the ideal "pasture" for "capitalist relations."

The role of agriculture in Yugoslavia, as well as in the Soviet Union, was to provide the basic capital for rapid industrialization. This is not surprising if we think of the agricultural share in the national income. In the system of "primary socialist accumulation" peasants were legally obliged to "sell" a certain quota of crops (farms being treated singly) at a price that was lower than the price in the free market system would be. At the same time, they had to buy manufactured goods which were overpriced, if they were available at all. Industries using crops could be set up with the surplus product extracted by the state. The low prices of farm products encouraged peasants to leave the overpopulated rural areas for towns where they hoped to get employment. The cheapness of agricultural produce was at the same time intended to improve the Yugoslav position in the export of manufactures. The first post–World War II decade in agriculture can, therefore, be best described as a period of fighting against the peasants and their private initiative. This battle was the more severe because the agricultural policy as conceived by the Communists could not be implemented except by force.

The system of "socialist accumulation" is bound to find itself in a double bind. It will work only until agrarian production falls sharply, resulting in a decrease in the accumulation of capital in agriculture. This imperils the position and development of industries and can, if farm products remain undervalued, result in the collapse of the national economy. At some stage it becomes clear that a different policy, granting peasants more independence, has to be undertaken. Only agriculture with a solid position and a status equal to that of the other sectors of the economy can satisfy the demands of both industry and the town population (Veselinov 1987).

The ill effects of the socialist accumulation policy were felt in Yugoslavia in the early fifties, when statistics revealed a considerable decline in agriculture compared to the prewar period. In 1953 the authorities, troubled by food shortages, permitted the coexistence of state and private sectors on a larger scale. To prevent excessive expansion by diligent entrepreneurs, however, several restrictions were enacted. Peasants were, for example, prohibited from buying machinery and the maximum land area of a farm was reduced by two-thirds. Besides, peasants depended more on the cooperatives; these had effectively become social-sector enterprises and could now dictate the conditions of farming.

From the fifties onwards the state, investing heavily in agriculture, tried to achieve self-sufficiency in food. But all the investments went into the state-run farms. In the sixties, however, the position of private landowners began to change for the better; peasants were, for example, allowed to buy various machines. After 1974, when the private sector received more support from the state, peasants could also enlarge their farms, though only by lease.

CONCLUSION

In the course of the twentieth century, Slovenia turned from an agrarian into an industrial country and is at present undergoing a slow and weary transformation into a postindustrial society. To assess and compare the three periods of twentieth century economic development is a rather delicate task because economic views prevalent in the market economy phase (1900-45) differed vastly from those characteristic of the socialist economy (1945-1991). In the first half of the twentieth century the Slovene economy made relatively slow, but harmonious progress; no oppressive measures were employed and domestic needs as well as potentials were accommodated. The process of industrialization was constantly checked and adjusted on the basis of sound economic logic. A completely different standard prevailed after 1945. The new communist state was to be industrialized as soon as possible; unfortunately only by extortion and the imposition of a fast tempo of industrial expansion was this feasible. At the beginning, favoring heavy and basic industries impeded balanced economic development. The disequilibrium continued even after processing industries, which alone can adequately meet the needs of the people and advance their living standard, were shown more attention. From the mid-70s, industrial and agricultural production stalled; their only means of growth being through improved efficiency.

At this point, the socialist economic system in Slovenia and other socialist countries came upon an insurmountable obstacle. Trouble erupted openly in the 1980s, when foreign loans, which had fed the apparently successful economic projects, became unavailable. Realizing at the end of the eighties that their power was jeopardized by economic failure, the monopolistic political structures threw the doors wide open to private enterprise. But it was already much too late to lessen the severity of the crisis that is still reigning in ex-Yugoslavia.

In conclusion, it should be emphasized that today, for all the reforms and all the freedom Yugoslavia and Slovenia were famous for, the inherited economic structure of Slovenia does not differ much from that of other former eastern bloc countries. Many reforms in the second Yugoslavia, however, facilitated the establishment of republic, that is, national economies, ensuring a comparatively smooth transition for Slovenia to independence, both political and economic.

BIBLIOGRAPHY

Bilandžić, Dušan (1985). *Historija socialističke federativne republike Jugoslavije 1918-1985* (A history of the socialist federal republic of Yugoslavia 1918-1985). Zagreb: Školska knjiga.

Čepič, Zdenko (1992). "Agrarna reforma po drugi svetovni vojni—značaj, učinki, posledice" (The agrarian reform after World War II—its character, effects and consequences). *Prispevki za novejšo zgodovino,* 1-2: 173-90.

Deset let socialistične graditve v Sloveniji (Ten years of socialist construction in Slovenia) (1955). Ljubljana: Predsedstvo glavnega odbora Socialistične zveze delovnega ljudstva Slovenije.

Đurović, Smiljana (1986). *Državna intervencija u industriji Jugoslavije 1918-1941* (The intervention of the state in the industry of Yugoslavia 1918-1941). Beograd: ISI.

Dvajset let graditve naše socialistične domovine 1945-1965 (Twenty years of the construction of our socialist homeland 1945-1965) (1965). Ljubljana: Založniški zavod Življenje in tehnika.

Gestrin, Ferdo and Vasilij Melik (1966). *Slovenska zgodovina od konca 18. stoletja do 1918* (Slovene history from the end of the eighteenth century to 1918). Ljubljana: Državna založba Slovenije.

Gestrin, Ferdo (1969). "Oris gospodarstva na Slovenskem v prvem obdobju kapitalizma (do leta 1918)" (Economy in Slovenia in the first phase of capitalism [to 1918]). *Kronika* 3: 129-138.

Gnjatović, Dragana (1991). *Stari državni dugovi* (The old state debts) 1862-1941. Beograd: Jugoslovenski pregled.

Grafenauer, Bogo (1968). "Privredni razvoj od 1800-1918" (Economic development from 1800 to 1918). *Enciklopedija Jugoslavije,* 7: 353-63. Slovenija, Zagreb: Jugoslovenski leksikografski zavod.

Janša-Zorn, Olga (1964). "Agrarna reforma v Sloveniji med obema vojnama" (The agrarian reform in Slovenia between the two wars). *Zgodovinski časopis:* 173-89.

Kresal, France (1974). "Oris gospodarskega razvoja Slovenije in ekonomski položaj delavstva, 1918-1941" (The economic development of Slovenia and the economic position of the workers 1918-1941). *Delavsko gibanje v Sloveniji 1918-1941* (The Workers Movement in Slovenia 1918-1941): 80-115. Ljubljana: Center za obveščanje in propagando pri RK ZMS.

Kresal, France (1976). *Tekstilna industrija v Sloveniji* (The textile industry in Slovenia). Ljubljana: Borec.

Kržišnik-Bukić, Vera (1988). *Seljaštvo u socializmu 1945-1948* (Peasantry in socialism 1945-1948). Biblioteka "Studije i monografije," 6. Banjaluka: Institut za istoriju u Banjaluci.

Kukoleča M., Stevan (1941). *Industrija Jugoslavije 1918-1939* (Yugoslav industry 1918-1939). Beograd: Balkanska štampa A.D. 13.

Lazarević, Žarko (1987). "Začetki uvajanja telefonije v Ljubljani" (The introduction of telephony in Ljubljana). *Kronika,* 1-2: 97-100.

Lazarević, Žarko (1989). "Analiza kmečkih dolgov v Sloveniji 1918-1941" (The analysis of peasant debts in Slovenia 1918-1941). *Prispevki za novejšo zgodovino* 2: 349-383.

Lazarević, Žarko (1992). "Kmečki dolgovi v Sloveniji 1918-1941" (Peasant debts in Slovenia 1918-1941). Ph.D. diss., University of Ljubljana.

Mirković, Mijo (1950). *Ekonomska struktura Jugoslavije 1918-1941* (The economic structure of Yugoslavia 1918-1941). Zagreb: Nakladni zavod Hrvatske.

Mirković, Mijo (1958). *Ekonomska historija Jugoslavije* (The economic history of Yugoslavia). Zagreb: Ekonomski pregled.

Narodna banka 1884-1934 (The National bank 1884-1934) (1934). Topčider: Zavod za izradu novčanica.

Petranović, Branko (1981). *Istorija Jugoslavije 1918-1978* (A history of Yugoslavia 1918-1978). Beograd: Nolit.

Prinčič, Jože (1992a). *Slovenska industrija v jugoslovanskem primežu 1945-1956* (Slovene industry in the clutches of Yugoslavia 1945-1956). Seidlova zbirka 2. Novo Mesto: Dolenjska založba.

Prinčič, Jože, Maruša Zagradnik, and Marjan Zupančič (1992). *Viri za nacionalizacijo industrijskih podjetij v Sloveniji po 2. svetovni vojni* (Sources for the nationalization of industrial enterprises in Slovenia after World War II). Viri 5. Ljubljana: Arhivsko društvo Slovenije.

Slovenci v desetletju 1918-1928 (The Slovenes in the decade 1918-1928) (1928). Ljubljana: Leonova družba.

Slovenija 1945-1975 (Slovenia 1945-1975) (1975). Ljubljana: Zavod SR Slovenije za statistiko.

Šorn, Jože (1959). "Razvoj industrije v Sloveniji med obema vojnama" (The development of Slovene Industries between the two wars). *Kronika* 1: 10-21.

Šorn, Jože (1979). "Slovensko gospodarstvo med vojnama" (The Slovene economy between the two wars). *Zgodovina Slovencev,* 686-699. Ljubljana: Cankarjeva založba.

Spominski zbornik Slovenije (The memorial miscellany of Slovenia) (1939). Ljubljana: Založba Jubilej.

Tomašević, Jozo (1935). *Finansijska politika Jugoslavije* (The financial policy of Yugoslavia) *1929-1934.* Zagreb.

Tomasevich, Jozo (1955). *Peasants, Politics, and Economic Change in Yugoslavia.* Stanford: Stanford University Press.

Trideset let socialistične Jugoslavije 1945-1975 (Thirty years of socialist Yugoslavia 1945-1975) (1975). Beograd: Monos.

Veselinov, Dragan (1987). *Sumrak seljaštva* (The twilight of the peasantry). Beograd: Ekonomika.

Vučković, Miloš (1976). "Uticaj svetske privredne krize 1929-1932 na privredu stare Jugoslavije" (The effects of the world economic crisis 1929-1932 on the economy of Yugoslavia). *Svetska ekonomska kriza 1929-1934 godine i njen odraz u zemljama jugoistočne Evrope* (The world economic crisis 1929-34 and its expression in south-eastern Europe), 197-227. Beograd: SANU, Balkanološki institut.

Vučo, Nikola (1968). *Agrarna kriza u Jugoslaviji 1930-34* (The agrarian crisis in Yugoslavia 1930-1934). Beograd: Prosveta.

4

Culture, Politics, and Slovene Identity

Ervin Dolenc

Since Slovenes spent more than a thousand years as part of some larger state unit, their history is mostly the history of their culture. Just as the political history of the states Slovenes lived in typifies *Mitteleuropa,* the cultural development of Slovenes does not differ much from the contemporaneous development of central Europe.

The education of Slovenes was closely connected to the Catholic Church from the early Middle Ages until almost the twentieth century. The first educational records in Slovene can be traced to about the year 1000. The first schools in Slovene ethnic territory were established in the seats of dioceses and monasteries, and in individual larger parishes in the twelfth and thirteenth centuries. From the Middle Ages on, Slovenes undertook university studies mostly in neighboring Italy and in Vienna.

The Protestantism of the sixteenth century brought essential progress. The Protestant demand that everyone recognize and comprehend the word of God made it possible for Slovenes to get their first Slovene elementary schools. Even more important, however, were two rank schools in Ljubljana and Celovec/Klagenfurt—five-class grammar schools that educated and prepared pupils for direct matriculation to university and approximately corresponded to the program of Protestant grammar schools in Germany. In the middle of the sixteenth century, the first books were printed in Slovene, satisfying elementary pedagogical and Protestant religious needs.

After the victory of the Catholic Counter-Reformation in the beginning of the seventeenth century, Jesuit grammar schools took over Latin lessons from the

Protestants in Ljubljana, Celovec/Klagenfurt, Gorizia, and Trieste. Slovene elementary schools, however, were extinguished together with the Lutheran church. Only a few students could attend elementary lessons, taught in high German, the language of the ruler and aristocracy, in parish, municipal, and especially private schools with very different academic standards. With time, Jesuit grammar schools incorporated superior studies (*studia superiora*), bringing elements of university knowledge in philosophy, theology, and church law to the Slovene ethnic territory. However, they never developed into a real university. In the middle of the seventeenth century, after the banishment of Protestants, printing works were gradually renovated. Individual intellectuals, especially among the aristocracy, began to take an interest in the past and present of their countries. Record makers of such knowledge, including Martin Baučer (1595-1668), Janez Ludvik Schoenleben (1618-81), Janez Vajkard Valvasor (1641-93), and others, left us important and still usable books on the history of the Slovene territories. In the first quarter of the eighteenth century the scientific association Academia Operosorum Labacensium was active in Ljubljana. Its members, about 40 lawyers, theologians and medical students from Carniola and the neighboring provinces, opened the first public library in the Slovene ethnic territory.

The opportunities for education remained almost unchanged in the Slovene ethnic territory until the reforms of enlightened absolutists Maria Theresa and Joseph II. The Order of the Jesuits was abolished in 1773, and their schools were taken over by the Austrian state. The next year, general and compulsory elementary education, partly in Slovene and partly in German, was introduced by statute. At grammar schools and *lycea* (the former *studia superiora*) German was used along with Latin; it was valued as a more developed and more usable language in the whole empire. Slovene was pushed out into countryside schools, the so-called *trivialke,* from which it was impossible to enroll even in secondary school. Students from the middle class *hauptschule* or *realschule* in bigger towns could go on to more advanced studies.

The second half of the eighteenth century, filled with developments in the natural sciences, the philosophy of the Enlightenment, and administrative needs for secular intellectuals, brought about the beginnings of the Slovene national self-consciousness and renaissance as well. In the sense that they had a national consciousness, Slovene "renaissance men" can be said to be the first Slovene intellectuals. In the last third of the eighteenth century they began systematically researching their ethnic hinterland, from the linguistic and historical aspects. Consciousness of the ethnic unity of Slovenes (who lived in seven different nationally and linguistically mixed provinces of the Habsburg monarchy), definitely asserted itself at the end of the eighteenth century and beginning of the nineteenth century.

Because of the dangerous impacts of the French Revolution, the nationalized educational system, which Theresian reforms trusted to laical state control, was, with the Elementary School Act of 1805, very quickly returned to the control of the Catholic Church.

In the years 1809-13 most of the territory settled by Slovenes was under French occupation. The French established the "Illyrian provinces" spanning three Slovene provinces (Istria, Carniola, and Carinthia), Dalmatia, and parts of civil and military Croatia. In the Illyrian provinces, with their seat in Ljubljana, elementary schools—previously of three different types—were unified. Slovene was introduced in the four-class elementary schools (*écoles primaires*), which were to be in every commune. The mother tongue was to be the basis of all education, not just the means for a more effective religious upbringing. The same approach was tried in secondary schools as well: in grammar schools and *lycea*.

In addition to advancing the Slovene language against German and French liberal legislation, Slovene intellectuals asserted their national identity by attempting to establish a university in Ljubljana. The university had a more direct political intention, however—to prevent young intellectuals from attending school in Austria (Ciperle and Vovko, 1987).

The memory of four years under the French remained strong among Slovene intellectuals and bearers of the nationalist standard for a long time. The short-lived community with the linguistically very close Croats in the Illyrian provinces gave rise to the Illyrian movement, which aimed at cultural rapprochement between the two peoples. However, Illyrianism provoked objections by its rejection of Slovene cultural language, whose value had just been appreciated. There is no doubt that this first Yugoslavism was subverted by the already strongly developed Slovene consciousness, and by the prevailing romantic search for the original ethnic culture of every nation.

After Napoleon's defeat and the restoration of Austria, the educational and administrative system returned to their previous shape. Fear of growing revolutionary and antifeudal movements throughout Europe made the control of the Church and state over spiritual life even stronger. A great majority of lay intellectuals were in some way tied to the state administration and therefore dependent on the ruling regime. The Austrian government, however, was opposed to new ideas, and consequently also to nationalism, both Slovene and German. Nevertheless, the German cultural foundations of the state were emphasized.

Advocates of national awakening tried pragmatically to take advantage of this dual approach by using Slovene to communicate with the masses. In 1843, following several short-lived attempts to publish a newspaper in Slovene, dating back to 1797, a Slovene newspaper, *Novice* (News), began regular publication. Slovene literature got its first works of importance, especially the poetry of Francè Prešeren. Slavic linguistics and cultural studies, connected with the national movement, reached a high level with the works of Jernej Kopitar, Matija Čop and Fran Miklošič. Growing interest in history and natural science was responsible for the establishment of the Provincial Museum for Carniola (1831), the Museum Association (1839), Natural Sciences Museums in Trieste (1825) and Celovec/Klagenfurt (1844), and Historical Associations for Carniola, Styria and Carinthia (1843). Those institutions began to edit expert reviews. The first Slovene-language expert literature was produced in the form of agricultural and health manuals. Throughout this period, Slovene national consciousness grew stronger relative to provincial consciousness, until it definitely prevailed in the 1860s.

The distinctly conservative regime of the post-Napoleon European order was overturned in the revolutionary year 1848. Slovenes took advantage of the short-lived political opening not only for antifeudal demands, but also for the first publicly and clearly stated national-political demand for uniting the Austrian provinces in which Slovenes lived (Carniola, Gorizia district, Trieste, northern part of Istria, southern parts of Styria and Carniola, as well as Slovenes in Venetia and Hungary) into a unique administrative unit within the monarchy. The program of *Zedinjena Slovenija* (United Slovenia) received only partial support from the conservative wing of the Slovene national movement. The supporters of the program were Slovene liberal intelligentsia, students and most Slovene intellectuals, living in the capital, in Vienna.

In the proposed administrative unit, shaped by following the ethnic border, with its own parliament and administration, Slovenes would use their own language in offices and schools, and a Slovene university would be established. This new administrative unit with the name "Slovenija" was to establish ties with Croats and Serbs within the monarchy. With the suppression of the revolutionary movement in Vienna and the gradual restoration of absolutism, Slovene demands and hopes failed, unlike much stronger national movements in Italy and Germany (*Zgodovina Slovencev* 1979).

In 1848 the draft of a state elementary schooling reform had been prepared in Austria, providing universal education, establishing the mother tongue as a teaching language, and separating school from the Church. The reform's implementation, however, was prevented by the restoration of absolutism. Church control became even stronger with a concordat with the Vatican in 1855. Only grammar schools were reformed, and secondary schools with more practical subjects, the so-called *realke,* were introduced. General two-year philosophical studies were transferred from universities and *lycea* to grammar schools, where schooling was extended to eight years. Natural sciences subjects and German benefited at the expense of Latin. This reform abolished *lycea* in Ljubljana, Celovec/Klagenfurt, and Gorizia. Of superior studies in Slovenia only theology at Ljubljana, Celovec/Klagenfurt, Maribor, and Gorizia remained, resulting in increased numbers of priests in subsequent generations, the majority of peasant sons being unable to afford studies at universities far away from home.

After the defeat in the war with France and the unification of Italy, the absolutist Austrian regime was forced, in 1860, to allow formation of a parliament and to grant certain forms of autonomy to provinces through provincial assemblies. Among Slovenes, political groups began to emerge: the Catholics came together around the review *Zgodnja danica* (Early morning star) and its editor, poet and religious writer Luka Jeran. The center conservatives associated with *Novice* (Janez Bleiweis, Lovro Toman, and Etbin Costa) remained the strongest group for a long time, with its leadership of national organizers and politicians. The liberal group rallied around the poet, writer, and critic Fran Levstik. In the sixties the national movement became very prominent in cultural associations—called *čitalnice* (a sort of reading room)—where entirely political activity was not allowed. As the culture was subjected more to national enthusiasm, it became indirectly associated with politics. With the same intention as its Czech model—national defense against German associations—a scouting and sport society *Južni Sokol* (South Falcon) was founded in 1863. *Slovenska matica* (Slovenian Literary Society), formed in 1864, provided a forum for Slovene serious belletristic and scientific literature, and *Dramatično društvo* (Dramatic Association), founded in 1866, for theater. Ljubljana, administrative center of Carniola, with a predominantly Slovene population (95 percent), was developing into a national center as well, from which intensive association activities were spreading. By organizing open air camps (1868-71), liberals took over the initiative in the Slovene national-political movement.

After repeated defeat in the war with Prussia and Italy in 1866, Austria had to withdraw from the German Alliance and Venetia. Defeat weakened the empire's inner stability as well, and the question of disintegration emerged. At the expense of an agreement with the Hungarians and the establishment of the Dual Monarchy, the ever-stronger German liberal bourgeoisie wrested the majority in the parliament and government from the aristocracy. Liberal legislation, referring to general rights of citizens, state representation, and judicial and executive authority, began to be introduced. In the framework of the new legislation, aimed against the concordat to a great extent, a school reform began. The state was given direct control over elementary and secondary schools; the Church was left with only religious instruction. In spite of the fact that the reform neither abolished religion lessons nor excluded the clergy from school councils, it meant quite a loss for the Church. The concordat stipulations regarding Church rights were limited also by the Marriage Law Act and the Interconfessional Act. All three "atheist acts" were condemned by the Pope, who began the so-called *kulturkampf* (cultural struggle) within the monarchy. Elections to provincial assemblies in 1867 brought about the first Slovene political victory. Slovenes appeared united at the elections and won a majority in the Carniolan provincial assembly. From then on, despite the declared equality of rights of all nations and languages, Slovene had to make its way into representative state bodies, offices, law courts and schools, especially at the secondary level, gradually and forcibly. The Church's rights were also limited by a special Elementary School Act of 1869, which, at last, practically established universal education and radically diminished illiteracy in subsequent generations (Melik 1970).

Of course, the struggle for and against the 1855 concordat, symbolizing absolutism and the reaction against bourgeois revolutions, could not be ignored by Slovenes who were fighting for their rights in those years. Liberal *mladoslovenci* (young Slovenes) wanted to persuade the Catholic wing that nationality was in greater danger than Catholicism. They were even prepared to give up their principled liberal position and publicly declare themselves Catholics. However, the great *kulturkampf* between liberalism and Catholicism in the monarchy, as well as the growing organization of the conservative Catholic wing pressed upon Slovenes and encouraged extremism. The powerful role of the clergy in organizing the Slovene national and political movement gave extreme political Catholicism the power to be more and more persistent in its demand that the movement define its religious-political stream. The Slovene liberals opposed the explicitly German liberal government on principle, demanding a policy of abstention from Slovene delegates along the same lines as that followed by the Czechs. The ultimate result was political disunion in the national movement at the elections to the federal parliament in 1873 and the beginning of a real *kulturkampf* in Slovenia itself. Catholic and conservative groups were united against liberals (Melik 1970; *Zgodovina Slovencev* 1979).

Due to the split among Slovene political groups, Slovenes lost ground numerically in relation to Germans in the federal parliament and provincial assemblies. Those failures and the weakness of the liberal wing facilitated renewed agreement after three years. The period of *slogaštvo* (a sort of concord) in national affairs lasted from the end of 1876 until the nineties. In the federal parliament and provincial assemblies, Slovene delegates appeared more or less united under conservative Catholic cover.

In other fields, especially in cultural life, the contrasts between factions became sharper and sharper. Due to the general renaissance of the Catholic Church under Pope Leon XIII (1878-1903), a new bishop in Ljubljana, Jakob Missia, and especially Catholic neoscholastic ideologist Anton Mahnič, a real Catholic offensive against liberalism and for renewed Christianization of Slovene society began in the mid-eighties. Under the influence of the Second Austrian Catholic Assembly, *Katoliško politično društvo* (Catholic Political Association) was founded in Carniola in 1890. It soon changed its name to *Katoliška narodna stranka* (Catholic National Party) and in 1905 to *Slovenska ljudska stranka* (Slovene People's Party [SPP]). The first Catholic assembly in Ljubljana in 1892 was a real turning point in the Slovene Catholic movement. Education and instruction, science, art, information media, social and political work according to Catholic principles were the demands of the meeting; henceforth, cooperation of all Slovenes was to be possible only on a Catholic basis (Pirc 1986).

In the eighties and nineties, the press and associations mainly divided into two conflicting camps. The Catholic side was more aggressive and mostly newly organized. They left most of the old *čitalnice* and the Južni Sokol organization to the liberals. Their common activities continued only in rare, narrowly focused expert associations. The liberals' answer to the Catholic organization in Carniola was the political *Slovensko društvo* (Slovene Association), founded in 1891, which was renamed *Narodna stranka* (National Party) three years later, and then *Narodno-napredna stranka* (National-Progressive Party). At the turn of the century the liberal party split in the Gorizia district, and in 1906 in Styria, too. Due to the predominance of German and Italian political parties, Slovenes in Trieste, Istria, and Carinthia cooperated politically until the collapse of the monarchy. Owing to nationalist tendencies, in the nineties Austrian social democracy also reorganized according to nationalities. In 1896, the *Jugoslovanska socialno demokratska stranka* (Yugoslav Social Democratic Party) was founded. It was meant to include Croats as well; however, it remained mostly Slovene. With a relatively weak electoral base, social democracy remained just a marginal political force until the collapse of the monarchy.

Elections to the Carniolan provincial assembly in 1895 represented a definite political separation between Catholics and liberals in the Slovene ethnic territory, as the Church openly engaged in the election campaign. Because of the total victory of the Catholic Party in the peasant curia, the liberals made an agreement with Carniolan Germans and maintained a Slovene-German liberal coalition in the Carniolan provincial assembly for the next 12 years (1896-1908). That was the crowning moment of principled weakness of the Slovene liberals.

Mostly thanks to Catholic activism, division deepened and spread from politics into culture, where it had actually begun with Mahnič in the eighties. After Anton Mahnič left for the island Krk to take the post of bishop, ideological leadership of the Catholic wing was taken over by his pupil, Aleš Ušeničnik. In 1896 Ušeničnik began a dispute with the Teachers' Association, criticizing it as unfaithful to the idea of "a national school on a religious basis." He charged the teachers with more or less consciously promoting the liberal spirit and leading the Slovene educational system astray, on the path of "pure humanity." The polemics deepened divisions, especially among teachers; until World War I, teachers remained the most bitter ideological opponents of radical Catholicism in the countryside.

The struggle over the schools was the focus of public attention. The Church had kept education and teachers within its purview for centuries. For teachers, buoyed by the great progress of pedagogy and the liberalization of education, the issues were, on the one hand, attaining professional independence from Church control, and on the other, control over the minds of the young, and, consequently, the future (Pirc 1986).

As universal and equal suffrage were finally introduced in 1907, the SPP, after ten years of widespread organizational work in the Slovene countryside, won an absolute majority in the 1908 elections to the Carniolan provincial assembly. They ruled alone until 1918. Unlimited Catholic rule in Carniola meant that the interests of the party more and more prevailed to the detriment of general Slovene benefit. The SPP took advantage of all the means at its disposal as the ruling party. Liberal teachers were exposed to persecution. In ten years of Catholic rule in Carniola, many teachers seemingly changed their political persuasion or left their profession.

The main principle of the Catholic movement in Slovenia was, according to its ideologist Ušeničnik, to put the leading role of Catholic principles in cultural strivings into effect at any price. Along with radicalism of principles he demanded also radicalism of organization—putting Catholics' social, political, and cultural activities on an uncompromising confessional, that is, Catholic, basis. In 1899 Catholic teachers resigned from the Slovene Teachers' Association and established the *Slomšek* union a year later. Catholic politically-oriented members left Sokol and founded their own supporting units in 1906. In 1907 a split occurred in the Society of St. Cyril and Methodius, which maintained private kindergartens and elementary schools in nationally endangered territories; in three years a Catholic National Guard appeared. The Leon Society, founded in 1896, was reorganized ten years later as the Catholic Science Association, in competition with the Slovenian Literary Society. Catholic intellectuals, however, resigned from the Society only in 1914.

The *kulturkampf* in Slovene ethnic territory, therefore, meant something more than the *kulturkampf* in Austria, Germany, and Switzerland in the seventies. It was not only a struggle against the Catholic Church, but a struggle for the leading place in culture. The spiritual division and *kulturkampf* before the First World War in the Slovene ethnic territory brought, at first, renewal and competition into cultural life. To a degree, competition improved the quality of cultural activities. In final perspective, however, competition led neither to a mature and constructive pluralism of ideas nor to political forms. Though competition might have been necessary at a certain point or maybe even essential, with time, especially after 1908, it began to impede the self-assertion of Slovenes in the mostly German monarchy (Pirc 1986).

Until the World War, Slovene science and art met European standards, though not in all branches and areas. Owing to low levels of industrial development and national assertion, the humanities had the advantage over the natural sciences; literature and painting predominated among the arts. The Slovene language completely made its way into elementary schools in Carniola, Gorizia district, and Trieste, was less successful in Styria and fared most poorly in Carinthia, where the German pressure was strongest. The situation was similar with Slovene in secondary schools. Only a private Catholic grammar school near Ljubljana was entirely Slovene; six secondary schools were Protestant; seven, however, were German. In state offices, the higher the office, the smaller the possibility for Slovene to assert itself. The question of a Slovene university in Ljubljana or Trieste appeared repeatedly from 1848 on as a political issue parallel to United Slovenia, but without success, thanks precisely to its political significance. However, a plan for the education of Slovene students at universities abroad did succeed. When the University of Ljubljana was founded in 1919, educated Slovene scientists took a substantial majority of professorships (Zwitter 1969).

Because, to a great extent, cultural workers themselves were the bearers of Slovene political tendencies before the foundation of Slovene political parties, we can talk about relations between culture and politics more definitely only when a Slovene professional political stratum emerged.

In the nineties a younger Christian social movement in the Catholic Party, personified in Janez Evangelist Krek, turned its organizational propaganda work to the widest, but therefore relatively uneducated and poor, strata of the Slovene population. The intelligentsia remained neutral, remembering the sharp, Catholic exclusivist attacks of Anton Mahnič on Slovene literati. Those who were university educated especially resisted the narrow Catholic criteria of Church ideologists. The Catholic party achieved a special anti-intellectual reputation during its rule in Carniola. We have mentioned the pressure it put on liberal teachers. It made efforts to create a Slovene university impossible, and it contributed a great deal to the decline of Slovene theater in Ljubljana.

Toward the end of the century, the liberal party, with its elitism, agitation against parishes, antidemocratic sentiment, lack of principles, and vexation of social democrats, was losing its connection with the Slovene masses and was going through an inner crisis. Therefore, younger Slovene intellectuals began to opt for social democracy. A greater number of students in Vienna, Graz and Prague, however, decided on independent political action. From 1905 on, national radicals began establishing economic cooperatives in the countryside under the slogan "From the nation for the nation!" They set up their party organizations there as well. However, after the victory of political Catholicism in Carniola, they reconciled themselves with the liberals, because of the external danger. The leader of the radicals, Gregor Žerjav, became a secretary of their common party.

In the decade before the First World War an important group of young non-Marxist intellectuals joined the Social Democratic Party. Under the influence of the Czech philosopher, Tomáš Masaryk, they were enthusiastic about organizational work among the lower strata of the population. Within the political party, however, they remained in opposition to the rigid Austro-Marxist leadership, especially on the national question. Like the liberals, the Austro-Marxists advocated a culturally unitary Yugoslavism.

The Slovene question in the Habsburg monarchy was, from the very beginning, primarily a cultural-linguistic question. It was formulated this way by the first Slovene cultural workers and remained in the same form when it was taken over by professional politicians. But when the politicians entered the scene, especially after the idea of a Yugoslav solution to the Slovene question had been raised, the majority of cultural workers and politicians parted ways. Politicians simplified their work, equating the political solution with a cultural one. At the end of World War I, after the collapse of the Habsburg empire and the establishment of a new "national" state, the Slovene cultural-linguistic question remained unsolved, to the great surprise of the majority.

After the formation of the first Yugoslavia, Carniola and the southern part of Styria, along with a very small part of Carinthia and part of the former section of Hungary annexed in 1919 were the only Slovene-inhabited Austrian provinces that came into the new state. The German minority in these territories was quickly pushed to the margin of events and played no further role in the main cultural-political struggles.

Transition to a new state community caused culture shock among Slovenes. Slovenes, with about 90 percent literacy, came into a community where the average literacy was only approximately 40 percent. Along with the cultural struggle inherited from the past, the fundamental issue of Slovene cultural politics became the relation to Slovenism and Yugoslavism.

Although Slovenes lost a third of their already small national territory, and were cut off from the sea and Trieste, their economic center, they benefited in other ways. A new great southern market brought prosperity to Slovene industry in the first decade after the war and the national state gathered most of its intellectuals, who had been scattered all over the empire, especially in Vienna. In the first years most schools were completely Slovenized. The Slovene language at last entered secondary schools, in which classes had been conducted mostly in German.

In the field of culture the laws of the old states in this territory remained in force throughout parliamentary rule (1919-1929), due to the lasting political crisis. The equalization of legislation throughout the country that occurred under the royal dictatorship meant a decrease of quality for Slovenia, because of low levels of education in the southern parts of the state.

Most significant, however, is the establishment of the University of Ljubljana in 1919. Although it had only five faculties, it enabled systematic, universal, and continual Slovene science. In addition to the university, the new state enabled Slovenes to have two state professional theaters (Ljubljana and Maribor), a state academy of music with a theater school and, at the end of the thirties, an Academy of Sciences and Arts and a university library. The National Gallery was maintained on the private and local level. Fine artists, however, were still getting their education abroad or in Zagreb (Croatia).

The unification of the Southern Slavs—though incomplete—and the centralist Vidovdan Constitution meant triumph for Slovene liberals. Their strivings for ethnic and, from this time on, cultural fusion with the other Yugoslavs aimed toward creating a united, firm polity that would finally stop the danger from the north (Germans) and west (Italians). It now resulted in concrete political advantages. The centralist state order, designed to advance this fusion, also made the predominance of political Catholicism impossible. The new state, in which Catholics became a confessional minority, had its center in its Orthodox part. Centralist regulation would thus weaken the extremely strong Catholic Church in Slovenia, which tenaciously resisted reduction of its influence and laicization of public life.

In the Catholic party, views on this question were confused in the first two years of the new state. The pro-Austrian or at least pro-Habsburg policy of the Slovene People's Party until the change of its leadership in 1917, favoring trialism, dictated a pronounced Yugoslav orientation in the new circumstances. Only after elections to the constituent assembly, with proposed constitutional changes emerging in spring 1921, did the latent autonomist and federalist

political orientation of the party get its full value. In opposition to the orthodox majority and the ruler, and with the presumption of majority electoral support in Slovenia, the Catholic party would secure an advantage in the
religious-cultural struggle as well. The distinctiveness of Slovene culture and
language from Serbo-Croat Yugoslavia justified administrative-political
autonomy, consequently cultural autonomy.

The third Slovene political group, espousing social democracy, went
through great ideological and organizational stresses in the first five years after
the overthrow of the Habsburg empire. The political power of its remnants in
the Socialist Party of Yugoslavia diminished after the consolidation of the new
state. The socialists, together with the liberals, advocated as great a separation
of the Church from the state as possible and the prohibition of Church intervention in politics. During the constitutional debate in spring 1921, social
democrats became more and more autonomist—in accordance with Slovene
public opinion. After the autonomist circle resigned from the party, the party
turned back to the concept of a centralized and unitary state as a better basis
for class struggle. Their position came very close to the liberals' attitude
about the cultural struggle. However, they usually did not take part in cultural
battles, because they considered them the concerns of the bourgeoisie.

The linguistically conditioned question of cultural policy concerned Slovene
literati more than the politicians. Those in the arts, social sciences and humanities, as well as publicists, who were earlier more or less united bearers of the
Slovene national movement against German cultural pressure, found themselves facing a dilemma in the new national state. The political dilemma—how
to enter Yugoslavia and yet uphold Slovene identity and autonomy—in its ori-
gin and nature primarily political, involved great cultural consequences.
Namely, most Slovene authors had rejected the Yugoslav linguistic integral-
ism of the old and new Illyrian movement even before the First World War.

The question of Slovene cultural identity had been addressed earlier by
about 30 eminent Slovene intellectuals, who assembled as a temporary National
Council for Slovenia, in the time between the decay of Austro-Hungary and the
establishment of the first Yugoslavia in November 1918. After two days of discussion a resolution was drafted, demanding Slovene cultural autonomy in the
new state. It was signed by 45 important culture creators of all ideologies.
Liberal politicians, however, prevented its publication. In the next four days,
the liberals collected 44 signatures on the Declaration of Mental Workers,
which denied the main contents of the resolution and advocated unconditional
political and cultural integration with Serbs and Croats as quickly as possible.
In this the democratic party demonstrated its exceptional power among Slovene
intellectuals, for 17 of them signed both, mutually contradictory, documents.

Much of the confusion among Slovene intellectuals about the linguistic question in the first years of the new state was due to the fact that, thanks to Catholic radicalism, most of them were attached to the national liberal political group. The liberals, however, tried to silence any autonomous movement, even cultural. The severely centralist and monarchist orientation of the Democratic Party (liberals) produced growing disenchantment among Slovene intellectuals, especially after they realized that Belgrade's state administration was worse than Austria's. Having no other real alternative, and because the accomplishment of self-determination for most Slovenes in the national state indicated that their national-political work was done, more and more intellectuals were withdrawing from direct political activities and dedicating themselves to their professions. Most Slovene intellectuals stated their autonomist standpoint again in the constitutional debate in spring 1921. "The Autonomist Declaration of Slovene Cultural Workers" was signed by 43 intellectuals, among them 10 university professors and quite a few with liberal views, who thus indicated their separation from Slovene liberal politicians. The agitation and debate lasted for some years and made it clear that the great majority of Slovenes preferred to keep their national individuality. The majority sentiment was confirmed by the words and actions of the Slovenian Literary Society, Association of Slovene Belletrists, and most professors of the University of Ljubljana. In parliamentary elections in 1923 the autonomist policy of the Slovene People's Party brought it 21 out of 26 Slovene mandates (Dolenc 1992).

In 1922 and 1923, liberal and pro-Yugoslav-oriented Slovene intellectuals, cooperating with a Zagreb review, *Nova Evropa* (New Europe), rejected the possibility of a quick fusion of Slovene culture into Yugoslav culture. They foresaw at the utmost the possibility of gradual, natural unification in a remote future (Nećak 1992). A divergence between culture and politics was also seen in the break-up of the Social Democrats, especially the exit of the former followers of Masaryk, mostly because of the rigid unitarist national policy of the party (Erjavec 1958). Two years later, however, the Communists, who split off from the Social Democratic Party in 1920, changed their centralist-unitarist view of the national question. The influence of Moscow can be seen on this decision as well (Perović 1990).

The Catholic Party began gradually to get rid of its anti-intellectual reputation after 1914, when the editorship of the Catholic art review *Dom in svet* (Home and the world) was taken over by Izidor Cankar. He broadened the narrow standpoint of Mahnič and included general aesthetic criteria in his evaluation of Slovene art. The new generation, which expressed itself in the review in those years raised the esteem of intellectuals for Catholic ideology. In spite of the Church's efforts to maintain its influence on Slovene spiritual life, especially on the educational system, the new generation of intellectuals of the beginning of the twenties was relatively open to new ideas, modern art, democracy, and Slovene cultural tradition.

The Church itself was adjusting to new times as well. In spring 1922, the conference of archdeacons and deans of the Ljubljana diocese allowed, from the "standpoint of priests referring to art movements," a certain autonomy for art and humanist science. The minor aggressions of Catholicism in those years were probably a result of uncertainty in the new, predominantly Orthodox state. Irrespective of that, right after the formation of Yugoslavia, Cankar felt that he had carried out his task; in 1919 he left the leadership of the party. Some years later he left the priesthood, dedicated himself to art history, and got married. The Catholic youth movement, formed around the reviews *Križ na gori* (Cross on the mountain) and *Križ* (Cross) represents a similar deviation from politics in the middle of the decade. A reverse process of politicization and profounder divergences was experienced by the Catholic group after the imposition of royal dictatorship in the thirties.

With essentially changed political and economic conditions—dictatorship and economic crisis—the second half of the first Yugoslav state was quite different in intellectual life as well. Political parties were forbidden. Ideological-political struggles moved into journalism. The daily press presented unchanged the views of old political groups on current political questions. Economic crisis and political developments in western Europe led to growing politicization of broad strata in Slovenia as well. This political pressure was transformed by politicians into populism and radicalism, which promised quick solutions. As in western Europe, extreme left and right-wing positions were gaining more and more popularity. Demagogy, radicalism, and the lack of principles of mainstream political circles forced intellectually more demanding strata into independent political action. They founded a series of new "cultural" reviews, behind which critical political concepts hid.

The aggressive Serbian unitarist regime, joined by some Slovene liberal politicians in 1931, challenged liberal intellectuals. With a demand for preservation of Slovene cultural specificity a crisis erupted at an old liberal art review, *Ljubljanski zvon* (Ljubljana bell) and liberals established their own journal—*Sodobnost* (Contemporaneity)—in 1933. A similarly liberal and Slovene, but even more politically engaged, faction founded *Slovenija* (Slovenia) in 1932. Due to the cooperation of Catholic politicians with the regime, conflict over social policy questions in the Church grew and was addressed in a papal encyclical in 1931. Christian socialists separated from the Catholic party, and were joined by Catholic intellectuals of formerly non-political Christian youth movements. In 1932 they issued the review *Beseda o sodobnih vprašanjih* (A word on contemporary questions). Communists reached into the field of culture with the review *Književnost* (Literature) in the same year. After it was banned, they wrote for *Sodobnost* (Prunk 1992).

In the first half of the 1930s, Slovene liberal policy was nearly completely compromised and had very little electoral and intellectual support left. As Slovene liberals in the Belgrade government were replaced by Slovene Catholics in 1935, even greater radicalism became possible for them. Italian fascism put pressure on the numerically strong Slovene minority in Italy, and German nazism, after annexation (*anschluss*) of Austria in 1938, reached the Slovene minority there. These movements represented dangerous national enemies for all Slovene political forces. However, Vatican policy, as outlined in the 1937 encyclical Divini redemptoris, dictated an explicitly anticommunist and undemocratic orientation. A radical struggle for re-Catholicization of Slovene society, following the example of Anton Mahnič from the previous century, was revived, but this time a special emphasis was placed on the role of intellectuals in this struggle. To organize an intellectual stratum, in the framework of Catholic Action—an organization fighting for re-catholicization among laity—special groups were founded for students, who, however, were outstanding for their juvenile enthusiasm and devotion to authorities. The final split among Slovene Catholic intellectuals was caused by the Spanish civil war (1936-39). The Slovene Catholic leadership's endorsement of Franco, who was clearly supported by fascist Italy, Germany, and, through the Spanish Catholic Church, also the Vatican, brought about a crisis at *Dom in svet* in 1937. In the next year, a new review, *Dejanje* (Action), was founded by writer Edvard Kocbek in opposition to the ruling leadership. The Communists, with their policy of making the Popular Front a meeting place for those who were not satisfied with the existing policy, increasingly came to represent an important political alternative in the Slovene part of the state.

After the German, Italian, and Hungarian occupation in April 1941, the old political groups in Slovenia found themselves without any real leaders. In organizing the resistance they were overtaken by the communists, who, in the coalition organization *Osvobodilna fronta* (Liberation Front), gathered also the majority of groups that had seceded from the old political parties. This resoluteness, the strong pressure of occupation authorities on Slovene intellectuals as bearers of national consciousness, and later on also the collaboration of some older politicians with the occupiers on the basis of anticommunism, contributed greatly to the decision by a large part of the Slovene intelligentsia to cooperate with the Liberation Front. The Front was joined also by some anticommunists for whom the liberation element was more important than the fact that, with time, Communists had uncontested leadership in the organization.

Undoubtedly there were many more intellectuals of liberal than Catholic persuasion in the Liberation Front. Slovene Catholics were represented by Christian socialists and intellectuals from Kocbek's circle. However, the predominant part of the clergy, especially from the diocese of Ljubljana, supported the activity of occupation forces (Godeša 1993).

In spite of the presence of numerous "fellow travelers" in the victorious Liberation Front (LF), the Communist Party of Slovenia (CPS) began to implement its "revolutionary" system of authority even before the end of the war. To direct and control cultural creations, a Commission for Agitation and Propaganda, called Agitprop, was formed, which after the war was structured hierarchically, from the local level through the whole chain of administrative authorities, to the very political summit of four or five people, who comprised the political bureau of the Communist Party of Yugoslavia (CPY). In the first two postwar years, real and potential opponents of the new authority were incapacitated and a state administrative and political apparatus was restored, making untroubled implementation of the new policies possible. Due to the predominance of the Communists, liberals and Catholics in the LF had to give up their ambitions for postwar political and organizational independence in the middle of the war (1943). The majority of Catholic politicians and intellectuals, including 260 priests, having actively opposed the LF during the war, emigrated in spring 1945 to the West; later on an important center of Slovene political emigration developed in Argentina. Schools were nationalized at once, and by 1952, religion lessons were completely banned. Ecclesiastical secondary schools (theological seminaries) and the theological faculty, which was removed from the University of Ljubljana, lost their right to be public. Diplomatic conflict between Yugoslavia and the Vatican in the beginning of the fifties was used for a final settling of accounts with the last ideological influences of Christian socialists and Edvard Kocbek as well. The Catholic Church in Slovenia was considered the greatest potential enemy of the state until the very end of Communist rule; consequently it was carefully watched.

The new authority eliminated remnants of liberal policy and terrorized intellectuals with show trials (for example, the Nagode trial in 1947). After political stabilization, deep social alterations in the fields of economics and culture were to be brought about by the Five-Year Plan of National Economic Development of Yugoslavia in the years 1947-51. Educational system reorganization, which lowered the standard already achieved in Slovenia, was based on the increased need for technically educated experts. In cultural creation the *Petletka* (Five-Year Plan) brought about a stronger ideological tilt toward the Soviet Union. In art only socialist realism was allowed and propaganda was directed against "decadent" Western art. Control over the university was intensified.

The conflict of the Communist Party of Yugoslavia (CPY) with Stalin in 1948 altered this trend. After a year's delay, cultural change was seen. At first contemporary, politically relevant Soviet authors were not translated any more, only older, generally acknowledged authors of both European cultural poles. At the end of 1949 the door was slightly opened to American film and popular music. Greater changes in the field of culture were not made until 1952. The Third Congress of the Union of Writers of Yugoslavia in Ljubljana, in October 1952, spearheaded by the report of Miroslav Krleža, a Croatian left-wing writer who had quarreled with Yugoslav defenders of rigid socialist realism even before the war, officially abandoned socialist realism and instituted decentralization in political dictation of cultural creation, which meant a certain degree of loosening, too. The most significant event of the period was the Sixth Congress of the CPY in 1952, which changed the name of the Party to the League of Communists of Yugoslavia (LCY) and formally altered it from the only political party in the country to a movement. Consequently, Communists also abolished all direct control bodies, like the Agitprop. The whole society was already so infused with the new spirit, it was said, that it would be possible to direct and control society less brutally (Gabrič 1991).

Owing to resistance to military and economic pressure from the Soviet Union, along with the simultaneous external political opening toward the West, a shift could be felt in culture. At the beginning of the fifties, poetry, prose, theater, and film began to drop their propagandistic political function and turn gradually to intimacy and experiment. Among young intellectuals, who had grown up after the war, the impact of existentialism was felt, especially in the review *Beseda* (Word) in the years 1951-1957. Satirical reviews with very gentle political humor were allowed. Critical intellectuals among Communists got their own review *Naši razgledi* (Our views). Polemics in the years 1956-58 between the then leading cultural-political ideologue Boris Ziherl and Josip Vidmar, the pre-war liberal literary critic, were a swan song for guided socialist realism. Vidmar, founder of the LF in 1941, who, after the conflict with Stalin, joined the CPY, advocated a certain autonomy of art in contrast to the limited sovereignty and subjection of art to ideology and politics still advocated by the old Communist Ziherl (Rupel 1989).

A "too intensive" loosening in the spiritual sphere of public life was, after the restoration of friendly relations with the Soviet Union in 1955, partially reversed with the foundation of an Ideological Commission in 1956, although this body did not work directly on the local level, as the Agitprop had done. The commission determined the maneuvering room of Slovene intellectuals, who, with their social criticism, represented a substitute for a real political opposition, inside and outside the Communist organization. The commission intervened especially against the younger generation's reviews *Beseda* (1951-57), *Revija 57* (Review 57, 1957-59), *Perspektive* (Perspectives, 1960-64) and experimental theater *Oder 57* (Stage 57, 1957-64). All these reviews and the theater were abolished.

The Seventh Congress of the LCY in 1958, besides ideological loosening, acknowledged again the existence of the national question in the second Yugoslavia, which had been declared solved after the war, following the Soviet example. A discussion referring to the national question was started in 1961 by the polemics of Slovene university professor Dušan Pirjevec and the Serbian writer Dobrica Ćosić; behind them hid the interests of political elites of both nations. The debate focused on old conflicts between the Serbian centralist concept on one side, and the wide autonomy of individual national units in the state—strongly advocated by most Slovenes—on the other. Apart from their principal standpoint concerning the right of nations to self-determination with a possibility of secession, the Communists never allowed questioning of the centralist unity and supernationality of the LCY, which exercised explicitly centralist regulatory authority in spite of the federal state order. Irrespective of the result of the polemics themselves, a division of united state funds for science and film production into individual republic funds the very next year meant a victory for the decentralizing, national principle, confirmed also by the Eighth Congress of the LCY in 1964.

In the fifties, parallel with this liberalization, an extensive school reform took place, which, however, did not remove that important public sphere from control. The elementary school became a united, eight-year compulsory elementary school. Classical grammar schools were abolished and a common four-year program introduced. More natural sciences and technology were introduced into school programs, remnants of humanist sciences were consistently pervaded by Marxism. At the university and research institutes, technical sciences gained support at the expense of the humanities. Some non-Marxist professors (e.g., Anton Slodnjak) were eliminated from the university. New sociological institutions were founded, under severe ideological control: the Institute for the History of the Workers' Movement (1959), Institute for Sociology (1959), and the High School of Political Sciences (1962) (Gabrič 1993).

The ouster of the main Serbian representative from the top leadership of Yugoslav Communists, hard-liner and centralist Aleksandar Ranković in 1966, cleared the way for liberalization of Communist policy in the economy, on the national question and, of course, in culture on an even larger scale. The opening of borders, which was to make the prosperity of tourism possible, facilitated direct contacts with the art and science of the Western Europe as well. This was a particular advantage for Slovenes living along the borders with Italy and Austria. In Slovene art, new modernistic avant gardes came to life. The first postwar generation of Slovene intellectuals, presenting an alternative to institutional culture in the fifties and at the beginning of the sixties, began to join national cultural institutions. Parallel with events in the West, a student movement arose. Younger Communist functionaries in the individual republics, especially in Slovenia, Croatia, and Serbia, advocated more intensive pluralism within the socialist political stream and a definite break with the old rigid political praxis of the Soviet Stalinist type. This movement, which was, especially in Croatia, also tinged with nationalism, began to slip out of the hands of old Communists, who had led the revolution during Second World War and still controlled the state political summit. In the years 1971 and 1972, a differentiation among leading politicians was gradually carried out in all three reformist republics, and leading positions were entrusted to conservative, hard-line politicians.

A new Yugoslav constitution in 1974 emphasized the integrative role of the LCY in the state order. The extensive autonomy of six federal units and two autonomous provinces within Serbia was to make Serbian hegemony impossible. At the same time, however, secessionism of Croats, Slovenes, and Albanians was ruled unacceptable. Ideological control over education, science and, to a minor extent, art intensified once again. Four professors were removed from the university, some intellectuals were sentenced as an example, propagandistic agitation against the writer Edvard Kocbek began again. In school policy the concept of educating and training an independent complete personality was defeated, and ideology as the main criterion for syllabi and teachers themselves prevailed. Verification of the political orthodoxy of personnel was conducted out from elementary schools to the university. In the context of a policy of instituting social and hence also educational equality, a reform of secondary schools was executed at the end of the seventies and at the beginning of the eighties. Common gymnasia, giving a broad educational basis to the majority of university-bound students, were replaced by "directed education" of restricted categories of secondary schools with an emphasis on ideological education and training (Repe 1992).

When the indisputable political authority, Josip Broz Tito, died in spring 1980, Yugoslavia was already in the middle of a deep economic and political crisis. Due to the repeated outbreak of unrest among Albanians in the autonomous province of Kosova in 1981 (a repetition of disturbances in 1968), national relations among individual Yugoslav republics were worsening. Serbs, who considered themselves forcibly divided by the 1974 constitution, began to make efforts for a recentralization of the state. The main initiatives came from the Serbian intellectual opposition.

In Slovenia 60 intellectuals of the younger middle-age generation (born mostly in the forties) took advantage of the crisis after Tito's death to press the authorities to permit a new review for cultural questions. "*Nova revija* (New review) is a result of holy anger over the barbarity of the seventies," one of its founders wrote nearly a decade later (Rupel 1989). From art criticism and wider social critique in the framework of socialism, a relatively large and heterogeneous group moved in a few years to openly advocating parliamentary democracy and free market. Thus Slovene culture entered more actively into politics again, this time on the side of democratization and political pluralism. Nationalism continued to predominate among Serbian intellectuals, and especially the Serbian Academy of Sciences and Arts and its outstanding figure, Dobrica Ćosić; Slovene and Serbian intellectuals, who had frequently cooperated in the postwar period, parted ways by the mid-1980s at the latest. The pressure of more and more numerous intellectual and other political groups in Slovenia—the weekly *Mladina* (Youth), peace and ecology movements—and the appearance of the crisis of the federal state with no prospects for solution, led the Slovene Communists to undertake political reforms, giving in to demands for democratization. (See the articles by Mastnak and Rupel in this volume.) However, the first free elections in Slovenia in April 1990, as well as the attainment of independence a year later, were probably only made possible by the fall of the Berlin Wall.

The question of Slovene culture and history was, until the First World War, mostly a question of language, the struggle for Slovene linguistic equality in the multinational state community. To the extent that this struggle continued in the time of Yugoslavia, it was partly influenced by the old feeling of smallness and threat. During the last three quarters of a century Slovenes have successfully rejected more-or-less concealed attempts to assimilate them into a wider national community. Slovene cultural creators, as the main bearers and maintainers of national consciousness, still remained in the front lines against such attempts. Furthermore, an important part of the Slovene intelligentsia remained opponents of different totalitarian ideologies through the whole twentieth century.

Slovene cultural creators were politically more active in times of political crises. First, when the political demands of Slovenes as an independent nation had to be formulated (1848-71), in the crucial historical moment of the disintegration of the Hapsburg Empire (1917-21), during the time of political crisis and repeated threat to their nationality (1932-45) and when totalitarian ideology and its administrative system were falling apart, thus making conditions for attainment of state independence possible (1980-91). In the latter process, their most important role was, perhaps, bringing courage to a broad range of the population who were tired of everything. However, this enduring role of support for politicians results, after each stabilization of political conditions, in traumas of a narcissist type. The road from the dizzying importance of politics back to quiet cultural creation is much more difficult and painful than the road there.

BIBLIOGRAPHY

Ciperle, Jože and Andrej Vovko (1987). *Šolstvo na Slovenskem skozi stoletja* (The educational system in Slovenia through the centuries). Ljubljana: Slovenski šolski muzej.

Dolenc, Ervin (1992). *Kulturni zamisli slovenskih političnih strank in skupin ter njihove kulturne organizacije v letih 1918-1929 (Kulturna politika in kulturni boj)* (Cultural concepts of the Slovene political parties and groups and their cultural organizations between 1918 and 1929 [cultural policy and cultural struggle]). Ph.D. diss., University of Ljubljana.

Erjavec, Fran (1958). "Avtonomistična izjava slovenskih kulturnih delavcev leta 1921" (Autonomous declaration of Slovene cultural workers in 1921). In *Historical Miscellany.* Buenos Aires.

Gabrič, Aleš (1991). "Slovenska agitpropovska kulturna politika 1945-52" (Slovene agitprop cultural policy 1945-52). *Borec* 7-9. Ljubljana.

Gabrič, Aleš (1993). "Slovenska kulturna politika v času 'socialistične demokracije' 1953-1962" (Slovene cultural policy in the period of "socialist democracy" 1953-1962). Dissertation, University of Ljubljana.

Godeša, Bojan (1993). "Slovenski intelektualci med okupatorji, Osvobodilno fronto in protirevolucionarnim taborom" (Slovene intellectuals among occupiers, liberation front and antirevolutionary stream). Dissertation, University of Ljubljana.

Melik, Vasilij (1970). *Slovenci in nova šola* (Slovenes and the new school). In *Miscellany Osnovna šola na Slovenskem 1869-1969* (Elementary school in the Slovene ethnic territory 1869-1969). Ljubljana: Slovenski šolski muzej.

Nećak, Dušan (1992). "Revija 'Nova Evropa' in Slovenci" (The review "New Europe" and the Slovenes). *Zgodovinski časopis* 46 (1).

Perović, Latinka (1990). "Dve koncepcije jugoslovenske države u shvatanjima jugoslovenskih komunista u debati 1923. godine" (Two conceptions of the Yugoslav state in considerations of Yugoslav Communists in a debate in 1923). In *Razprava o nacionalnem vprašanju v KPJ leta 1923* (Discussion on the national question within the CPY in 1923). Ljubljana: Partizanski knjiga.

Pirc, Jožko (1986). *Aleš Ušeničnik in znamenja časov* (Ales Usenicnik and the signs of the times). Ljubljana: Družina.

Prunk, Janko (1982). "Politične koncepcije slovenskega meščanstva v stari Jugoslaviji" (Political conceptions of the Slovene bourgeoisie in old Yugoslavia). *Prispevki za zgodovino delavskega gibanja* 22: 1-2.

Prunk, Janko (1992). "Slovenski narodni vzpon" (Slovene national ascent). In *Narodna politika 1768-1992* (National policy 1768-1992). Ljubljana: Državna založba Slovenije.

Repe, Božo (1992). "Liberalizem' v Sloveniji" ("Liberalism" in Slovenia). *Borec* 9-10.

Rupel, Dimitrij (1989). *Slovenski intelektualci (od vojaške do civilne družbe)* (Slovene intellectuals [from military to civil society]). Ljubljana: Mladinska knjiga.

Zgodovina Slovencev (1979). (History of the Slovenes). Ljubljana: Cankarjeva Založba.

Zwitter, Fran (1969). "Višje šolstvo na Slovenskem do leta 1918" (Higher education in the Slovene ethnic territory to 1918). In *Miscellany Petdeset let slovenske univerze v Ljubljani* (Fifty years of the Slovene university of Ljubljana). Ljubljana: University of Ljubljana.

SECTION II:

Movements

■ ■ ■ ■ ■ ■

5

From Social Movements to National Sovereignty

Tomaž Mastnak

In Slovenia, as in other parts of Yugoslavia, the liberalization of the sixties was stifled at the turn of the decade. A systematic and massive purge of economic, political, and cultural apparatuses marked the dawn of the leaden seventies, the era of the cultural revolution Yugoslav style. The first real breach of that settlement occurred in the late seventies in Slovenia, and with the take-off of the democratization process the unitary state began to crumble away. Yugoslavia was created in two European wars and accommodated more to the Western power calculus than to the interests of local peoples; in addition it was ruled for much of the time, covertly or overtly, by a military hand in Belgrade. It could not survive democracy and was therefore determined to prevent it from developing. In the yet unfinished drama generated, in its final acts, by the conflict between democracy and permanent revolution, Slovenia is (with a grain of salt) the only success story.

The story began some fifteen years ago with the emergence of a "punk" movement.[1] It was only later, in the mid-eighties, that it was called the first new social movement in Slovenia. When it came into existence it was a youth subculture—tiny and marginal as such phenomena usually are, yet spread from the Hungarian to the Italian border and from the Austrian in the north to the Croatian in the south, and crossing Croatia to extend into Istria. Its protagonists were the first generation free from the socialist ideology that dominated society at that time. They renamed the world they lived in and articulated new

cultural codes, *altri codici* (Melucci 1984, 1985). Their action is better understood as production of society (in Touraine's sense) than confrontation with
the system. But they were not spared confrontation by the system. As ideology is a bond that holds society together, the punk's symbolic challenge in a
way unbound society, and the system could not tolerate this affront. In 1980-
81 the authorities used police repression to try to eliminate the punk movement, yet finally had to retreat.

The conflict and its outcome had far-reaching consequences. State repression failed for three main reasons. First, the protagonists of the punk scene were
intelligent enough to succeed in initiating a public discussion on the accusations that were used to legitimize the repression against them. This displace-
ment of the conflict from the repressive to the ideological level was made
possible by the second reason: A number of intellectuals lined up behind the
persecuted punks, suspending their ideological divisions in order to publicly
oppose the use of violence as a means of resolving social problems, in general,
and to reject the absurd allegations, offensive even to common sense, which
were meant to justify its use in this particular case. And third, the official youth
organization, the League of Socialist Youth (LSY), unexpectedly decided to listen to its social base rather than to blindly follow police instructions. When the
public debate, for which it provided the political space, proved that no evidence
could be brought against punks, LSY refused to participate in the repression.
From the point of view of a democratic system as it is customarily imagined,
there is nothing earthshaking about these structural elements. In an undemocratic system, however, they represented a democratic breakthrough. Moreover,
they shaped the pattern of the democratization of Slovenia.

The actors who initiated the democratization process were the actors in the
new social movements, and they continued to be its principal protagonists until
the formation of political parties and the first free elections. The movements
emerged after the repression against the punk scene had failed. In retrospect,
it was the democratizers who styled punk a movement and recognized its pri-
macy in the kind of "history" they created as their life-world. In the first half
of the eighties, pacifists, antimilitarists, environmentalists, feminists, gays, and
seekers of "new spirituality" all appeared in public. With other youth subcultures they formed a network that called itself the "alternative scene" or simply the "alternative." The protagonists were young people, mostly under 20.
The intellectuals involved in the scene were the post-1968 generation. Their
great concern was to avoid vanguardism, and they became a group among
other groups. As a result, the most propulsive social and political theory from
that time was a constitutive part of the alternative culture. The distinctive characteristic of the alternative scene was that it was free from the figure that played

a central role in other socialist countries: the dissident. The alternative understood its own action as the production of the social sphere, the creation of social spaces of otherness, and would refuse to be characterized as dissent or opposition. Slovene counterparts of East European dissidents entered the democratization process only after it had been through its formative phase, and if they ever gained hegemony it was only after the time approached to reap the fruits of the democratic transformation.

On the one hand, the democratic movement in Slovenia was not deduced from a general idea of democracy and it was certainly not led by an oppositional politburo that would place on the agenda particular issues and concerns. On the contrary, it was a plurality of struggles for a number of concrete, everyday, particular, specific issues and concerns. On the other hand, ideas were of greatest importance for the movement, which was, consequently, characterized by a high intellectual profile. It was intimate with what was intellectually and politically happening in the world and was distinguished by a sophisticated analysis of the socialist system at home and in the broader region, as well as by the ability of critical self-reflection.

Another important feature of the movement was its subtle sense of media. In the *intermundia* of political power blocks, or in their niches, it created its own, alternative media. It published leaflets, fanzines, bulletins, books, tapes and records, organized concerts, exhibitions, public discussions and happenings, and used modern technologies (especially video and computers) as soon as they were available. A crucial role in the formation of the alternative scene was played by the local radio station, Ljubljana based Radio Student, which successfully combined punk rock, New York underground and similar music with the issues of new social movements, political analysis, and theoretical work ("post-Marxism," Lacanian psychoanalysis, semiotics, etc.) The alternative public sphere provided the foothold for influencing the established media. The greatest success was the transformation of the LSY's weekly, *Mladina,* in the early eighties, into the forum of the independent society and the most influential political magazine in the country. In the mid-eighties, a number of discontented journalists in the central media organized themselves, giving priority to the professional ethical codex over the party line. Their not unsuccessful struggle for the freedom of press and information was of greatest importance for the democratic transformation in Slovenia.

The key achievement of the alternative scene was the formation of a new political culture with a distinctive political language at its core. A fair account of this achievement, and of how it was brought about, would require its own book; in a crudely simplifying summary, one could talk about a discourse of civil society. This discourse was related to similar discourses of Polish, Czech, and Hungarian democratic oppositions, with which it was familiar, yet there were aspects in which it differed from them (Mastnak 1992b, chapter 1). As a regulative idea, *civil society* was conceived of as a sphere distinct from, independent of, and opposed to the sphere of state action. As such, in principle exclusive of any total (itarian) community, it was understood as a necessary yet not sufficient condition of democracy. It was opposed to socialism, which in both Soviet statist (Leviathan-like) and Yugoslav self-managerial (more Behemoth-like) versions aimed at overcoming the state-civil society difference, thereby theoretically and practically leaving no prerequisites or guarantees of liberties and rights. In practical terms, the idea of civil society implied the junction of a pluralist society, an accountable state bound by public laws (there was, in Yugoslavia, a whole body of secret laws for political usage authorizing the army and the political police to take "exceptional measures," that is, to act freely in an emergency situation), and institutional mechanisms to articulate diverse social needs and interests and to mediate unavoidable conflicts between civil society and the state. The idea of state was closer to the *Rechtsstaat* than to the rule of law, and much prominence was given to the implementation of human rights and political liberties; society, if it was to be democratic, was an open space characterized by autonomous institutions, and central to the idea of plurality were the rights of minorities: of the largest minority—women—and of sexual, ethnic, religious, and other minorities. The multiparty system was seen as the necessary mediating mechanism, but not sufficient: there was a role to be played by social movements and civic initiatives.

In theory, all this meant a departure from Marxism in its many forms, and the departure itself took on many forms—none of them was emotional. (The emotional rejection of Marxism and of the reality shaped on its principles appeared much later: when neither existed any more.) The new discursive framework was also the framework of action: civil society was not only a norm and analytical tool but actor as well. It was the descriptive term encompassing, in this case, new social movements and protagonists of the alternative culture, which were gradually joined by citizens' initiatives, human rights groups, professional associations (of writers, philosophers, sociologists, and journalists, and later by lawyers, doctors, and others), and, cautiously, by the Catholic Church. In this "second wave," understandably, a greater role was played by older generations, especially intellectuals who were more or less established in the system yet critical of it, or simply unhappy with their position in it. Activities were only loosely organized and loosely connected to each other, dispersed and protean; there was no privileged actor or field of action; actions were typically issue oriented and most had an ad hoc character; yet there was a permanence of activity.

Having outlined some general characteristics of the democratic movement that developed in Slovenia in the early eighties, I can turn back to the narrative of events, and first of all to the campaign against punk in Slovenia, to point out another dimension of the story: the Yugoslav dimension. There was a double framework to the democratization in Slovenia. One was Slovenian—the struggle between democratic and antidemocratic forces inside the republic. This struggle took place in the Yugoslav framework, which had more than one aspect and the significance of which shifted. The most important aspects were: First, that there was a unitary organized antidemocratic interest, a Yugoslav alliance of antidemocratic forces, so that Slovene opponents of democratization always worked in a federal context and with Yugoslav support; and second, that there was no comparable unity of democratic forces. The fraternity of the student movement was by then dead and could only feed the politics of nostalgia; there was no common language left, nothing like the humanist Marxism of the sixties.[2] There were democratic groups in other Yugoslav regions yet the contacts between them and the alternative movement in Slovenia had not amounted to much more than occasional individual communication. The hegemony of new social movements in initiating and directing the democratic transformation was a unique Slovene phenomenon; and it was only in Slovenia that the alternative to the existing system was explicitly articulated in terms of civil society. This concept effectively hegemonized the field of democratic communication and action—in other parts of Yugoslavia there were only phenomena that could sociologically be described as elements of civil society. As a consequence, the democratic forces in Slovenia had no real counterpart elsewhere in Yugoslavia. Moreover, they were opposed not only by antidemocrats at home and in the unitary state but more than once also by what counted as the Yugoslav democratic opposition. Successes of the democratization in Slovenia and equally successful antidemocratization in the Yugoslav center gradually disentangled the overlapping and cross-cutting frameworks into two opposing blocs—into a conflict between Slovenia and Yugoslavia.

In the antipunk campaign, accusations against the subculture were first launched by the Slovene yellow press; their attacks were not only promptly assisted but by far exceeded in Zagreb and especially Belgrade newspapers. The charge was fascism, which was a new tone, and if one would have believed *Politika ekspres* (a sensationalist Belgrade daily) one would think that Ljubljana was little short of being taken over by Nazis. The accusation was as absurd[3] as it was dangerous: it meant putting an end to discussion before it could even begin. Because the label was never retracted or disputed (except in Slovenia itself) it conditioned the view that something was deeply wrong in the north of Yugoslavia. It represents the first exercise in postcommunist irrationalism. I agree with Svetlana Slapšak that the "destruction of the balance of public discourse" was the necessary condition for the destruction of Yugoslavia;[4] however, one should look for the beginnings of this destruction in the antipunk campaign. Moreover, other disruptions of the discursive balance had followed before nationalism, which is now blamed for everything, actually emerged.

In the years that followed the Nazi-punk affair a major restructuring of the Yugoslav system started: one could observe the repressive apparatus of the state progressively assuming the role of the ideological apparatus of the state. Ideology continued to be of central systemic importance, yet as the Yugoslav Communist Party fell into decline, the repressive apparatus that were designed as instruments of its power began to take over the Party's historic role. When public prosecutors and ultimately army generals started to play the role of the ideologist, ideology was more and more immediately becoming material force until it finally coincided with it. *Corpus ideologicum,* a body of ideology, commenced to exist as a military formation, as officers' corps. When it had definitively gripped the masses, it also armed them. This final stage was reached at the beginning of the nineties, yet the process started in its early years, and in 1985 the new, greater, role of the army (and the repressive state apparatus in general) was well established.

The early eighties were marked by a number of political trials, culminating in 1984 with the trial of the Belgrade six (intellectuals charged with "counter-revolutionary organization" for running a free university in private apartments and with "hostile propaganda" for publishing abroad neo-Marxist articles critical of Yugoslavia). The reaction to the trial was not limited to Belgrade. Common actions were taken around it that represented virtually the last common cause, which brought together a truly pan-Yugoslav opposition. Some of the legal and financial help (and moral support) for the defendants was provided from Slovenia; of greater importance, however, was that, in Slovenia, the information blockade over the case was broken. Journalists who slandered the accused and prejudged their guilt were sued by a group of professional colleagues. As a result, reporting became much more balanced and the defendants and their lawyers could publicly present their arguments. Since then, the press in Slovenia has not been instrumentalized in the execution of political justice, and the public learned an excellent lesson in legal culture. The action in Slovenia did help the defendants in Belgrade. Its achievements, particularly a better press and improved sense of legality, however, seem to have remained confined to the northern republic.

In Slovenia, the most important developments in those years were, first, the state's delegation of repressive action against the alternative scene to civil society itself, and, second, the formation of an alliance between new social movements and the LSY. The former was significant because it ended the illusion that civil society is per se, and necessarily, democratic. It was a warning that, when civil society takes to making its own laws and justice, the danger of a new kind of totalitarianism emerges (Mastnak 1989). The contract between the movements and LSY, by which the movements became attached collective members of the youth organization without giving up their autonomy, provided these vital actors of democratic transformation with legality and thus relative safety. At the same time, the LSY acquired a growing legitimacy, and the very fact of basing political authority on legitimacy was a major change in the political system.

The mid-eighties were characterized by an increase in the intensity and scope of autonomous social action. Actors oriented their activities to the public, presenting their ideas, programs and initiatives and arguing with both misunderstandings and misrepresentations of their deeds and aims. Numerous open letters, petitions, and public statements were written, mainly concerned with human rights and political liberties. Independent demonstrations were organized: the first among them protested against what turned out to be the last May military parade in Belgrade; another the bombing of Libya, international terrorism, and the Yugoslav arms trade and the training of Third World soldiers; and a big one protested local authorities' playing down of the dangers of the Chernobyl nuclear plant explosion. In 1984, homosexuals organized the first week-long celebration of gay culture in Ljubljana; feminists aroused great interest (and some complaint, not least from liberal intellectuals) with the "women only" happenings among their activities; the first successful ecological campaigns occurred. The real triumph in popularizing alternative ideas, however, was the peace movement's initiative for the recognition of the right to conscientious objection and the introduction of civilian service, as an alternative to the mandatory military service. The minimalist and reformist proposal was furiously attacked by representatives of the Yugoslav People's Army (JNA) and a number of (mainly federal and Serbian) political bodies. The issue continued to be raised in the media for a number of years. The initiative failed to achieve its aim and religious objectors kept serving repeated prison sentences, but it succeeded, quite unintentionally, in revealing the ultimate truth about the Yugoslav system: that it was armed (and did not care about truth). The alternative, as articulated by the movements and the alternative scene, was much more attractive than the existing system. Opinion polls showed that a great majority of Slovene society supported the new social movements and what they represented.[5] They became what Kant (in *The Contest of the Faculties*) called *signum rememorativum, demonstrativum, prognosticon* (signs of historical progress).[6]

In 1985, the term civil society appeared in the discourse of the ruling party, which indicated that the League of Communists of Slovenia (LCS) had started to change its attitude toward the new reality. After its functionaries cosponsored the "Nazi-punk affair," the party for some time ignored the new social movements, hoping they were only a passing Western influence. This proved to be a vain hope and LCS began to look for ways of getting a hold of the new concepts. Its ideologists, on the one hand, tried to reintegrate the concept of civil society into Marxist political language, to interpret it with the help of Gramscian neo-Marxism, and to prove that civil social issues were "organically" linked to self-management, that the existing socialist model was in fact genuine civil society coming true—that civil society in that sense was indeed the party's programmatic aim. On the other hand, they applied the method of "ideological differentiation." They recognized the movements as, in principle, a positive phenomenon and then proceeded to refute some negative features— everything that would escape integration and pacification. This was a great leap for the party yet too small a step for it to catch up with the democratization process. While the Communist old-timers and hard-liners were losing ground in the internal Party debate, LCS was losing control over social and political developments. In 1987 it had to organize a plenum under the slogan of "the struggle for the youth." This was a belated recognition of the fact that the young generations had been lost from both the actual day-to-day politics and from the future base of the Slovene party.

In its congress in 1986, LSY departed definitively from the role of the "youth transmission party" designed for it by the party-state (Mastnak 1987). It declared itself an organization in civil society, founding its politics not on the program of the Communist Party but on the achieved level of social self-organization: this was understood as the only real basis for democratization of the country. LSY ceased to be the umbrella organization for the alternative movements. It adopted the issues put on the agenda by them and transformed itself in a way that made it the counterpart of the alternative scene (indeed, of the independent society) in the political system. The era of political monolithism had been ended as a result of the pressure of the relatively strong and clearly articulated civil society, of the loss of the youth for official politics, and the abandonment of the party by ever greater number of intellectuals. LCS stepped up its course of reforms and modernization. It got rid of the old guard and chose to become a social democratic party.

The hard core of the Yugoslav system was quick to respond. In 1985, the JNA's counterintelligence service started the operation *Mladost* (youth, in Serbo-Croat) the target of which was democratization in Slovenia. Those activities, however, were kept secret. It took some years before the army appeared in public. The tensions between the northern republic and the center, however, grew in proportion to the proneness of the system in Slovenia to democratic reforms and transformation.

A major upheaval was caused, in 1987, by LSY's proposal to put an end to the relay of youth. This was a ritual in the best tradition of the socialist-realist mass manifestations. Young people all over the country had to carry around a phallic symbol to celebrate Tito's birthday. After it had passed from hand to hand for about two months, the baton was handed over to "our dearest Marshal Tito" on May 25 in the JNA stadium in Belgrade, with thousands of disciplined young bodies prostrating themselves at the leader's feet. The hollow baton held a letter swearing to the leader the eternal loyalty of the young generation to the triple legacy of the "liberation struggle," their Yugoslav fatherland, and communism. The ritual was meant to symbolize brotherhood and unity and was permeated with militarist spirit. It grew more and more absurd and grotesque after Tito's death. After its proposal to end all this (for economic, if not for other, reasons) was rejected, LSY refused to take part. Their stance was vilified as destroying Yugoslav brotherhood and unity, and LSY was finally compelled to participate. Consequently, it tried to deconstruct the ritual from within. Among other things, *Neue slowenische Kunst,* a group of artists which was in the first half of the eighties persecuted by the Slovene authorities, designed a poster for the event which was happily endorsed by the federal organizational committee. The young functionaries obviously thought that the poster well expressed the spirit of the relay of youth. However, when it was soon disclosed that the piece of art was a remake of an old Nazi poster, a great scandal broke out. That was the last relay and Tito's symbolic, and final, death.

The cult of the dead leader could not endure as a unifying bond of the imaginary Yugoslav society, yet no other ties really existed. In Slovenia, at that time, no positive reasons were seen for the existence of Yugoslavia. There was, of course, brute force. At first, there were ceaseless press campaigns against the democratic menace. Certainly, in those campaigns, which intensified in 1985 only to escalate in the years to follow, never a word was said against democracy, for the Yugoslav system had self-evidently accomplished democracy. Targets of the verbal aggression were protagonists of democratization. However, because it was out of the question to generally describe them as "democrats," another collective term had to be invented; and because democratization was easily associated with Slovenia, the solution was at hand. The democratization process was described by its antagonists in national (actually ethnic) terms. It became Slovene national deviation. When a Belgrade newspaper thought that the worst thing it could say about the alternative scene was to call its protagonists "queers," the logical consequence was to denounce Slovenes as "queers." More conventional denunciations were used, too: antisocialists, anti-Titoists, anti-Yugoslavs, counterrevolutionaries, etc. Two among them were, so to speak, organizing principles: that Slovenes were anti-army and anti-Yugoslav. They were used as virtually synonyms: being anti-army had meant being anti-Yugoslav years before the JNA moved to wage war for "Yugoslavia."

The initiative for the recognition of conscientious objection was still being debated, underpinned by then by the peace movement's growing criticism of the militarization of society, when, in spring 1988, Slovene newspapers criticized the JNA's scandalous arms trade (selling arms to famine-stricken Ethiopia). *Mladina* followed this story by disclosing the abuse of power and corruption in the army (conscripts building a private villa on the Adriatic coast for the Secretary of Defense). The generals construed these reports as "attacks on JNA," and they inspired the federal political authorities to make a statement that a counterrevolution was taking place in Slovenia. This was clearly an emergency situation and the statement empowered the army to act. In spring 1988, Slovenia was on the verge of military intervention.

Soon after the federal government's response, a military trial was held in Ljubljana in summer 1988. Two editors of *Mladina*, a contributing author (a good opposition organizer), and a sergeant-major of JNA, a Slovene, were charged with divulging a secret military document. The military court found them guilty without ever having proved the case. The show-trial blatantly violated a number of laws, procedures, and the Slovene constitution. The fact that it was not held in Slovenian (along with Italian and Hungarian one of the official languages of the republic) additionally accentuated its politically provocative nature (see Mastnak 1988). It was generally perceived as an attempt to crush the process of democratization, and the public reaction was unexpectedly swift, massive, and resolute. The nationwide mobilization was coordinated by the Committee for the Defense of Human Rights (CDHR), founded in Ljubljana after the arrests, and attracted more than a thousand membergroups and more than 100,000 individuals. For weeks, throughout the duration of the trial, there were demonstrations in front of the military court and military prison and a number of other activities, all showing determination to resist the armed counterdemocratization.

CDHR was formed at the point when a cycle of the new social movements was coming to an end. They had been legalized, their ideas had become a common good, and their issues a matter of public concern. A debate on their future was interrupted by the military trial and the *levée en masse* against it. Naturally, all the movements joined the CDHR and many of their protagonists began to play an important role in it. The committee successfully capitalized on the experience and achievements of their predecessors, but the movements had to suspend their proper activities when joining it. CDHR caused a complex shift in the structure of independent social action. In contrast to the movements, which had pursued their positive programs, CDHR's activity was defensive, negative. Of still greater importance was the shift from independent social to independent political action. There was a discussion, in the formative phase of the alternative, on whether movements were political, unpolitical, or "antipolitical." CDHR clearly was political and it unified the field of independent action into a field of political action; it also homogenized it. In the Slovene framework, the very existence of CDHR pluralized the political space. Strictly speaking it bipolarized it, for CDHR was facing the official political organizations that were weakening and being transformed. Further changes were imminent. In autumn 1988, when democratization in Slovenia appeared to be saved, the process of forming political parties started.

The creation of political society, in which the emergence of political parties was a key moment, has to be seen in the double framework of Slovenia and Yugoslavia. In Slovenia, it was the growing autonomy and strength of civil society as well as its inner differentiation and pluralization that created the need for political representation. In the political system, the demonopolization of power took place. LSY declared a "struggle for power" in 1988. This was an unprecedented step—when Communist rulers (who claimed that they had the historical mandate to govern) wished to eliminate their opponents they used to accuse them of struggling for power. The declaration was more than simply a challenge to the Party, it was a redefinition of the nature of power. Only a little later LCS began to talk about its "descent from power." It was as if it recognized that its monopoly of power was generating the crisis and at the same time blocking any attempt to solve it. It was not too late for LCS to realize that it had to share power in order not to lose it completely. What both approaches to the demonopolization of power had in common was the modern democratic concept of power as an empty space (see Lefort 1981, 1986)—as opposed to the real estate model of power that had existed in the communist old regime—and both consequently helped to constitute the democratic political space.

The fact that, in Slovenia, the Party transformed itself into a party contributed considerably to a nonviolent transition to democracy. Nothing analogous had yet happened elsewhere in Yugoslavia and the trends in Serbia, in particular, did not bode well. In 1985 the Serbian Academy of Sciences and Arts started to work on the Serbian national program containing the plan for Greater Serbia. In 1986 the anti-Albanian mobilization of Serbs in Kosova began. In spring 1987, Slobodan Milošević visited Kosova to give full support to Serbian militants there, and in autumn he took over the Serbian League of Communists. He first established full control over the media and purged the party of liberal elements. In 1988 he moved to constitutionally annul the autonomy of the provinces of Kosova and Vojvodina. With the so-called antibureaucratic revolution (mass raids of the chauvinist mob) he changed the leadership in Vojvodina, Kosova and (early the following year) Montenegro. As a result, Serbia gained control over the federal institutions, successfully blocking democratic reforms and building up its power. The creation of Greater Serbia was well under way.

The repressive restructuring of the Yugoslav system and the revolutionary coup and totalitarian mass movement in Serbia determined the broader framework of democratization in Slovenia. Not surprisingly, such developments were perceived as an outside threat to the realistic prospect of a better life. This prospect was increasingly the common aim of both the democratic movement and those in power and an impetus to the formation of connections between them. It was CDHR that established regular contacts with the authorities who for the first time recognized a declared oppositional organization as their dialogue partner. The results of the contacts were unsatisfying for both sides and they ceased when the trial came to the end, only to be resumed under the pressure of Yugoslav developments. In February 1989 Albanian miners in Kosova went on a hunger strike in a desperate attempt to reverse the demolition of the political autonomy of the province. The alternative in Ljubljana took the initiative to manifest solidarity with them and their cause. Not only all major opposition groups but also the official political organizations supported the initiative and took part in a joint public meeting, the first of its kind. The Serbian leadership went mad, calling people onto the streets and threatening that the storm troopers of the antibureaucratic revolution would invade Ljubljana. In order to prevent this from happening the protagonists of the solidarity meeting continued to convene and coordinate activities. When the first danger of a Serbian raid passed,[7] meetings of this coordinating body concentrated on the political future of Slovenia. These roundtable talks did not bring spectacular results. However, they quasi-legalized the opposition (formal legalization followed with the passage of a new law on political organizations) and paved the way to free elections, which were held in April 1990.

Demos, the coalition of six opposition parties, won the elections with a 55 percent majority and formed a center-right government with a Christian Democratic prime minister. However, the two strongest single parties in the new Parliament were the Party of Democratic Renewal (formerly LCS), and LSY, transformed into the Liberal Democratic Party. The new social movements that ran as the Independent List failed to get any members elected to

Parliament. Slovenia would have quickly developed into a boring democratic country had it been left to develop freely. In the last two years, one could have observed phenomena that are typical for postcommunist democracies: much entropy in the work of the political system; tendencies toward the building of new power monopolies; difficulties in finding the just measure of economic reforms and means of implementing them; the decrease in the intellectual level of public discussion; all sorts of characters entering public life, not always with impeccable agendas; the advent of traditionalist, undemocratic and antidemocratic social groups; intolerance and vengefulness. In many aspects Slovenia was better off than other East European countries in a similar position, thanks mainly to the achievements of a long democratization process, the relatively viable economy and the low influence of the fundamentalist free market ideology, and to the country's open borders. Among encouraging things that have happened (the preservation of a liberal abortion law and the succession of the center-right by a center-left government formed by the Liberal Democrats, who also won the elections in December 1992). However, it is not only the free choice of its population, but also Yugoslav and international constraints, that have determined developments in Slovenia, and the country has had to live under the curse of interesting times.

In Yugoslavia, all attempts to reform the system were blocked by the fascist regeneration of Serbian communism, incompatible with the creation of any democratic settlement and unscrupulous in choosing means with which to pursue its aims. In March 1989, an emergency situation was declared in Kosova, due to pressure of "the people" in the streets of Belgrade; a year later, the JNA's intervention in the province was followed by the institutionalization of an apartheid system. In summer 1989, Serbs in Croatia were organized and soon announced that what they had in mind was the formation of a "Serbian autonomous province"; by summer 1990 this had become a rising of the "people in arms"—armed and protected by the JNA. After the victory of the Party of Democratic Action in the first multiparty elections in Bosnia-Hercegovina in November 1990, Serbian extremists there started to prepare for war—with the help of Belgrade and the JNA. The rise of Serbian power was complemented by the decline and fall of federal institutions. The federal presidency virtually ceased to function as such when Serbia gained control over half of the votes; the federal government was powerless and enjoyed credibility only in the West; the federal assembly was discredited. In January 1990 the Yugoslav League of Communists dissolved and the JNA started to claim that it was the only remaining Yugoslav institution—although it sided with Milošević and was a major actor in the politics of the dissolution of the federal state. In June 1991, it intervened in Slovenia; in ten days of relatively low level warfare it failed to achieve its objectives. Immediately after, a most destructive war against Croatia began. The horrors of that war have been surpassed by the war against Bosnia-Hercegovina, launched at the beginning of 1992, carrying out genocide on the Muslim population.

The contours of these politics were visible in the mid-eighties, and the illusion that they might be reconcilable with democratization perished in Slovenia in 1988. However, there still was hope that they might not prevail in Yugoslavia and some kind of *modus vivendi* in a common state would eventually be found. (As late as October 1990 Slovene and Croatian authorities proposed a confederal model for Yugoslavia.) Mixed feelings gave rise to a contradictory politics. Under the menace from outside—of which political and ultimately military justice was one most pressing aspect and the systematic misrepresentation of the developments in Slovenia, and slander in the Serbian press,[8] another—politics in Slovenia became homogenized. The democratic movement, under CDHR, joined forces and found common interests with the reformers in power. The democratization was increasingly perceived as a national project: on the one hand, it was nationwide, on the other, it was seen as pertaining to the nation.

Political language changed as civil society began to be nationalized. The constant flow from Belgrade of accusations formulated in ethnic terms, and the need to defend democratization against them, determined the field of discussion. In this atmosphere Slovenes whose thinking was bounded by much the same mental horizons as the accusers gained more prominence than they would have normally enjoyed. It was in the circle of Slovene literati around the journal *Nova revija,* not in the alternative scene, that Ćosić, still a patriarch of Serbian opposition, looked for kindred spirits (yet failed to find allies). When *Nova revija,* in 1987, published "Contributions to the Slovene National Program," the publication made a much greater impact in Yugoslavia than in the democratic movement in Slovenia. Only later, when, with Demos, people from the journal's circle came to power, did the "Contributions" become an historic event.

With the military trial, the cause of democracy was linked to the question of national sovereignty. Yet even then, with democracy becoming national, the main concern was to develop and preserve a democratic society. The aim of democratization as it was understood in its formative phase—a society independent of the state—had not been abandoned. At that time, an independent state had not been an issue. In 1988, however, under the mounting antidemocratic pressure from the Serbian Yugoslav capital, it became one. It was almost impossible to avoid the conclusion that sovereignty was required in order to have a democratic society. The idea of sovereignty was initially very "soft" (a sovereign Slovenia inside a democratically renegotiated Yugoslavia), and nation was juridically (not racially) defined.[9] And yet this triggered developments that escaped control.

First, the logic that followed from the concept of national sovereignty was as binding as that which led to the embrace of the concept. The idea of a sovereign Slovenia in Yugoslavia was not insincere but unrealizable. It could not be blamed for the failure to democratize the Yugoslav center yet it certainly did not contribute to democratic developments there. Because sovereignty is, strictly speaking, indivisible, its politics are bound to be exclusionary; the fact that democratic society as it was formed in Slovenia needed national sovereignty in order to be able to survive was detrimental to its communications across internal Yugoslav borders. To a degree, Slovene politics became the mirror image of Serbian exclusivism.

Second, while the homogenization of politics in Slovenia took place on a democratic basis, it still could not fail to influence the nature of that basis. The homogenization was necessary in order to protect, not to advance, the democratic movement, and this kind of protection actually impoverished democracy. The democratic movement became less alternative and more oppositionist, less pluralist, and more efficiency oriented, and neglectful of ideas for the sake of expediency. Some made a virtue of necessity, and in its prevalent Demos version democracy was reduced, in the internal proceedings of this coalition, to unanimous party discipline, and in its dealing with the world outside, to anti-communism (when communism had already ceased to exist) and incantations on national sovereignty. For a powerful group in Demos, which debased nationalism to ethnic thinking, Slovenia was no more than non-Yugoslavia. Fortunately, Slovenia has survived Yugoslavia while Demos has not.

Third, as soon as the idea of national sovereignty was uttered the democratization process in Slovenia got caught in webs of meaning which were beyond its control. The democratization at a certain point in time became nationalist because the independent society needed to constitute an independent state in order to be able to have control over its own destiny, so that citizens of that state, and not an external power, could ultimately determine what was to happen to their lives. In the political languages that dominate in the international community, however, nationalism means chauvinism, xenophobia, and racism, if not purely and simply fascism. Internationally, the Slovene case has met both with little understanding and much hostility. In Europe, in particular, which has thoughtlessly declared the nation-state obsolete, Slovenia would be, if taken seriously (which it is not), at best considered a killjoy. Besides, it was held to be separatist, and separatism is generally seen as only causing trouble and as something that is usually fought against with arms. A really unnecessary illusion of the democratic movement in Slovenia was that Europe cares about democracy and that set of values that were used as ammunition in the cold war. The West, on the contrary, has had an attentive ear for Serbian political propaganda. The Western attitude toward the Yugoslav crisis has been disastrous. In embracing the Belgrade view of events and prospects for the future, the West has only heard what it wished to hear and taken notice only of what it wanted to know. It has constantly interfered with developments in the region, in a way that was detrimental to the advancement of democracy and consistently supportive of the Serbian political elite. By insisting on what it found convenient to call a "unitary Yugoslavia" it encouraged Milošević and company to resist a possible reform of the federation. When Slovenia and Croatia, in June 1991, decided that there was no other option left to them but to declare independence, they were accused of separatism and of destroying Yugoslavia. In fact, Yugoslavia had already been destroyed and they were trying to escape the deadly embrace of Serbian communism going fascist. Slovene nationalism was a response to the collapse of the federal state—an alternative aimed at preserving the civil order and preventing the lapse into the state of nature. What destroyed Yugoslavia as a state was not nationalism but the devolution of power to the people: the Serbian nation becoming people[10] and building their empire on blood and soil.

A public secret in ex-Yugoslavia is that the U.S. secretary of state, during his visit to Belgrade in June 1991, gave carte blanche to JNA to sort out things in Slovenia in 48 hours. I have no means of checking the truth of the rumor. The fact is, however, that JNA did intervene in Slovenia immediately after the American politician had left, and that the West abided by his declaration that no "unilateral acts of secession" will be recognized. The Western Yugoslav policy that has followed has led, inevitably, to the escalation of violence and to the holy war Serbs are fighting for Europe in Bosnia. The London-Paris-Belgrade-Pale[11] axis seems to have succeeded in founding the new Europe on genocide and destruction.

Mladina (Milharčič 1991) was quick to comment that the European policy on the Balkans would fill the encyclopedia of political idiocy[12] and that the graffiti in Ljubljana celebrating the beginning of the European "peace efforts" reads "Van den Broek Go Home!" The understanding of what was happening was a bitter consolation, if any, for it could put no brake on events. In particular, the political and economic isolation with which Slovenia was punished after the secession did little to enhance democracy. Instead, it promoted persons who had never, in thought or action, depended much on the world outside. In a country deprived of contact with an international political community, the atmosphere was favorable to those who wished to turn politics to inner, ultimately ethnic, resources and would only rejoice if the stately framed political community imploded into a *Gemeinschaft.* The exhausted economy inherited by the new state had no prospects of recovery as long as it was excluded from the international system and could not sustain the old system of social security. This alone would be very difficult to cope with and would become the breeding ground for all sorts of sinister phenomena.

Recognition came too late, and where creation could have but failed to take place, one has instead to be happy and grateful for the chance of restoration. Wounds that were inflicted, even if only symbolic wounds, will contain poison long after they have healed. In addition, the war in Croatia and Bosnia has affected Slovenia in many ways, but above all in terms of security and the 100,000 refugees who have fled from active Serbian fascism to Slovenia. In such a situation, with hardly any help coming,[13] it is easy to forget that fortune smiled at Slovenia when it fought its short war of independence and to blame the less fortunate for the miseries the powerful in Serbia and the West have created. This frustrated nationalism is finally starting to bear the fruit that Western antinationalists have been looking for all these years. Slovenia now has its chauvinist and xenophobic party. This may be an encouraging development. For after neither persistent striving for democracy nor political realism have gained much international status for Slovenia,[14] the existence of a potentially fascist party may be the required qualification for really joining Europe.

ENDNOTES

I am grateful to Lynne Jones for reading and commenting on the first draft of this text.

1. For a more detailed reconstruction of the story see Mastnak (1991 and 1992) and Jones and Mastnak (1991).
2. This, to be sure, still existed—yet not as a common language. One of the last attempts to recreate Yugoslav opposition on, broadly speaking, Praxis philosophy occurred at the 1983 summer school in Komiža (an echo of the banned Korčula summer school). When participants from Slovenia, already ideologically alienated, refused to follow the guidelines for political action in Slovenia as formulated by their Belgrade and Zagreb colleagues, they were dismissed as Austro-Marxists, that is, nationalists. The loudest and most aggressive in the Belgrade contingent was Vojislav Šešelj.
3. The corpus delicti in the prosecution of Igor Vidmar, a *spiritus movens* of the punk scene, was in one case a Dead Kennedys' button "Nazi punks—Fuck off" and in the other a Campaign for Nuclear Disarmament "Crazy Governments" badge with a crossed off swastika. Documents are collected in Maleckar and Mastnak (1984).

4. Slapšak (1992, 53). I cannot agree either with the author's egalitarian distribution of guilt for the destruction of Yugoslavia on its former constituents or with her leveling description of the present situations in all of them as equally bad— as if, for example, Croatian state censorship could be equated with the Serbian genocide, which is not even mentioned.

5. According to 1986/87 polls, about 45 percent of the Slovene population were willing to participate in the new social movements while about 75 percent were sympathetic to their ideas and actions.

6. Kant says that certain events can be taken to prove that humanity makes progress. "Therefore, an event must be sought which . . . would allow progress toward the better to be concluded as an inevitable consequence. This conclusion then could also be extended to the history of the past . . . in such a way that the event would have to be considered not itself as the cause of history, but only as an intimation, an historical sign (*signum rememorativum, demonstrativum, prognostikon*) demonstrating the tendency of the human race viewed in its entirety. . ."(Kant 1963).

7. Those in Belgrade responsible for this kind of politics insisted on the realization of a Serbian visit to Ljubljana (called in the newspeak the "meeting of the truth") and finally scheduled it for December 1, 1989. It is significant that they chose the date of the formation of the first Yugoslavia (a kingdom ruled by a Serbian monarch) and not November 29, the founding day of the federative Yugoslav republic. When Slovene authorities banned the meeting and were ready to use force to prevent it, Serbian power holders, in a secret decree by their assembly, enacted an economic boycott of Slovenia.

8. The Belgrade press was distributed and read in Slovenia (much more than the other way around) and articles from it reprinted in Slovene newspapers. Slovene authorities, however, were anxious to prevent any response to Serbian hate speech which could be accused of spreading "anti-Serbian" sentiments.

9. Consequently, this was not the phantasm of nineteenth-century nationalism. Compare Emmerich de Vattel (1758, Preface, p. xiii): "Nation is here a sovereign state, an independent political society."

10. "Volkwerdung der Nation" was the name given the concept invented in Germany in the thirties. Compare A. Rosenberg (1932, 532).

11. Pale is the capital of the Bosnian Serb forces.

12. The idiocy of Western diplomacy has possibly been surpassed only by that of Western non-governmental organizations.

13. In 1992, Slovenia applied to the United Nations for $135 million to help the refugees but was granted only $35 million. Much more money, in relative and absolute terms, went to Montenegro, the aggressor state on the Serbian side. International agencies have also refused to provide help for refugees who live with private families (which is the majority of the refugee population in Slovenia)—they were only financing camps.

14. That it is too small to exist as an independent state was the thesis of a lecture given by the foreign minister of Luxembourg.

BIBLIOGRAPHY

Jones, Lynne and Tomaž Mastnak (1991). "Behind the ethnic rivalry," *Times Literary Supplement,* July 19.

Kant, Immanuel (1963). "An Old Question Raised Again: Is the Human Race Constantly Progressing?" from *The Contest of the Faculties.* In Lewis Beck, ed., *On History: Immanuel Kant.* New York: Bobbs-Merrill.

Lefort, Claude (1981). *L'invention démocratique* (The democratic invention). Paris: Fayard.

Lefort, Claude (1986). *Essais sur la politique XIXe-XXe siècles* (Essays on politics in the nineteenth and twentieth centuries). Paris: Seuil.

Maleckar, Nela, and Tomaž Mastnak, eds. (1984). *Punk pod Slovenci* (Punk under Slovenes). Ljubljana: KRT.

Mastnak, Tomaž (1987). "Even the future is not what it used to be." *Across Frontiers,* 3: 3.

Mastnak, Tomaž (1988). "The Night of the Long Knives." *Across Frontiers,* 4 (4/5): 1.

Mastnak, Tomaž (1989). "Modernization of repression." In Vera Gathy, ed., *State and Civil Society: Relationships in Flux.* Budapest: Hungarian Academy of Sciences.

Mastnak, Tomaž (1991). "From the New Social Movements to Political Parties." In James Simmie and Joze Dekleva eds., *Yugoslavia in Turmoil: After Self Management.* London: Pinter Publishers.

Mastnak, Tomaž (1992a). "Civil Society in Slovenia: From Opposition to Power." In Paul G. Lewis, ed., *Democracy and Civil Society in Eastern Europe,* Basingstoke and New York: Macmillan/St. Martin's Press.

Mastnak, Tomaž (1992b). *Vzhodno od raja: civilna druzba, pod komunizmom in po njem* (East of Eden: Civil society under communism and after it). Ljubljana: Državna Založba Slovenije

Melucci, Alberto, ed. (1984). *Altri codici: Aree di movimento nelle metropoli* (New cultural codes: Arena of metropolitan movements). Milano: Il Mulino.

Melucci, Alberto (1985). "The symbolic challenge of contemporary movements." *Social Research.* 52 (4).

Milharčič, Ervin Hladnik (1991). "Za čast in plen" (For honor and plunder). *Mladina,* Sept. 17.

Rosenberg, A. (1932). "Europa in Rom" (Europe and Rome). *Nationalsozialistische Monatshefte,* 3.

Slapšak, Svetlana (1992). "Serbian Alternatives: Are There Any?" *East European Reporter* 5.

de Vattel, Emmerich (1758). *Le Droit des Gens ou principes de la Loi Naturelle, appliqués à la conduite & aux affaires des Nations & des Souverains* (The rights of man or principles of natural law, applied to the conduct and affairs and nations and rulers). London.

6

The Politics of Punk

GREGOR TOMC

Youth movements can be differentiated into subcultures, subpolitics, and counterculture (Tomc 1989, 8). In *subcultures,* young people emphasize specific forms of artistic creativity (music, dance, etc.) and cultural innovation in general (life style, image, slang, etc.) in contrast to the prevalent ones. A young Berlin jazz fan, described by Egon Monk, listening with zest to "Tuxedo Junction" on the American army radio station in the closing operation of the Second World War, oblivious to the fact that these same Americans were bombarding his parents' house, was a member of the jazz subculture (Ascherson 1970). The hippies of the sixties held a similar disassociating orientation when they were "freaking out," a process that Frank Zappa defined as "casting away old-fashioned and limiting standards of thought, dress, and morals by adopting a creative relationship with your environment" (Zappa 1970). A rocker of a very different temperament expressed his experience of life in a "subcultural ghetto" in the following manner (Reed 1969):

> *There are problems in these times*
> *but none of them are mine.*

Members of a youth *subpolitics* perceive such an attitude as escapist and defeatist. The position of the person in a subcultural enclave who recognizes prevalent social phenomena but declines to interpret them as his problems is unacceptable to members of youth subpolitics. They feel at home in the world their parents have created, basically accepting the values on which it is based, but are highly critical concerning implementation of those values. The student movement in Slovenia in the late sixties and early seventies, for example, criticized the ruling party for inefficiency in carrying out the socialist revolution—there was not enough egalitarianism, self-management, or solidarity with other revolutionary movements. (The same, by the way, was also true of the American student movement, which criticized the involvement in the Vietnam war in the name of traditional American values, of the "American dream.") Members of subpolitics are culturally conformist, they accept the dominant goals of the nation as their own. But because the solutions offered to existing problems are unacceptable to them they turn to political innovation, to more radical means of resolution. For the authors of the movie *The Strawberry Statement,* political radicalism becomes a crucial point of identification (Dolar 1971): Strike to prove yourself alive!

Theodore Roszak attempted to integrate both aspects of youth movements, subcultural and subpolitical, in his analysis of the American situation in the sixties (Roszak 1978, 50). In his opinion, the apparent weakness of the interrelation between the two sides of youth rebellion, the perception that lunatic bohemian beatniks and hippies lived in a world separate from the sober political activism of the student New Left activists, was specious. While the subculture was at the time still closer to Ginsberg and the subpolitics to C. Wright Mills, Roszak claimed that it would not remain so. Sooner or later the capitalist civilization as a common antagonist would unite them into what he labeled a counterculture. A *counterculture* is a youth movement in which both subcultural and subpolitical considerations are prominent sources of orientation in the social life of their members.

Today we know that Roszak was mistaken in the sense that the counterculture that he envisaged never emerged in American society—the hippie emphasis on tribal community and psychedelic religious personal change, on the one hand, and student activism with its emphasis on mass movement and social reform on the other, could find no common interest. Had the counterculture evolved and then succeeded to political power, America today would be a very different place indeed. A totalitarian regime would be trying to carry out a cultural revolution—no more cities, no more high technology, no more rationalism, individualism, and utilitarianism; instead, thousands upon thousands of small communes might have offered a choice of Zen, yoga, drugs, occultism, astrology, free love, the simple life in tune with nature, and obligatory participation at the progressive rock concerts of bands like the Mothers of Invention or the Grateful Dead. The transition period would have involved enormous hardship of Kampuchean dimensions (200 million Americans could not live off the land) and innumerable personal dramas (the great majority of the people—despite all their hesitations—still feel at home in the modern world).

Slovenes, together with other people of Eastern Europe, were not so lucky when a communist counterculture emerged as a ruling political party after the Second World War. In its initial phase, the communist movement was a youth counterculture. The majority of its members were young people: in 1945, 64 percent of the representatives at the First Congress of the People's Front 61 percent of the Communist Party members, and 72 percent of all political representatives were young people (Hafner Fink 1987, 229). And they were most certainly also a counterculture. Capitalist society had to be transformed in totality—market replaced by state regulation, parliamentary democracy by avant-garde party rule, society by community, intimacy of family life by growing up in public, bourgeois culture by socialist realism, jazz music by revolutionary songs depicting the struggle of the proletariat and other nonantagonistically disposed working people. With such views, communists were extreme marginals before the war. As such they were also an extreme minority—immediately before the outbreak of the Second World War, there were some one thousand Communists in Slovenia (Kos 1984, 56). Such extreme enclaves are of course not exceptional in modern society. In prewar Europe, there were also, for example, fascist subpolitics, bohemian and jazz subcultures, religious cults and other avant-garde countercultures beside socialist realism. Communists were exceptional in the sense that they combined the general strategy of a future total denial of existing society with the tactic of concrete methods of seizing power in the present (Bolshevism). Their strategy, moreover, was exclusivist (they were the only ones in possession of the Truth) and universalist (they would improve the lot of everybody, even of those who are too alienated to want it).

When the communist counterculture became the ruling class, the once exotic dogma was imposed on all. If they were once hostile toward the modern world, the modern world now became hostile. If they were once problematic inside the context of modernity, they now redefined modernity as problematic. Things that were taken for granted yesterday became questionable, if not counterrevolutionary, today: everything from playing jazz to listening to classical music, from uncombed hair to fancy clothing, from trying to make a profit to traveling abroad, from meeting with a group of friends on a street corner to expressing your political beliefs.

Trying to abolish everyday modern life is a gigantic task. It is an exploit worthy of gods, whereas the Party only had a handful of semi-intellectuals at its disposal. A defeat was inevitable—it was only a question of when, how, and at what cost to the innocent bystanders of this experiment in revolutionary innovation on the macro-level.

In Slovenia, the march of the Party from defeat to defeat toward the final disaster lasted for 45 years. The utopian project was first abandoned in the sphere of culture, of creating the "new man." In the sixties and seventies, there followed the abandonment of specific economic policies (reforms of ownership, regulation, motivation, etc.). Finally, in the eighties the Party monopoly on political power disintegrated. As our topic of interest is (sub)cultural, only the process of cultural disintegration will briefly be discussed.

After about a decade of this party time, Russian and Russian-inspired socialist realism (an avant-garde art trend generally favored by Bolsheviks) was gradually abandoned and Western (both elite and mass) art was slowly reintroduced. Classical music could once more be heard on the radio, non-Russian films could be seen in the movies, books neutral on the subject of class struggle and revolutionary strategy and tactics could be purchased in bookstores. People could once more determine how to spend free time—there were fewer and fewer compulsory work brigades and indoctrination meetings where the new man was to have been forged.

This loosening-up was highly significant for the revitalization of Slovenian youth subcultures. In the first postwar period, members of the jazz subculture could not meet freely, perform publicly, or listen to their favorites on the radio. Accusations of "vagrancy" by plainclothesmen could result in sentencing to forced labor. The saying of the day was "he who plays jazz today will betray his country tomorrow." Subcultural images were not tolerated, and bands of zealous young communists patrolled the streets cutting off improper elements of image. After approximately five years jazz music was slowly reintroduced to dance floors, but bands were closely monitored by the police and official youth organization members. If music became too "decadent," (meaning, for example, boogie-woogie) authorities could stop it immediately. Image was still hard to cultivate because subcultural commodities were unavailable in shops, borders were effectively sealed off, and the standard of living was lower than before World War II.

In the sixties jazz became a legitimate form of musical expression, but by then, of course, it no longer functioned as a part of the youth subculture. This was the age of rock'n'roll. The first generation of rockers in the fifties was numerically, creatively, and otherwise insignificant in Slovenia. As a matter of fact, the only youth subculture with an elaborate image and life style was a fabrication of the police. The authorities took advantage of gossip circulating in Ljubljana concerning a group of young people who called themselves Black Cats and partied in an empty apartment. It was said that they listened to rock'n'roll and jazz, dressed in black, indulged in free sex and heavy drinking, and practiced ritual killing and then eating of cats. But despite hostile media coverage and police harassment, the group was never taken to court.

The rock subculture became numerically significant in the sixties, when two factors coincided—a period of liberalization of the Party, marked by attempts at economic reform, greater political tolerance, and artistic autonomy, with the creative impact of the Beatles and the Rolling Stones. Almost every street had its own rock band that played cover versions of rock standards. Most people could, for the first time, freely travel abroad, where young people could buy records and cultivate a rock image. Discos opened and bands played on a regular basis, some even became professional. Although there was still a lot of negative coverage of the rock subculture in the press, it came mostly through opinions expressed by individual citizens. Negative reactions no longer functioned as part of some coordinated campaign of the authorities. The Party was more or less neutral on the question of rock'n'roll.

In the beginning of the seventies, a new attempt at cultural revolution was staged. The Party tried to reconsolidate its power with the ideology of global self-management, on the one hand, and confederalization of party organization (effectively abandoning the idea of *Jugoslovanstvo* [Yugoslavhood]) on the other. All political opposition was eliminated, notwithstanding the student movement as a very active youth subpolitics of the time, but the rock subculture managed to survive undamaged. Even more, this was the time when the first truly creative bands emerged in Yugoslavia playing their own versions of rock'n'roll—for example, a hard-rock group from Sarajevo called *Bjelo dugme* (White button) and a progressive-rock group from Ljubljana called *Buldožer* (Bulldozer).

By and large rock was regarded by the authorities only as a threat to the symbolic order (Hebdige 1980, 128) and no longer as an actual threat to the existing order. As such it was uneasily tolerated in its subcultural ghetto. Every now and then, however, an overzealous party official would translate the symbolic threat into an actual one and a ban would result. An annual festival of rock bands from all over Yugoslavia was banned in Ljubljana in 1974, for example, because somebody discovered that its date coincided with a Party and secret police celebration. Another time, the band Bulldozer was prevented from performing in Ljubljana by a top city youth organization leader who considered them politically and otherwise suspect.

When punk rock appeared in the late seventies it was initially tolerated as just another rock style. But because of its aggressive message and its visibility in everyday life through public meeting places, graffiti, and personal image, the authorities attempted to suppress it in the early eighties. State opposition began with an attempt to associate punk with Nazism and culminated with harassment as an everyday aspect of being a Slovenian punk. The punk subculture never quite managed to recover from this encounter with the repressive apparatus of the party state, but then, neither did the Party.

The repression of the punk scene was the last feeble attempt of the Slovenian party to legitimate its role as the agent of cultural revolution. Not even the official youth organization backed it in this policy. After 45 years of political defeats, the Party had lost its language, its ideology, its culture, its economic policy (but still not its privileges!). In short, the League of Communists of Slovenia (LCS) had lost its identity, and as a final consequence also its will to power. It turned out that socialism was a formation sui generis only if we include progressive disintegration as one of its basic characteristics. Or, to paraphrase Mao Zedong: All revolutionaries are paper tigers. They seem horrible, but are, in reality, not so powerful. Looking backwards, it is capitalism that is strong and not the communists.

THE CONTRIBUTION OF PUNK TO THE DOWNFALL OF THE SOCIALIST REVOLUTION

When considering the position and role of punk in Slovenia, three actors have to be taken into account—the Party (the League of Communists), the youth organization (the League of Socialist Youth), and of course punks themselves.

The Party defined the social context. In its leadership were the hard-liners who had purged it of its liberals and carried out a failed attempt at a cultural revolution in the early seventies. The experiment ran out of steam when the emphasis on amateur cultural activity met the resistance of the elite cultural establishment, global self-management and social property led to the gradual collapse of the economy, and critics challenged the power monopoly hidden behind the institution of indirect democracy called "the system of delegates." Despite this, the Party was, at the end of the seventies, still the key if not the exclusive political actor.

Forgetting their own evolution from a youth counterculture, Communists were extremely mistrustful of the youth phenomenon. Like all other totalitarian movements, they subordinated everything to one principle—just as fascists had to the nation and Nazis to race, so Communists to class. From the perspective of a person indoctrinated with communism, the youth question is simply insignificant, a residual category, something which will be resolved automatically with the victorious class struggle. It is thus not surprising that Marx and Engels did not have much to say regarding the youth question. When they did address the issue, it was to decry the exploitation of children, their poverty and delinquency (Marx and Engels 1973a, 26-50), criticize student factionalism inside the party (Marx and Engels 1973a, 163) or praise the role of young workers (Marx and Engels 1973a, 169). In the future socialist society, young people would be brought up in special institutions at state expense (Marx and Engels 1973b, 44) where they would learn the complete production system (Marx and Engels 1973b, 45-46).

In the Soviet Union, first land of socialism, these extremely vague directions had to be operationalized. On the eve of the October revolution, Lenin believed that extreme exploitation of children and young workers was progressive because it would make them more susceptible to communist ideas (Hafner Fink 1987, 13). He perceived young people as mere objects of communist indoctrination and leadership. For Stalin the young are at the same time a reserve army of peasants and workers and an instrument for exerting influence on the masses of young people (Hafner Fink 1987, 32). In the company of such classics, Tito contributed nothing original to the Marxist analysis of the young generation: immediately after the war he stressed the need to reeducate the young (Broz 1971, 45). Twenty years later, however, all he could do was express his disappointment at the failure of this process (Broz 1973, 133).

Changes in party orientation toward the young generation were also reflected in the role of the official youth organization, the only unspecialized political organization to survive the Communist takeover in Yugoslavia. Immediately after the war it was directly subordinate to the Party—it followed the party program, its function was to aid the Party in the accomplishment of its goals. It would achieve this with a "struggle for the youth"—the indoctrination of young people with communist ideology by means such as brigade work and special seminars. In 1949, 95 percent of the young people in Slovenia were members of the youth organization. In the fifties, the party leadership articulated the possibility of depoliticizing the youth organization—it had no specific function in the system and thus represented a potential political rival (Hafner Fink 1987, 341).

The role of the youth organization should, according to these critics, be limited to cultural, sports and similar activities. In the next three decades the fate of the organization depended on power relations in the parent party organization: in more dogmatic periods it had to serve as a mere transmission of party will, while in more liberal periods it functioned as a semiautonomous organization for leisure activities of the young. Thus, a relatively autonomous League of Youth of the liberal late sixties was transformed into a mere extension of party will in the early seventies as the League of Socialist Youth (LSY). At the end of the seventies the Party, preoccupied with its own crisis, was once more losing its interest in the organization, and as a result loosened its grip.

How did the punks of the late 1970s perceive the youth organization politicians? They mostly ignored them. As cultural conformists, the "official young people" publicly validated by the Party as worthy of the revolutionary project were utterly uninteresting to their subcultural counterparts—they cultivated the image of their parents, they had their parents' tastes, they had

similar expectations in life, even the goal of their political activity was to realize the dreams of the older generation. For punks, taking any politics seriously
was ridiculous, and taking "youth" politics seriously would be piteous and a
sign of bad taste. The only important things were happening in the parallel
world of subculture: a new record by a favorite band, a night on the town, a
new image, writing graffiti, playing in a band, etc. These are the creative outlets at the disposal of a member of a subculture, filling an otherwise boring
everyday life of school or work drudgery with interesting activities. If punks
were an autonomous rock subculture, then youth politicians were a dependent
counterculture. If punks were a subculture on the rise, then the youth organization was without its own identity and direction.

In this sense punks were not a youth movement critical of the official youth
organization. The youth organization was a disintegrating counterculture disinterested in the subcultural scene. They were simply living in parallel worlds.
The two sides would never have met had the Party not willed it to be so.

The Communists decided to translate the symbolic threat of punk into an
actual threat to the existing regime when France Popit, the influential general
secretary of the Party, disclosed at a conference of communal party secre-
taries in 1981 that punks publicly "throw up," take drugs, and in general
behave in a tasteless manner (Bakše 1989, 61). Franc Šali, who was at the
time in charge of cultural affairs in the party, was surprised and replied that
Popit's opinion was not the official attitude of the presidency of the Party.
Popit conceded that he only expressed his private opinion, but by then it was
already too late. For the communal officials present, his every word was law.
The only problem was that the great majority of them had never heard of
punk. So, on arriving home the next day, they turned to the only reliable
source of information in a still semitotalitarian context: the police. But the
police were also largely uninformed, so they started an investigation. It was
then that the highest party circles decided to discredit and then destroy punk
by connecting it to nazism.

In November of the same year the weekly newspaper with the largest cir-
culation in Slovenia, *Nedeljski dnevnik* (Sunday daily), published an article by
its editor, Zlatko Šetinc, the son of a high-ranking Communist official and a
man with close connections to the police, entitled "Who Draws Swastikas?"
(Šetinc 1981). Šetinc arbitrarily connected two otherwise independent events:
the arrest of three teenagers for torturing a schoolmate and the presumed
organization of a Nazi Party. The article was accompanied by pictures of a
young man in a Nazi uniform (taken from an English magazine) and a punk
graffito. Among other things, Šetinc wrote:

> The damned kids. Where exactly do they come from? Who gave us
> these spurious seventeen year olds who torture a schoolmate for the
> fun of it, and boys who kill their peers? Who steal cars, get drunk and
> even take drugs. Where did the young people who draw swastikas,
> organize nazi socialist parties and who greet with a raised right hand
> come from? (Šetinc 1981, 3)

Three alleged Nazi punks were arrested and kept in prison during three months of investigation. After their release two were charged with creating hostile propaganda with a possible prison sentence ranging from one to ten years. The trial was held two years later and the two alleged Nazi punks were released because of lack of evidence.

During all this period, police repression on a wide scale was being waged against punks: there were raids on pubs and other meeting places, persecution of the punk image, interrogations, investigations, raids against graffiti writers, bannings of concerts, and censorship. Raids on pubs and other meeting places had the function of atomizing the punk scene. If punks developed a habit of meeting in a certain pub or disco, this was a sure sign that it would soon be closed down by the authorities—for renovation, because of neighbors' complaints, unsatisfactory sanitary conditions or some similar reason. In other cases, waiters obviously worked in close cooperation with the police. They would, for example, refuse to serve punks and would call the police with allegations of improper behavior. At Medex, a pub on what the punks called "Johnny Rotten Square" in the center of Ljubljana, the waiters refused to serve them, so punks would have other people buy them drinks. One day a waitress called the police because someone was supposed to have said "Heil Hitler" (Skupina avtorjev 1984, 488). Although she could not identify the culprit, the police nonetheless arrested all the punks present. One was slapped in the face while another was severely beaten at the police station.

Sometimes parts of the punk image were not tolerated. On two consecutive occasions, a well-known Ljubljana punk had problems with the police because of two buttons he wore. The first offense was a crossed-out swastika with "Nazi punks fuck off" written over it; the second button showed a swastika, hammer and sickle with "crazy governments" written across them (Skupina avtorjev 1984, 18). He went to court where he was sentenced to a 30-day prison sentence for offending the national and patriotic feelings of his fellow citizens.

Many punks, especially the younger ones, were "invited for a conversation" at the police station. One 16-year-old punk was questioned about Nazis among his friends and acquaintances (Skupina avtorjev 1984, 486). The police asked him to admit that he, too, was a Nazi. Then they beat him with bare hands and truncheons, threatened and insulted him until he finally confessed and signed a document to that effect. After that he was released. Some days later he told a social worker what had happened to him. The social worker convinced him to put his story down on paper and took it to the boy's school. From there a letter of protest was addressed to the police authorities but the only consequence of this was a visit to the school by a group of policemen to inquire whether the letter was by any chance not forged.

Investigations were as a rule carried out without search warrants. The police came to the apartment of a punk at 7:30 A.M. when she had already left for school (Skupina avtorjev 1984, 16). They searched her room and confiscated some pictures of German generals, addresses of people, and papers with slogans. With the owner of the items gone, the police arrested her roommate!

Police action against graffiti writers was also ruthless and swift. In a couple of weeks the authorities managed to do what the Fascists did not achieve in three years of occupation of Ljubljana in World War II—they arrested 18 graffiti writers. They even used lie detectors in the campaign. One of the writers who admitted that he wrote swastikas and slogans against the red bourgeoisie was sentenced to three days in a detention center for minors (Skupina avtorjev 1984, 487). Others were fined.

The authorities also found ways to prohibit concerts. A band called Laibach (the German name for Ljubljana) was the main target of this repression (Skupina avtorjev 1984, 19-20). Members of the parliament of Ljubljana decided that a group with that name could not be allowed to spread fascist ideas. They passed a resolution stating that the use of this name is an infringement of law. The band was forbidden to play in Slovenia as long as it used that name.

Censorship was widespread. An example is the case of a fanzine banned from publication in Ljubljana (Skupina avtorjev 1984, 22). The punks who conceived the fanzine also wanted to publish some documents concerning police repression. The authorities decided that the fanzine could give the impression that the system was repressive and could be interpreted as an appeal for help. They insisted that changes be made before it could appear in public.

How did the official youth organization react to these campaigns against punk? In accordance with their powerless position, they were proliferate in articulating standpoints but only seldom even attempted to act upon them. These standpoints, as the prevalent reaction to the punk phenomenon, will thus be described first.

At the cultural plenum of the League of Socialist Youth (O kulturni politiki 1981, 3-21), Mile Šetinc criticized mass culture as "opiate of the masses" and then rebuffed definitions of "so-called" punk either as an example of class struggle in music or as an import of a social force hostile to socialism. In his opinion

Punk is above all what a discussant has called a symptom indicating undeveloped self-management relations, social alienation, rule of mass culture of a commercial type, inefficiency of our "abstract ideological-political discourse," conformism and careerism in the youth organization and its alienation from young people. Now that we are striving for the youth organization to establish a more intensive connection with young people and their problems which are intensifying in the crisis situation we are going through, it will be more useful to fight against the reality which manifests itself in a deformed way by the punk symptom than to alienate punk from the young with an aprioristic opposition. (P. 17).

In Article 12 of Standpoints and Directions of the plenum (O kulturni politiki 1981, 92-100), members of "official youth" decided to offer concrete support to mass culture as well as to the "so-called" punk:

The LSYS will encourage amateur mass music of the young and offer its assistance in assuring possibilities to practice and to perform for music groups. It will simultaneously strive for a more coordinated and responsible program policy in record production, recording and airplay of Slovenian youth mass music on radio and television as well as for a more creative treatment of manifestations of these music in mass media, above all on television. (P. 97)

Judging from the discussion that followed, punk was not on the priority list of most of the discussants on lower levels of the organization. A member of the official youth from Postojna recounted past success in library science, restoration of cultural institutions, and other endeavors. In the future they would have to put greater emphasis on ideological-political work, the relay of youth (a celebration of Tito's birthday with young people running all over the country), and cultural cooperation with the Yugoslav army. Representatives from Nova Gorica and Tolmin near the Italian border stressed that their greatest problem was that many young people were watching commercial Italian television stations instead of the socialist-oriented television from Ljubljana. In Celje professional youths were offering young people an alternative to cheap culture in the form of readings of lyrical poetry or theater plays.

There was little talk at the plenum concerning the police repression of punk, which was at its peak. Mile Šetinc was cautiously against it:

Numerous discussions in youth publications and also in a wider context were recently dedicated to the phenomenon of the so-called punk. This phenomenon in musical creativity undoubtedly deserves attention as it became so popular among the young that the otherwise few attempts at administrative intervention of distribution of products of this musical orientation in the past were totally inefficient. (O kulturni politiki 1981, 20).

There were also those who welcomed the state repression, among them Andrej Perko, president of the Ljubljana branch of the LSY:

> But when it comes to excesses with swastikas the president of the Ljubljana youth is categorical. "There is no room for them, not in punk and not in society. We have to be rigorous." (Skupina avtorjev 1984, 271)

Srečo Kirn, a high-ranking youth functionary on the level of republic, responded even more categorically. He distinguished two camps in the punk movement, anarchist and rightist. He first discounted the anarchists because they dared to deny the role of the youth organization in society, but he was even more critical of the rightist deviation.

> The other tendency which manifests itself inside the punk "movement" is of course more dangerous and the one to which we should dedicate our attention. This tendency is connected with what I mentioned previously, to nationalist excesses. It is of interest that these tendencies appeared to be analogous to the rightist movement in Great Britain also. In our context it manifests itself above all in slogans for a "clean Slovenia" in which workers from other republics are enemies who have to be defeated. A tendency to adore certain historical monsters, such as Adolf Hitler, has also appeared. In such cases we will of course be merciless. There can be no compromise in this case and we will struggle with all our power and resources against such a black reaction, destroying the conditions as well as the manifestations of such and of similar attitudes. (Skupina avtorjev 1984, 217)

Kirn claims that he initially sympathized with punk and even published punk writings in the student newspaper *Tribuna*. But later he came under the influence of the Slovene chief of police, Tomaž Ertl, and became convinced that punks are in reality the class enemies of socialism. He went through another transition when two other youth activists, Igor Bavčar and Tomaž Mastnak, convinced him that he was in the wrong. Kirn describes the whole episode of becoming a "born again punk" in the following manner:

> To understand my position I have to tell from the start that I believed in the conception of classes. Now: at the outbreak of the nazi punk affair Ertl with his famous little hand-bag came to the secretariat of

the Presidency of the RC [Republican Committee] LSY and drew out some papers to prove that rightists stand behind punk and other such things. I honestly admit that he convinced me at the time. I started making connections with the English National Front and said to myself that something has to be done in connection with this, and it has to be done publicly. I wrote [my opinion] at home and when I had it in handwriting, Bavčar and Mastnak visited me. I read the text to them and I have to say that they were amazed, above all Tomaž, by what they had just heard: namely I expressed a certain support of the police. A discussion followed in which Tomaž and of course also Igor convinced me that my attitude was completely wrong, and I accepted this! I tore the manuscript and said: You are right, I was too faithful. And from that moment on my attitudes were more or less identical [to theirs]. (Bakše 1989, 61)

So it came about that the youth organization did not express support for police repression of punks. Perhaps their silence had some influence regarding the extent and the intensity of the persecution. What we do know is that the Nazi punk affair definitely had an influence on the youth organization itself. On this matter, Igor Bavčar said:

This was one of the essential things. This is when we got the idea of pluralism, that is, of a front-type youth organization which was later articulated in the congress documents. With the Nazi punk affair we were faced with a dilemma. They wanted us to renounce a part of the youth population, that part of Slovenian youth which was obviously going somewhere else and was not interested in what we were doing. (Bakše 1989, 43)

And Srečo Kirn on the same topic:

In the last analysis I agree with you that intrigues in connection with punk represented a sort of a turning point. It was then that many youth functionaries realized that they can all of a sudden find themselves in a very extreme situation in relation to authority, when the question of legitimacy and legality is put forward—not yours but the authorities! (Bakše, 1989: 63)

It is only with difficulty that one can discover traces of this newly discovered autonomy in the documents of the Eleventh Congress of LSY in 1982. On the one hand, the party had numerous suggestions for improvement of the draft version which had to be considered, but basically the problem was that LSY was still an organization of young Communists. The conflict was still one within the party. The whole discourse was predominantly communist—a lot of reference to Tito and Kardelj, revolutionary traditions, working class, avant-garde party, and other cliches.

The authors of the documents warn that sectarianism of the youth organization in relation to the culture of the young is an unwarranted reaction to mass culture as an "opiate of the masses" (Dokument 11. Kongresa ZSMS 1983, 70). The only way to resist various deviations in culture is by widening cultural horizons and not by prevention. The president of the republican LSY, Darja Colarič, even expressed official support of punk:

> And this (front-type organization of LSY) has in reality been strengthened, however strange this may sound. Nobody succeeded in driving a wedge between the young and their organization; the greatest danger of this happening was precisely the threat with regard to punk. But precisely here, without intending to institutionalize this new wave among the young, we have succeeded in maintaining its autonomy and rebuffing all attempts to confront our organization with thousands who identify with punk. (Dokument 11. Kongresa ZSMS 1983, 9)

Four years later, at the Twelfth Congress, members of LSY still clung to the self-management socialist discourse despite the deep crisis of the Communist regime. The days of the Nazi punk affair were long over and, as a result, there was little talk of culture among the young. Punk was of interest to professional youth only as long as it appeared to be a political excess. When it was pushed into an artistic ghetto it became invisible for the young activists. As a result, most talk of culture was on a very general level (Dokument 12. Kongresa ZSMS 1986, 29-30): LSY must not limit its activity to funding of sports, culture, and recreation but must also be active in finding solutions to basic problems of social development, economic progress, and everyday life of young people, and so on. The only exception was the band Laibach, whose name, totalitarian image, and ideology (a combination of Stalinism and nazism) provoked the authorities. As a result the band had problems playing concerts in Slovenia (but not in other parts of Yugoslavia!) as well as a lot of hostile press coverage. The LSY quickly reacted to the political excess and wrote in the conclusions of the congress: "We demand that initiatives and adopted attitudes for the legalization of the name and activity of the band LAIBACH are immediately realized." (Dokument 12. Kongresa ZSMS 1986, 38)

If the relation of top LSY officials to the punk subculture was more or less limited to declarations of intent, it was for the simple reason that punks were of no "use value" to them. Laibach, however, became a love at first sight for the official youths. Laibach and *Neue Slowenische Kunst* (NSK), a group of painters (IRWIN), a theater group (Scipion Nasice), and a group of designers (New Collectivism) were more an artistic avant-garde than a rock movement. Seeking inspiration in historical avant-gardes (above all socialist realism and Nazi art), they used mass culture as a medium to reach a wider audience with their countercultural messages. They preached that the West is decadent and the "new man" is needed to save it; that collectivism will triumph over individualism as a result of a cultural revolution spearheaded by NSK shock troops. All this rang a familiar bell for official youths, reminding them of their own not so distant countercultural past. On top of that, NSK ideology could always be interpreted as a critique of, rather than an apology for, totalitarianism. Better still, as artists, Laibach and their comrades could represent, as punk rockers could not, a legitimate cultural platform for LSY. Soon the youth organization began to finance numerous projects of the avant-garde as parts of LSY alternative cultural policy, setting it apart from the party's political activities.

To maintain this newly discovered boundary, official youths, for example, hired artists to conceive an image of the relay of youth, an institution that had existed ever since the end of World War II, to celebrating Tito's birthday, which—on his initiative—also became the official Day of Youth. Young people from all over the country would, as already mentioned, run for months, gradually approaching Belgrade where a rally would be held on May 25 at the Stadium of the Yugoslav People's Army. No serious objection to the event had ever been voiced (Mekina and Zapečnik 1989, 105), but, in the early eighties, youth officials from Slovenia started expressing their first, more or less cautious, objections regarding its meaning. Was not this sort of worship appropriate only for deities and not for Comrade Tito? Its bad (socialist realist) taste and its cost (some local LSY organizations spent up to 80 percent of their annual budgets to finance their part of the event) were cited. In 1986 all these objections culminated into a suggestion by a group of students from Ljubljana, supported by the University Committee of LSY, to carve a gigantic baton for the relay of youth from a four-meter-long tree trunk. On what was once Johnny Rotten Square in the center of Ljubljana, a group of sculptors from the Academy of Arts started to work while students voiced their opposition to the relay and a petition against the relay was circulated for signatories. In the evening when the baton was at last carved and appropriately painted, funeral rites were held in its honor. The authorities, who criticized the whole happening as tasteless, as an act of despair and an abuse of democracy, nevertheless did not intervene. The next morning, garbage collectors took the work where it really belonged, in the opinion of the demonstrators—to the dust-bin (of Ljubljana, if not yet of history).

The majority of top LSY officials were at the time not so radical as the student branch of their organization and therefore decided to go through with the preparations for the relay which, in 1987, started from Slovenia. True to their nature, NSK avant-gardists conceived something so pompous and monumental that no previous celebration could compare with it. Fearing a new scandal (party ideologues opposed the project) and also in a dilemma because of its enormous cost, the whole project was eventually dropped. But despite this, a scandal was provoked: New Collectivism designed a poster which was a remake of an old Nazi poster on which the swastika was replaced by the Yugoslav flag. It took the authorities quite some time to catch on, and when they did, criticism of LSY for attempting to revive fascism spread like an avalanche throughout the country.

Despite the undoubted affinity between the LSY and NSK, the new avant-gardists could only offer the political youth an alternative cultural policy. What the LSY really needed at that point was an alternative political orientation, a way to create recognizable political borders in relation to the party. It thus comes as no surprise that the main interest of top officials at the 1986 congress was the new social movements (the peace movement, greens, gays, and feminists) which were evolving as characteristic youth subpolitics. Activists of the new social movements did not perceive their own autonomous political organization to be a real option until 1989, so they sought to penetrate the existing political organizations, above all the youth organization and the Socialist Alliance of the Working People. The peace movement, for example, functioned inside the LSY from the beginning of the 1980s—cautiously in the beginning, with general demands for world peace which were not problematic inside the existing political context, then growing more daring, with demands for civil service, civilian control of the Yugoslav military complex, and an initiative for demilitarization of the Balkan region. The relationships were symbiotic—the movements that worked inside LSY used it to gain access to political decision making and the media, while LSY acquired a new source of legitimacy through the movements when the disintegrating communist ideology no longer offered one. The new social movements presented a new possible source of orientation and activity for LSY. It is therefore no wonder that at the twelfth congress its leadership already demanded the integration of new social movements into LSY in order to ensure their legitimate and full functioning (Dokument 12. Kongresa ZSMS 1986, 29-30). But as far as punk or the rock subculture as a whole were concerned, LSY proceedings were of no significance—members of new social movements were a subpolitics and as such predominantly uninterested in the rock subculture.

Although the official youth mostly polemicized against punk, they sometimes also tried to act upon their words. The most prominent of the first generation of punk bands, *Pankrti* (Bastards), often had problems with LSY activists (Skupina avtorjev 1984, 219-220). In 1978 the band was prevented from playing at a Ljubljana high school because the LSY branch there sided with the teachers' view that the Pankrti were obscene. In that same year the president of RC LSY, Boris Bavdek, tried to prevent the band's first single from being issued by the Student Cultural Center. In 1979 the leadership of LSY prevented the band from playing at the Day of Youth and Tito's birthday celebration. Pankrti's problems culminated in their rejection for a prize by RC LSY in 1980. The youth organization also did nothing to improve the working conditions for the rock musicians as they boasted they would do in 1981—reneging on promises to organize places to play, provide more opportunities to record, and improve distribution and media coverage.

Youth organization attitudes toward punk were often uncoordinated. One manifest example of this was the concert in solidarity with the Polish people on the occasion of the Jaruzelski military coup. Only the youth organizations from the University and from two boroughs of Ljubljana gave support to the idea of the concert. Igor Bavčar recalls that "in preparations for the concert we had great problems above all with the Ljubljana youth team. Nijaz Smajič, a youth official from Vič was foremost among them" (Bakše 1989, 46).

Because an effective integrative mechanism was lacking (be it democratic centralism or democratic elections), youth organizations on lower levels were becoming increasingly autonomous. This sometimes had negative aspects, as in the above situation when Stalinist-oriented youth officials tried to prevent a public expression of sympathy with Polish Solidarity, but more often it had positive side effects. The majority of ideologically uninhibited young people were able to use local LSY organizations as a legitimate cover and a source of funding for the organization of rock concerts and other subcultural activities. Conflicts arose only when subcultural activities spontaneously evolving through local branches of LSY provoked hostile reactions from Communist authorities.

In 1980, for example, a group of young people in the coal-mining town of Trbovlje organized an art exhibition with a punk concert (Skupina avtorjev 1984, 149-155). The posters for the event reminded the authorities of Nazi art and as a result the whole event was prohibited. The local LSY branch had been the formal organizer of the event because it would have been much more difficult for an informal group of people to get permission. But when scandal broke out, the LSY branch immediately distanced itself:

> All that to which a young worker, peasant, miner, student strives toward is present in all working people, self-managers, in all those who build on the basis of our achievements. The goals of all are identical whereas the form may vary depending on the generation. All these people who in the rapid pace of life still find moments for

> relaxation, who seek and learn from the tradition of the nation are
> humiliated with the posters—their work was humiliated, their cre-
> ativity, their past. They were surprised by this propaganda material
> which was supposedly inviting them to an art exhibition and a punk
> concert and they publicly said that they do not want it in their midst.
> In relation to this young people have assessed that all, especially all
> that the older people went through during the war personally, can-
> not be stuck on walls and cannot be hidden behind the word punk.
> (P. 155)

Another characteristic example of punk-LSY relations is the case of the
already mentioned punk fanzine in Ljubljana. As it was next to impossible for
an informal group to issue a fanzine on its own, the Student Cultural Center
(SCC) was used as a front. When the first issue was supposed to see the light
of day, the city branch of LSY intervened. At a meeting of the authors, representatives of SCC, official youth representatives, and party members, the
publication of the fanzine was postponed until the questionable parts were clar-
ified (Skupina avtorjev 1984). Igor Vidmar, who was there as a representative
of SCC, described the behavior of youth officials at the meeting:

> There were quite a few of them but as is befitting in the presence of
> older people, they were mostly silent. Only one of them, I think he
> was from the republican conference, tried to be more papal than the
> Pope and used this "affair" in which SCC did not show sufficient
> instinct for "political security" to put us down. (P. 199)

A couple of days later, members of the city branch of LSY reproached the
creators of the fanzine because of the lack of a concept.

> We are not against this type of expression. What is needed is a pro-
> gram for which SCC gets the necessary space and finances from
> Slovenian culture, which is why a concept for the fanzine must be
> elaborated. . . . The fanzine, such as it is, is unacceptable but this does
> not render it impossible in the future. What is needed is a concept.
> (Skupina avtorjev 1984, 201)

To translate this demand into everyday language: what is needed is more
(self)censorship.

LSY held its last, thirteenth congress in 1989. An organization that for
decades had served as a transmission of party will, and that only recently had
started incorporating ideas and practices of new social movements as its own,
underwent a metamorphosis and became the LSY-Liberal Party (in the
European sense of liberal), interested above all in private property and mar-

ket regulation! As such, it of course showed little patience for cultural questions. Culture is only mentioned once, in the platform point that all cultural activities should have equal opportunity of access to the public (Programski dokument 13. Kongresa 1989, 32-33).

The story of two uneasy—and by and large mutually disinterested—fellow travelers through a rapidly disintegrating socialism was thus effectively ending. In the nineties, these two changed beyond recognition. LSY—Liberal Party renamed itself the Liberal Democratic Party, adopting a new name as well as a new party boss, thus abandoning its communist and revisionist past to lay claim to its direct opposite, the heritage of the European liberal tradition. As for punks, they became a part of rock'n'roll history. The rockers of today live in a very different sort of social environment.

One of the crucial consequences of the political democratization of 1990 was secularization. Ideology that had been withering away for decades at long last finally collapsed. This meant, among other things, that the ruling elite could no longer translate phenomena of everyday life into "problems of the transition period." Words lost their magic grip on reality and most aspects of everyday reality became "de-problematized." As a result, for some people democracy itself became a problem—they had difficulty adjusting to the mundane nature of everyday modern life. Just as socialism depended on faith, those who opposed it were also involved in events somehow transcending the here-and-now nature of everyday life. The fact that the whole political system was based on the belief in a certain scenario of a future "final solution" explains both why the party was so intolerant to opposition as well as why some people perceive postsocialist democracy as a loss. Such an attitude is most characteristic of dissident members of subpolitical movements; it is much less common among members of subcultures, who felt at home in the modern secular world even when they had to create their own version in marginal enclaves within everyday socialist reality. Just as they were indifferent to socialism then, they hardly noticed its demise now.

CONCLUSION

What can we say about the relationship between the official youth organization and members of the punk subculture in the eighties?

Sometimes members of the LSY perceived the rock subculture as a political movement, be it an ally or an enemy. Srečo Kirn, as we saw, for a time perceived it as a hostile movement, either anarchist or fascist. Igor Bavčar, on the other hand perceived punks as potential allies, saying, "I suggested a 'deal' to

Vidmar—punk is your concern, we recognize you as a part of Slovenian youth, I don't remember exactly in return for what" (Tomc 1988, 1360).

In both cases we have a misunderstanding of subculture—politicians ascribing their own political orientations inside the dominant culture to those who live a unique subcultural enclave and show little interest in politics. As we saw, members of the rock subculture are, above all, cultural nonconformists, putting their emphasis on alternative cultural practices such as creativity, life style, image, and slang. A political movement can narrow or widen the social space at the disposal of subcultural practitioners perceiving it as either a symbolic or an actual threat to the existing order, but it cannot use the subculture effectively for its own purposes. The conditions under which the Slovenian rock subculture functioned thus changed significantly over the years: from repressive tolerance in the fifties, to relative liberalization in the sixties, to a renewed period of intolerance and repression in the early seventies (mitigated by a more developed commercial music industry), followed by a period of gradual disintegration of the communist project in the late seventies and the eighties, and resulting in another "liberalization."

From the aspect of communist cultural policy these phases indicated oscillations between countercultural and political activity. Politics is understood as a goal-oriented activity in the mainstream culture whereas counterculture is understood as a combination of culturally deviant and goal-oriented activity, that is as a striving for the attainment of goals outside the mainstream. The communist cultural policy in the years immediately after World War II was itself countercultural, a cultural revolution for a "new man," and as such extremely intolerant of anything not in accordance with the postulates of socialist realism. An analogous process, but with a significantly lower degree of intensity, was attempted in the seventies. The sixties and the eighties were, roughly speaking, periods of greater tolerance of the rock subculture, if not exactly of its promotion.

Representatives of the youth organization more or less followed the oscillations in the "parent" party organizations as described. In periods when a more fanatical person was predominant in the organization, a person believing in the reference of internalized ideological beliefs to a particular social reality, youth organization members conceived an ambition to combine political activity with cultural deviation, that is cultural revolution. In these periods, they would perceive mass culture as the "opiate of the masses," a decadent import from the West. (Very rarely, a different strategy was at work and official youths would try to incorporate mass culture by defining it as the true culture of the proletariat, a culture consumed by the man in the street and thus friendly to socialism.) But in periods when a modern person became predominant in the organization, a person in tune with everyday reality and not hostile to it, cultural policy became more tolerant. Under the more liberal conditions, however, members of the LSY no longer had a mechanism at their disposal that could help them determine what was reactionary and what was progressive in culture. They were lost and could only plead for equal access for all taking part in cultural life. But if this was a return to normal for subcultural practitioners, it represented a problem for the members of the official youth. By renouncing their countercultural position, they were also losing their roots, their original identity and position.

As the youth organization was losing its countercultural characteristics, it was also losing its interest in questions of culture in general and in rock subculture in particular. Something similar can also be said of members of the rock subculture. Their interest in politics in general and in youth politics in particular was limited to extreme situations. One such extreme situation was triggered, as was seen, by the party boss France Popit. But when the campaign against punk ended, the punks' interest in politics also diminished. For them, the really interesting things are not happening in factories or at political meetings but rather in their free time, filled with subcultural self-expression.

BIBLIOGRAPHY

Ascherson, N. (1970). "Heretics." The *New York Review,* November 19.
Bakše, I. (1989). *Ne čakaj na maj* (Don't wait for May). Ljubljana: Karantanija.
Broz, J. [Tito] (1971). *Tito—omladina—mladost revolucije* (Tito—youth—youthful revolution). Zagreb: Biblioteka Centra.
Dokument 11. Kongresa ZSMS (Documents of the 11th congress of the LSY) (1983). Ljubljana: ZSMS
Dokument 12. Kongresa ZSMS (Documents of the 12th congress of the LSY) (1986). Ljubljana: ZSMS.
Dolar, M. (1971). "Prove Yourself Alive." *Tribuna,* no. 1.
Hafner Fink, D. (1987). *Odnos KPJ-ZKJ in mladinska organizacija* (Relations between the CPY-LCY and youth organizations). Ljubljana: FSPN.
Hebdige, D. (1980). *Potkultura: značenje stila* (Subculture: the significance of style). Beograd: Pečat.
Kos, S. (1984). *Stalinistična revolucija na Slovenskem 1941-1945* (The Stalinist revolution in Slovenia 1941-45). I. Rome: published by the author.
Marx, K., and F. Engels (1973). *Omladina I i II* (Youth I and II). Beograd: Marksistična biblioteka.
Mekina, I., and S. Zapečnik (1989). "Somrak Štafete" (The twilight of Tito's baton). In B. Leskovar, ed., *Kompendij za bivše in bodoče politike* (Compendium for past and future politicians). Ljubljana: ŽKZ.

O kulturni politiki ZSMS in dejavnosti mladih na področju kulture: Kulturni plenum ZSMS (On the cultural policies of LSY and youth cultural activity: Cultural plenum) (1981). Ljubljana: ABC 14.

Programski dokument 13. kongresa (Programmatic documents of the 13th congress) (1989). Ljubljana: ZSMS.

Reed, L. (1969). "Beginning to See the Light," *The Velvet Underground* (record album). New York: MGM.

Roszak, T. (1978). *Kontrakultura* (Counterculture). Zagreb: Naprijed.

Skupina avtorjev (1984). *Punk pod Slovenci* (Punk under Slovenes). Ljubljana: KRT.

Šetinc, Z. (1981). "Kdo riše kljukaste križe?" (Who draws swastikas?). *Nedeljski dnevnik* November 22.

Tomc, G. (1988). "Intervju z Igorjem Bavčarjem" (Interview with Igor Bavčar), *Nova revija* 80/81. Ljubljana.

Tomc, G. (1989). *Druga Slovenija* (The other Slovenia). Ljubljana: KRT.

Zappa, F. (1970). "Kaj je to 'Freaking Out'" (What is Freaking Out?), *Tribuna* 9/10.

7

Troubles with Democracy:
Women and Slovene Independence

Vlasta Jalušič

THE FIRST POSTSOCIALIST STRIFE

It was December 1991, more than a year after the first free elections in Slovenia. About two thousand women and men gathered in the front of the Slovenian Parliament demanding protection of reproductive rights within the new, postsocialist constitution. Thirteen women's groups, women's initiatives inside trade unions, and ten parliamentary and nonparliamentary parties organized the demonstration. The demonstrators shouted: Women's rights into the new constitution! Women's ministry! Women's parliament! Abortion without compromise! There will be new elections! If you decide without us, we will vote against you!

The paragraph regarding the "human right to decide upon the birth of one's own children" (reproductive rights) remained the last point of disagreement in the entire constitutional debate in Slovenia after independence. That outcome was no surprise for anyone who had followed the debate during the 1990 elections, when Slovenia was still a part of Yugoslavia. The reproductive rights debate raised open discussion about the role of women in the Slovene nation and included the issues of the birth rate and the supposed fear that the small Slovenian nation would die out. There were also ideological discussions about the foundations of the old, communist system and the necessary foundations of the new, democratic society. Strong pressure built up to omit the reproductive rights paragraph, on the basis of three main arguments:

First, Slovenia as a new state aiming at immediate international recognition, desperately needed a new, democratic constitution. The consent of all parliamentary parties was crucial. So, if agreement could not be reached on the human right to decide over the birth of one's own children, this paragraph should be left out in order to facilitate adoption of the new constitution and allow new elections.

Second, the conservative (especially Catholic) corner showed "wonderment over the fuss about this funny question." If the adoption of the new constitution could be endangered by "such a trifle," they declared, Europe would really "laugh at us." Another "argument" of the opponents of constitutional reproductive rights was that no European constitution guaranteed such rights.[1]

Third, some opponents saw the paragraph on reproductive rights as a remnant of the totalitarian communist system, which had dictated the "forced emancipation" of women. This totalitarian argument was connected with the question of democratic legitimation as well: it was not important what the rights were in fact, but simply that the rights had been given by the communists. Opponents tried to discredit the rights gained by women in socialism. They claimed that under socialism Slovene women were forced to work outside the home, given unwanted social equality, and prevented from playing the nurturing family roles assumed to be natural to them.

But what was the actual point of this struggle in Slovenia?

As a female, born at the end of the 1950s, I belong to a generation that grew up in a period of rather liberal attitudes toward contraception and abortion. During the last twenty years, decisions regarding one's own reproductive capacities were not questioned. Moreover, nobody would even have thought about questioning them—at least not in public. Perhaps it was an original solution, indeed, to have a paragraph guaranteeing reproductive rights in the Yugoslav federal constitution of 1974 (which was attacked later from all possible sides) and the republican constitutions, which inherited Paragraph 55 from the federal document. We can only guess whether it was the alertness of some Communist "state feminists"[2] to possible future transgressions against this right or the character of the socialist constitution that made such a solution possible.[3]

Many independent women's groups in Slovenia had publicly argued for the preservation of abortion rights in the new, postsocialist constitution. The 1974 constitutional right had served as the foundation for all further legislation on this subject, and many women believed that reproductive rights were the basis for women's political and social rights. Also, they had seen that previous liberal and social-oriented legislation on this question had achieved positive results.

Opponents of constitutional reproductive rights claimed that the defenders of this right were making abortion propaganda and that abortion is not a right but an "emergency way out" that does not belong in the constitution. Defenders replied that their plea addressed a set of rights, one of which was legal abortion, and that omission of these rights would put 51 percent of the population in the position of second-class citizens. If reproductive rights were not constitutionally guaranteed, pro-choice legislation could be abolished by a simple majority in the parliament. This right had extremely strong symbolic importance. As opponents clearly claimed that women should not decide for themselves, there existed the danger not only that abortion might be outlawed, but that women's equality might be abolished, at least symbolically.

Only 11 percent of the parliament elected in 1991 were women, and there was only one woman on the constitutional commission when the abortion discussion took place. Despite powerful pressure from the governing parties, the women MPs (25 of 240) made a joint statement supporting the retention of reproductive rights in the constitution. The women's campaign and the demonstration were successful: The paragraph remained, although not in the original form: defined not as a right, but as freedom to decide over the birth of one's own children.

The debate and demonstration answered an important question: in what situations are women in Slovenia ready to organize themselves? The answer, it appears, is that women will organize when their customary rights are endangered. And reproductive rights have already been understood as customary women's rights.

Back to the Past

The discussion of abortion rights illustrates how all the classical political and human rights dilemmas of the "new beginning" entered the 1991 transitional period from socialism to something else. Should there be a complete break with the old regime in all details? Should one change the entirety of legislation and all the beaten tracks of everyday life, too? Or is it possible to make compromises and not make a complete revolution?

Although Slovenia was known as a country in which the "softest" and longest reform within socialism took place, the new politicians were not able to avoid the classical dilemmas about the "new beginning." It was not only the "woman question" that was treated as suspicious and scrutinized as a part of the ideology of the old system. To understand the situation of women and women's initiatives in the postsocialist era, we have to take a short glance into the past.

There is still very little competent Slovene women's history.[4] The only works available are some contributions written between the two world wars, some ideological works based on the Marxist insistence that the woman question can only be resolved by the construction of socialism, and a very few new works from the 1980s, when neo-feminist women's initiatives appeared.

Slovene women have not had a long-lasting independent mass women's movement, at least not a movement separate from struggles for Slovene national interests, identity, and culture. However, instances of women's rebellion and mass self-organizing against their unequal position or against an unjust social order, as well as many women's social and political organizations, societies, and movements can be found in Slovene history.[5]

There is evidence of early women's membership in many religious sects during the reformation, where they enjoyed equal status as priests, too. Between the sixteenth and eighteenth centuries in Slovene territory the majority of victims of the inquisition were females. Women were allowed to attend school after the reforms of the Empress Maria Theresa in the eighteenth century. However, the struggle for women's right to attend school was connected to the struggle for schooling in the Slovenian language.

Organized women's movements emerged in the second half of the nineteenth century with the increasing numbers of educated women. The introduction of compulsory primary school for both sexes in 1869 brought women a chance to attend state teachers' schools. Female teachers, educated and literate, initiated the first women-organized campaign for equal pay and suffrage through their own organization. The first women's strike in Slovenia came in 1871 in the confectionery factory in Ljubljana. The raising of women's consciousness concerning their position in society was connected to the appearance of women's societies (the first one was founded in 1887) and women's presses. In 1897 *Slovenka* (the Slovenian woman), the first women's magazine with feminist ideas, was launched in Trieste. A study in 1926 about women in nineteenth century Slovenia claimed that the General Slovenian Women's Society founded in 1900, showed "clear feminist and social orientation" (Štebi 1926, 162).

But, above all, women played an important role within the Slovenian national movement at the end of the First World War and later. They demonstrated and gathered signatures for the so-called May Declaration in 1917-18.[6] Since women were a part of the movement against the Austro-Hungarian monarchy they were really

> entitled to expect human rights and equal citizenship in the new state. Unfortunately that didn't happen. On the contrary. Slovene women had better social position and citizenship rights in Austria than

> women in Serbia, Montenegro, Macedonia, Bosnia and Hercegovina. The old Yugoslavia never harmonized the legislation it inherited from its various parts—above all differences in women's legal position. Besides, the danger that Serbian laws would be extended to other parts of the state always loomed. (Muser 1972, 90)

After the formation of the Kingdom of Serbs, Croats, and Slovenes in 1919, women demonstrated again, this time against the Belgrade regime. In June 1925 the "united women of Slovenia" (12 women's organizations) held public women's meetings "regardless of party or class" against the extension of the patriarchal family law to the whole state. Meetings were organized in Ljubljana and other places in Slovenia. Women demanded equality in inheritance laws for women and children (including children born out of wedlock) and a woman's right to vote and campaigned against alcoholism and prostitution and for peace (Muser, 1972).

The Era of "State Feminism"

In spite of their loyalty to Yugoslavia, Yugoslav women did not gain formal equality until the end of the Second World War. Starting from Marxist analysis, communists had elaborated the whole ideological construct of the importance of women's emancipation for the proletarian state before the Second World War. Slovenian Communist Party activist Vida Tomšič provided the ideological basis for socialist legislation on women and gender relationships for all of Yugoslavia. As early as 1940, she listed women's demands for and of the Communist Party, from the protection of mothering to equal pay for equal work, from abortion rights to political equality and the right to divorce. But in the same text, she speaks against "bourgeois feminism" in a manner similar to Clara Zetkin.

Nevertheless, after the Second World War the legal equality of women began to be an important part of the legitimation of the socialist system. Women had participated heavily in the national liberation struggle. Lydia Sklevicky (1984a) writes of 100,000 active women participants in the whole of Yugoslavia, 34 percent of all combatants. A quarter of them died in the struggle. Women made up a third of all victims of the Second World War in Yugoslavia.

No less important was the founding of the semiautonomous women's organization in World War II, the Anti-Fascist Women's League. The organization was a broad front of women of different origins and political convictions, and united all the traditions of women's activism. It was the only successor to the "bourgeois" feminist and proletarian women's movements (Sklevicky, 1984b). The development of this organization, which was disbanded in 1953, was not without contradictions: although it was expected to serve as a transmission belt for the interests of the Yugoslav Communist Party and as an official women's movement, it showed tendencies toward independent women's political action.

> The picture of tasks and goals of the organization was confused: on the one hand, it attempted to mobilize women for difficult tasks in a country destroyed by war, and to liberate them from the patriarchal system. And, on the other hand, one expected neither independent strategies nor organizational strength. (Sklevicky 1984b, 89)

The Anti-Fascist Women's League was dissolved for two reasons: first, because of its potential for separatism and second, because of the conviction that the woman question was actually part of a broader social question and shouldn't be divided from it. After its dissolution, most "state feminists" lost their basis and professional status. Generally, only voluntary work was possible in the councils for social and political questions of women within the Socialist league; only a very small circle of women professional politicians were involved in decision making. This was one of the reasons for women's loss of influence at the state level (Sklevicky 1987).

Since the "equal legal status of women" was a basis of legitimation of the socialist system, it was necessary to put this image of equality into existence in the form of law. Emancipation was given from above without regard to the specific circumstances and differences in the whole Yugoslav state. As a consequence of enormous historical, national, religious, geographical, cultural, and economic differences, the right to work, and later, reproductive rights, never had the same meaning for women in different parts of Yugoslavia. Though women made up 39 percent of the employed in all of Yugoslavia in the mid-1980s, they were 46 percent in Slovenia, 42 percent in Croatia, between 35 and 37 percent in the other republics and 22 percent in Kosova. These differences were comparable with world North-South differences.

On the other hand, the official ideology proclaimed the nonexistence of the woman question, which would be solved simultaneously with the liberation of the working class. The fact that women enjoyed a good legal position in the second Yugoslavia was connected with the special ideological premise of the "role of woman in socialism" and not with the concept of women's politics. Ideologues argued that the woman question was not a separate issue, but only a part of a broader social question. Women in our country already enjoy equality, they insisted, at least formal equality; all we need to do to solve the woman question is to make some corrections (social measures) and perhaps some changes at the level of consciousness.

Even though the regime used women's issues for its own legitimation (women's work as an important contribution to the economy, the need to socialize the household and the "family functions") as well, women in socialist Yugoslavia did get formal rights, including some rights women in most western countries had never before enjoyed. Among these were the recognition of reproductive rights in the constitution, mentioned above; legal acknowledgment of marital rape; the opportunity for women to retain their family name after marriage, without adding the husband's family name; and long parental leave for both partners. Though in some parts of Yugoslavia there was a huge gap between the legal and real circumstances of women's lives, socialist "state feminism" created a system characterized by a relatively large degree of legal and social equality for women.

Generally speaking, everyday discrimination faced by women in Slovenia and the rest of Yugoslavia was not so very different from that in neighboring, nonsocialist countries. But

> there existed forms of inequality which are inherent in the policies of these states, often hidden behind formal equality . . . the persistence of a sexual division of labor and employment, in which the tasks allocated to women are less well rewarded . . . the failure to alleviate the burden of housework or to equalize the burden of domestic labor and responsibility between the sexes . . . the notorious "double shift" . . . the failure to redefine men's roles in a manner comparable to the redefinition of women's roles—so that even the latter becomes not so much a redefinition as the addition of a new role (participation in the labor force) onto an almost completely unreconstructed older one (mother and housewife). (Molyneux 1981, 29)

While there were a considerable number of women active in social care, local initiatives or self-managing interest councils for child care and schooling, representation was very low in higher posts. There was no quota system, at least none comparable to other socialist countries. Due to the special characteristics of the "self-management" system, the decision-making network was rather opaque and crucial decisions were not made in the lower-level bodies. For this reason, the percentage of female delegates in the "delegate system," which was at 26 percent at the beginning of the eighties, was not a good indicator of their political activity and influence.

Because self-management demanded that individuals be "socially active" (i.e., take part in hundreds of party or self-management organs), state feminists constantly complained about women's inactivity. Public opinion research in the seventies showed great disinterest among women in participating in self-management and the delegate system (Rener 1983). The paradox lay in the answers to the question "Why do you not participate in the delegate system?" Women answered mainly that they "do not have an interest" or that they "do not have time." Later, in the beginning of the nineties, they would answer that politics "is a waste of time." The answer shows the main problem of women in a system trying to actualize emancipation, namely, that the socialization (i.e., the industrialization) of the household doesn't bring more free time.

A further problem of political participation was that, in fact, the public space didn't exist as such, but was, a kind of enlarged household that also included the sphere of work outside home. So, if the percentage of women participating in the delegate system was higher than the percentage of politically active women in other nonsocialist countries, this was the result of entering only one part of the public space, the realm of socialized housework. This intermediate level of participation was not political, but social, a kind of "female semipublic kingdom," where women were left to themselves because they didn't disturb the established order too much.

Women didn't gain many benefits from access to the political public space. On the contrary, their political public space got smaller, indeed almost disappeared, and the social realm grew (perhaps this was one reason for the constant influence of "state feminists" in this area).

In addition, the spheres in which women were present lost importance and influence. One may even ask whether the national assembly lost its real political influence because there were too many women sitting in it (in 1982 about one-quarter of the delegates in the Slovene assembly and almost half of the leaders of the assembly were women) or whether women were elected to the assembly only because it had very limited influence. The "feminization" of a wide range of professions such as school teachers, judges, bank employees, lawyers, and physicians was a sign of the semipublic kingdom. Feminization (women were 60 percent of physicians and judges) meant at the same time decreasing professional status and salaries.[7]

The influence of "state feminism" at higher decision-making levels persisted until the beginning of the early eighties. "State feminism's" loss of influence was a consequence of systemic changes and growing economic difficulties, on the one hand, and of the beginning of disintegration processes in the whole state and society on the other. The legitimation function of special social polities, connected to the supposedly special role of women in socialism, became useless when a revised concept of the market system was introduced.

Besides, changes in Slovene society were very closely connected to the growing strength of nationalism. These developments showed how fragile women's rights and formal equality can be if there is no tradition of women's movements, or of independent women's political forms, and no women's public political consciousness about the meaning of their rights. The dominant "new democratic" discourse about women started to claim that 40 years' forced emancipation of women had destroyed socialization processes and even the family itself.

At the same time, this discourse contained a very strong ideology of progress and praise of "democracy and human rights." In spite of this, there was no questioning of these terms of debate and especially no questioning of the term "democracy," which was (as majority rule) used as cover for every possible action or argument (including the 1991 war). There emerged a paradoxical situation, in which one could use the "new democratic" discourse for both abolishing and restoring certain human rights.

Feminist Movements Emerge

We cannot speak about the women's movement and feminism in Slovenia in the eighties without discussing independent feminist initiatives in the seventies and eighties in Yugoslavia as a whole. Yugoslavia had several advantages compared to other socialist states. But the decisive one for the women's movement was open borders, which allowed the West to have an early impact on society in general and on women's movements in particular. Feminist literature, women's movement experience of Western countries and other feminist influences were brought into Yugoslavia very early.

The first academic women's group appeared in 1979 in Zagreb, spurred by a 1978 international feminist conference in Belgrade. It grew out of "the generation without its own tradition of organized women's activism," as Lydia Sklevicky (1987, 5) put it . Several groups appeared at the beginning of eighties, mostly in Belgrade, Zagreb, and Ljubljana, among them academic groups and, later, rape crisis centers. At first, there was a stronger connection between Zagreb and Belgrade than between either and Ljubljana. In Zagreb, the *Žena i Društvo* (Woman and Society) group had a strong academic interest. The group consisted of women philosophers, journalists, sociologists, and writers, who started to analyze different aspects of the so-called women question.

In Belgrade, feminist activists were never so homogeneous. Žarana Papić speaks about more informal groups, which were fluid and more radical in their feminist lifestyle. (Papić 1989). In both centers, activist groups appeared in the mid-eighties, partly in conflict with more academically oriented groups. In Ljubljana, the appearance of the first groups was associated with other new social movement activities, but in Belgrade and Zagreb only women's groups, unaccompanied by peace or ecology groups, were present. Thus, the independent women's network was the only independent new social movement spread across the three important centers of Yugoslavia.[8]

As Papić put it, the feminism of that time was not a movement in the broad social meaning. It was marginalized and bound to alternative cultural institutions. Nevertheless, if we believe that feminism is not necessarily a mass movement, but can also be an "intellectual tendency without a movement" (Delmar 1986), then we can see that this mixture of intellectual tendency and activism left some important traces in consciousness. Besides, when in the mid-eighties more radical groups such as Lilith in Ljubljana or lesbian groups appeared, the term feminism had been "legalized," so to speak. These groups did not suffer any direct party or state repression, though neither were they welcomed.

If we take a look at the situation in Yugoslavia during the interregnum of the mid-1980s, when some successful liberalization had occurred, we find many examples of rethinking women's position outside of the "state feminist" approach. Research was undertaken and some works published that we could call *women's studies*. Projects were few in comparison to Western activity. Characteristically, they were not institutionalized, but were either conducted as private research or hidden in other courses at the university. They grew out of very poor research infrastructure—almost all literature was in foreign languages and had to be bought with personal funds.

The main part of the very rich domestic literature on women from the nineteenth century to the Second World War was not evaluated and was left "hidden" in the libraries, mostly for ideological reasons. As late as the early eighties one of the very ordinary women's weeklies in Slovenia was censored because it reprinted material from some old "bourgeois feminist" texts. In the seventies and in the beginning of the eighties especially some studies could get past censorship under ideological cover (for example, the sociologists' conference about the social condition of women in the self-managing system in 1976 in Slovenia, articles in the Croat review *Žena* (Woman),[9] or the annual international women's studies seminars in Dubrovnik (discussed in Papić 1989, 194).

In the beginning, of course, everything published had to either spend a great deal of space condemning bourgeois Western feminism, or be presented in the more tolerated form of socialist feminism. In the 1970s, especially in Croatia and Serbia, discussion among some women scholars and journalists on feminism and its role got a lot of publicity and opened public space for discussion about women's issues.[10]

Up to the early eighties in Slovenia there were almost no independent studies that we could call women's studies, except some hidden studies at the university (especially in the realm of the sociology of family), and no independent women's groups. The beginning of independent studies and action was connected with the process of liberalization and especially with the rise of independent, women only, activities.[11] A very important element was the theoretical impact of women's studies in the Western countries. At the same time the concrete political influence of feminism in the West was also significant.

But the lack of diversity of forms and the low degree of political self-organization of women (and also other autonomous political initiatives) severely limited the extent of these studies. The influence of different feminist strands was quite obvious. The first independent publications emerged in 1982 (even before that year, although in the form of literature and not as studies): some translations and introductory studies were published,[12] two women's issues of the quarterly *Problemi/Eseji* (Problems/Essays), many articles published separately in various periodicals, and in the last two years some independent almanacs, about women and politics, family, and abortion.

Certain criticisms of oversimplification of the concept and construction of "woman" appeared, too. Some of this criticism was directed toward the official perception of the socialist, working class project of the emancipation of women, and some tried to rethink its own categories of woman, womanhood, feminism, etc.

To remedy the lack of independent women's political initiatives, a critique of the phenomena of "state feminism" was required. The new groups criticized the instrumentalization of women in politics, the "state feminist" practice of making decisions in small, separate circles, their aversion to feminism and women's movements (except the proletarian) and their antipluralist attitude. But they did not criticize the indisputably large legal achievements of the state feminists' actions.

The problem new feminists faced was a consequence of the means of achieving legislative equality: the laws came from the narrow circles above and not from below. Women had started to perceive law as something naturally given; they didn't expect to have to fight for their special concerns. At the moment when some rights and legislation were endangered, women didn't believe they could be taken away. And it was very hard for them to mobilize themselves again,[13] especially since they had to mobilize themselves to retain some good things from the discredited socialist system. The fight for preservation was perceived as suspicious.

A Part of the Civil Society Movement?

When the first public happening for women only in Ljubljana was organized early in 1985, Slovenia experienced a shock. First had come the Women's Section of the Sociological Society, which became active in 1984. Then Lilith emerged, a women-only society that organized happenings, meetings, and lectures. Lilith opened discussion on women's identity, women in the media, violence, and abortion rights.[14] At about the same time, some independent works and translations of feminist texts were published. There was now a perceptible interest in feminism among younger women, and the whole public space expanded. Despite the ambiguous attitude of some of the editors, the weekly *Mladina* accepted some articles on feminist issues.

A few other independent, new social movement groups were also emerging in the early 1980s: above all the peace group, the ecology group (with quite a number of women members) and the gay group. The first women's activities were partly coordinated with these groups. But, since women's groups were the only new social movement group with an all-Yugoslav network, and due to the latent antifeminist uneasiness among Slovene alternative circles, women's activities should be treated as a somewhat separate phenomenon.[15]

In order to organize "women's space" and a certain atmosphere for group work, socialization and solidarity among women, feminist groups had to be more or less self-sufficient. In 1989, they were among the first opponents of the military trial against three journalists and an officer accused of stealing military secrets, but they did not became a part of the ensuing national civil society movement. In the mid-eighties, long before the trial, however, there were some important common public actions with other groups.

One of them was the campaign against obligatory military training for women. The Yugoslav federal army had secretly proposed this policy in 1985, and in 1986, women from Lilith cooperated with the Peace Movement Working Group to expose the plan. The action got considerable coverage in the Yugoslav media and was understood as one of the Slovene "attacks" on the Yugoslav People's Army. With two groups and some unaffiliated individuals working for the campaign, there were a large number of signatures on the open letter sent to the Slovene and Yugoslav state authorities in April 1986. The letter demanded that the army declassify the proposal and allow public discussion. It also expressed opposition to any obligatory military training for women, not because women were unsuitable for such training but because there existed no need for further militarization of society and because women would not become more equal by this means. The campaign also supported the efforts of the peace group to introduce alternative civil service for men. The state and military authorities quickly abandoned the proposal for women's military training.

The second important common activity was the largest mass action since the student demonstrations of the sixties—the demonstration for a moratorium on building nuclear power stations in Yugoslavia, organized by the Working

Group for Women's Movements and Women's Studies, Ecology Group and the Working Group for Peace Movements one year after the Chernobyl accident, in April 1987. Some four thousand people joined in the protest. The meeting was reported extensively in both alternate and mainstream media outlets in the West, but no foreign report noticed that the demonstration was organized by women!

Still, mass campaigns and organized actions were only a part of the work done by the longer-lived groups. Lesbians began to organize themselves. A special group concerned with violence against women started the SOS hotline for survivors of rape and other violence against women. A series of five gatherings of a loose all-Yugoslav network took place, two of which were held in Ljubljana: the first one in December 1987 and the last one in January 1991.[16] Interestingly, a common document by Yugoslav feminists from the December 1987 meeting declared that the "various feminist initiatives and groups in Yugoslavia are legitimate and legal," which was partly a sign of their difficult position as something which had not been directly forbidden, but at the same time was not explicitly allowed and supported, either. Women at this meeting also appealed to all women "to join the existing feminist groups or establish new ones." It opposed population politics of any kind, which was very important in the face of intense public discussion about the "excessively high" birth rate of the Albanian population in Kosova.

At the same time, the common document urged that "lesbians should become publicly evident" and demanded "constitutional equality of all citizens irrespective of sexual orientation."[17] (Ženski skup 1987). The meeting was living proof that the most varied kinds of feminist initiatives were flourishing in the territory of Yugoslavia; the whole spectrum from radical feminists to academic and socialist feminists was represented. The presentations by constituent groups of their work and problems, about their ways of acting and organizing, showed the typical limitations with which feminism was confronted in the socialist system. The public announcement of the meeting itself showed how difficult it could be to restore historical memory: although it was presented as "the first Yugoslav feminist meeting," a participant reminded the group that fifty years before, a feminist alliance was founded in Ljubljana that joined together numerous women's associations from various parts of the kingdom of Yugoslavia. The 1987 meeting was, however, the first in the history of socialist Yugoslavia.

In 1987 there were four different independent feminist groups in Slovenia: the Women's Section of the Sociological Society, the Lilith group, and Lilith's two subgroups, the women's spiritual group and the lesbian group (LL). An attempt to gather all different initiatives under one umbrella in the Working Group for Women's Movements and Women's Studies in early 1987 failed.

There were actually not very many members to gather together, and also the usual differences of personality and principles emerged.

In 1988 the first Yugoslav lesbian camp took place on the island Rab, organized by LL and Magnus, the gay male society, both from Ljubljana. Several lesbian publications came out (e.g., *Lesbozine*), and the group made its coming out in the weekly *Mladina*. A lesbian and gay disco was opened once a week in Ljubljana. Later, a common periodical, named *Revolver,* was published by both groups.

WOMEN AND THE "SLOVENE SPRING"

What was going on at the state level at this time? Even in the late eighties the younger leading women within the League of Communists and Socialist Alliance were trying to modernize the state and party approach toward women and to bring new issues within the old system, trying to co-opt some new feminist initiatives. Some women from the independent groups joined their meetings and started to open questions of domestic violence, equal opportunity and other issues, although without much success. Some of the Communist women even ran for Parliament on their own women's list in the elections in 1990. But the specific form of organization for women in the framework of the all-embracing Socialist League of the Working People, councils for socioeconomic and political questions concerning women (organized after the women's organization was disbanded in 1953) ceased to exist with the official abolition of the one-party system in 1990.

The years 1989 and 1990 were the years of a mass movement in Slovenia, the so-called Slovene spring. This period has been connected to the military trial against "the Four." However, without the previous activities of various independent groups, which weren't connected to the national issue but to the question of making active participation in the public space possible, the Slovene spring wouldn't have occurred. The national issue was on the agenda of only one intellectual circle.

The trial of the Four allowed all questions on the public agenda before 1989 to be subsumed under the national question. All questions that did not fit well enough into this shape became unimportant. If in the mid-eighties issues such as conscientious objection, obligatory military training for women, and the rights of homosexuals had equal or greater importance than other issues, after the military trial everything changed. Everything and everybody was mobilized for "our boys" and against the Yugoslav military.

In June and July 1989 a great many women joined demonstrations organized to support the four accused men as well as to protest against the existing power elite and the regime. They set up separate meetings and tried to assume their "special," "natural" roles as "caring mothers and sisters." A group of women, self-described as non-feminists, visited the military chief of command of the Yugoslav People's Army in Ljubljana. Another group brought flowers, as a sign of protest against the military, to the soldiers who were guarding the military court.

On the other hand, very few women were members of the Committee for the Defense of Human Rights, which became the main source of personnel for the first postsocialist government and the new Slovene power structure. An extremely interesting logic could be seen: with the shift from civil activist politics to the power struggle, from nongovernmental action to pro- and antigovernmental actions, there were fewer and fewer women present within the competing groups!

Moreover, the feminist groups themselves begun to split, as a few women became caught up in the new parliament-centered politics while others rejected working within the system of political power. Little female membership could be seen in the first political parties that appeared in 1989. With the exception of the League of Socialist Youth (which later became the Liberal Democratic Party), where the demand for a women's ministry was added to the program by a small circle of women at the congress in 1989 (without real discussion), almost nobody took an interest in women's politics. Most new parties worked out planks in their programs to show their purported interest in female voters, but later did not take these declarations seriously at all.

A proposal by the old, socialist government for new population and family policies, including some mild restrictions of reproductive freedom, spawned an antiabortion campaign by members of the Christian Democrats and the Slovene Peasants' League (which became the Slovene People's Party). Simultaneously, many new independent women's groups—a second wave of Slovene feminism—appeared in 1989/90.[18] These groups were later (together with women from some previously left-oriented political parties) the main protagonists of the campaign for constitutional abortion rights.

Women's Politics and the Transition: Problems of Democratic Legitimation

The task of actualizing democracy as a sociopolitical system after the fall of socialism raised some new questions about the concept and practice of democracy. Women in Slovenia and other East European countries were faced, for example, with a situation in which the women's intimate right to reproductive choice could be democratically abolished by parliamentary majority! (In some other states this has already happened.) In other words, their freedom was challenged in a brutal and unexpected way. Indeed, as we already noted, those rights were not the achievements of democratic developments within socialist society, but a kind of gift paternally granted by the hierarchy. And exactly this atmosphere brings, of course, serious problems with legitimation.

Here, perhaps, lurks the answer to a major question for women in the transition: why were socialist women's emancipation and the rights women gained in socialism so brutally discredited and rejected in the East European new democracies? The paradox we are faced with is that the so-called velvet revolutions brought democracy to East European societies, and at the same time (at least in part) removed the legislative and legitimative bases of the status of women. Many women took part in oppositional activities under the socialist system. These oppositions were nonconformist and, despite of great deal of *machismo,* more open. By contrast, many women have been alienated from the new system of democracy—the parliamentary multiparty system—which seems to be both extremely ineffective and at the same time inimical to women's and workers' rights.[19]

POLITICS OF ANTI-POLITICS?

The first impression of democratic politics produced by the Slovenian experiences with free elections, parliamentary debates, and media battles for influence, is that the house of Parliament is a big disorderly house, in which argument and serious discussion is displaced by advertisements for different parties. Contrary to expectations, it seemed that in a democracy, parliamentary representatives are only able to talk about trivial matters.

Politics appeared to many women as a waste of time, as a privilege of those who have leisure time, which women certainly do not have. At the same time bad memories linger on from socialist times, memories of what was then called politics (usually equated with the state and state politicians). This is why some current analysts speak of the "dominance of political policy" (Dölling 1991, 10) in socialism and why oppositional, civil society movements in socialism regarded themselves as antipolitical. They defined politics as something ugly which should be reduced to the minimum necessary. The same applies to the state; there is usually still no differentiation between the state and politics in most peoples' minds. There was "too much politics" in the previous system, people say. It is time now to leave governing to the experts, to the technocrats—everybody else should take a break or be free to choose between activity and inactivity. This is especially appealing for those who suffered so much from compulsory "political activity" in the totalitarian system (for example, women). This notion of politics, which includes the abolition of most social policy institutions, has become widespread in postsocialism and symbolically produces and reproduces the old Rousseauian notion that the public space is immoral—and insofar as women want to stay "moral beings" they should not enter the space of "corrupt public matters."[20]

However, this is only the crudest picture of the general tendencies within the public space. The antipolitical attitude does not encompass only the female population and it is not only the result of the gap between expectations and the real picture of political development, but is also due to troubles with the democratic concept itself. Democracy as a state system does not necessarily bring welfare and happiness—but these were the guiding spirits of the East European mass upheavals.

Besides, contrary to expectations, the most successful East European democratizations took place within countries with the highest national homogeneity, with strong protectionism against the countries to the east of them and with compact borders. Slovenia became one of the best examples of this. The troubles women have are that sooner or later they are put in a role within the ideology of the closed national body. Above all, they must be mothers and the reproductive force of the nation. They are the means through which "national politicians" perform their macho-nationalist body-building exercises.

Women in Slovenia are in a much better position than women in any of the ex-Yugoslav republics, East European states and perhaps even some Western countries. First, they have inherited social legislation from the former socialist system; the products of step-by-step changes and the efforts of independent groups have not been destroyed. Second, the economic situation is still not as bad as in almost all East European states. Despite the very high percentage of unemployment, women are still 47.2 percent of the total employed population. Due to the more rapid increase in male unemployment, this percentage is even higher than before (see Report on the Position of Women in Slovenia from 1992 and the Preliminary Report from 1993).

Also, some new institutions of women's politics emerged from the independent activities of the eighties. Since the Youth Organization and its successor, the Liberal Democratic Party, served as umbrella organizations for oppositional activities in the eighties, their demand for a parliamentary body for women's politics could not be ignored in the first postsocialist government. The assembly established a Committee for Women's Politics. After the Liberal Democratic Party got the highest percentage in the 1992 elections, a Bureau for Women's Politics in the Government of the Republic of Slovenia was formed. Even though it is not a ministry, as was claimed when the idea emerged, its very existence is proof that women's groups and actions in the last ten years made some mark on public consciousness.

The bureau cooperates with all political parties[21] and various independent women's initiatives. There is not as deep a gap between the state institutions concerned with women's politics and the independent initiatives in Slovenia as in most other Eastern European states, where bad experiences with the "state feminists" and the general aversion toward the state create more problems.

Despite these positive signs at the state level, a new attitude that is not very "woman-friendly" is developing in the public space. This is partly due to the rise in blatant sexism, and partly due to the very raw economic liberalization, which relies on mass advertising with its stereotypes.[22] Ideology, including the ideology of democracy, now operates in its crudest form. We are faced not only with sweeping changes in political, social, group, or individual lives and rights, but also with an attempt to bring society back to the state of nature in order to build up a completely new system.

Again we are witnessing the disintegration and reintegration of the state, political mechanisms, social structure, and their connections. This inevitably involves change and suffering in the lives of individuals, as well as the redefinition or rebuilding of the "category" of woman at all levels. Formal legislation still has many advantages in comparison to other states, but with the revision of legislation as a whole there will be changes for women as well. There is no special male plot necessary in order for legislators to overlook and leave out some "small things" concerning the position of women in 450 laws that are going to be changed, as the current director of the Bureau for Women's Politics put it (Kozmik 1993).

It might be these omissions that present the biggest practical danger of the transition. A vast gap exists between the great, mass revolutionary purposes of the recent past and the daily politics among women for equal opportunity. Westerners often ask: is it better or worse (for you, for the people in general, for women) now that socialism/communism is over? There is no simple answer. It is simultaneously better and worse. The position of women in politics has changed inasmuch as the whole system has changed from socialist paternalism (taking care of women and their social position) to a system in which democracy is not legitimated by women's emancipation. Although the existence of independent women's initiatives is now legitimized, the role of independent and party-aligned women's groups has changed. We are faced with a situation in which the role of nongovernmental women's organizations in politics is smaller than in the last period of socialism.

Women in the postsocialist countries do feel a need to unite their different roles, but at the same time it seems that they remain antipolitical. Unfortunately, the dominant vision of equal opportunity politics is still the "socialized household." Experience shows that the socialist vision of the "socialist household" as a shortcut to equality had countereffects and that it didn't change the division of labor in the family. The whole concept should be questioned from its beginnings. Women's aversion to politics predicated on "not having time" or "having to work" reveals that the core of the question is how to change partner relationships, family conditions, and daily life, and not how to build huge social facilities to "solve" the problem of housework. The demand for equal opportunity policies should be applied toward legitimation of the new democracies. And the redefinition and rehabilitation of the term politics is necessary. An East German slogan encapsulates it: *Ohne Frauen kein Staat zu machen!* (No state without women!) The reasons for woman's participation in politics cannot be the utilitarian acquisition of power and influence only, but, above all, must be the principled actions that will validate women as political beings.

ENDNOTES

1. All parties agreed absolutely before the beginning of the constitution-making process in 1989 that the new constitution should not diminish existing rights in any way.
2. The term needs explanation. Seen in historical perspective, "state feminists" have done many good things for women in Slovenia, especially in social matters such as abortion rights and mother and child care. The Scandinavian welfare state was an influential model for the Yugoslav "experiment," and Scandinavian feminism is often called *state feminism*. But some other authors use the term pejoratively to label female politicians coming out of the women's movement.
   I try to avoid ideological polarization and show the paradoxical position of these Communist women "state feminists" who tried to do something for women while claiming not to have anything in common with feminists. Their power was small compared to male Communists, and they lacked a mass base of support after the disbanding of the official women's movement in 1953. Whether they were aware of it or not, they were feminists of some sort, and the old term *afežejevka* (member of the Women's Antifascist League) as well as *feminism* have been used as pejorative terms for every woman fighting for equality.
3. It is interesting to observe how positive concepts of women's rights are very easily turned into their opposite. The 1980s discussion of the implementation of the 1974 Yugoslav constitution's "right to decide over the birth of one's own children," initiated by certain demographers and "state feminists," turned into a discussion about population policy. Leading demographers argued that there was an urgent need to "balance demographic development in Yugoslavia." In practice, this meant an urgent need to stop the high birth rate of Albanians in Kosova (a non-Slavic population) and increase the birth rate of other nationalities (especially in Slovenia, Serbia, and Croatia). One can also see this subversion of women's

rights issues in the case of the Serbo-Albanian conflict where the question of rape has been politicized for nationalistic purposes.

4. In the eighties, some research was done for the whole of Yugoslavia, especially by Croat historian Lydia Sklevicky (1953-89). She concentrated on the interwar period and World War II and its aftermath, focusing on the only semiautonomous women's organization after the war. She wrote in 1984 that the "discussion about the 'invisibility' of women within Yugoslav history was opened very recently" but "outside professional historical circles" (Sklevicky 1987, 54). It is important to stress that, since then, the situation has not changed very much, even in Slovenia.

5. The early start of women's movements in Slovenia under Hapsburg rule was connected to other Austrian women's organizations. The most radical defender of women's rights and a subtle critic of circumstances was the writer Zofka Kveder (1878-1926), whose early, frequently attacked masterpiece was "The Woman's Mystery." I would like to stress, however, the opinion of Erna Muser, a feminist-oriented "outsider" from socialist times, "that the history of Slovenian women's movement cannot be compared to the history of women's movements of the big, politically independent and economically strong nations, as we usually do. Whilst experiencing social discrimination, the movement for defending national interests unavoidably prevailed in the public appearances of Slovenian women, being crucial for the Slovenian people" (Muser 1980, 90).

6. The May Declaration espoused the union of the South Slavic nationalities (Slovenes, Croats, and Serbs) living under the Austro-Hungarian empire. The South Slavic union would be a third unit in the empire, in addition to Austria and Hungary, hence the name *Trialism*.

7. No wonder that one of the postsocialist slogans was to bring back the status of these professions, meaning that more males should be employed. Banks, for example, currently prefer male white-collar workers.

8. A recently published book on women in east central Europe (Einhorn 1993), in which some brilliant analysis is developed, neglects entirely to mention the ex-Yugoslav feminist groups from the 1970s and 80s (in Zagreb, Ljubljana, and Belgrade), which were connected to many Western (American, German, French) feminists.

9. In the eighties we could find in *Žena* (Woman), a magazine that broke certain socialist principles very early on, feminist writers such as Juliet Mitchell and Ann Oakley published alongside officials and the Communist Party faithful.

10. The most influential group was *Žena i Društvo* (Woman and Society) in Zagreb mentioned above.

11. The women's section of the Sociological Society from 1985 was restricted to women only and represented the first study and consciousness-raising group here. The members were younger educated women, some scholars and students.

12. For example, an anthology of Alexandra Kollontai, anthologies of mostly radical feminist texts (Brownmiller, Millet, Atkinson, Irigaray), works by G. Bock, Olympe de Gouges, Mary Wollstonecraft, and original texts were published.

13. One of the reactions of women to the antiabortion campaign was anger: how dare they speak about such things as banning abortion? There was widespread denial of the idea that democracy could take away the right to choose.

14. The discussion about the low birth rate in Slovenia in 1987, which was not the first public discussion of the issue, was accompanied by a church campaign

against abortion rights that included showings of the American antiabortion film "The Silent Scream."

15. I can still remember quite well the discomfort of some very liberal younger Slovene intellectuals in the face of the women-only meetings of Lilith.

16. These meetings occurred every year from 1987 to 1991; the 1988 and 1990 meetings were in Belgrade, the 1989 meeting in Zagreb. The 1991 meeting was the last meeting organized by any alternative Yugoslav network.

17. There were differences in Yugoslav republican legislation concerning homosexuality: in Serbia, Macedonia, and Bosnia-Hercegovina male homosexuality was still a crime. This was not the case in Slovenia.

18. The Women For Politics group was founded in the spring of 1990, with the aim of helping women assert themselves in politics. It organized two colloquia; one on women's studies, and one on women, the family, and politics, and it published several publications, including "Abortion: The Right to Choose." "Initiative"—Society for Equal Opportunity for Women and Men—works with a more social agenda, encouraging and organizing programs and taking action to improve the economic, social and political position of women. It has a club for practical life, which offers psychological counseling, and publishes books including an anthology on *Women in Slovenia* (1992). The Prenner Club is a pressure group of female intellectuals. Initiative delle donne (Women's Initiative) was formed in Koper. The group has similar goals to the groups in Ljubljana. They are also very active within the women's peace network of the former Yugoslavia as part of the Women in Black movement and work with refugees from Bosnia. The SOS hotline for battered women and children was formed by members of Lilith. The Lilith group and the SOS hotline joined a campaign for the evacuation of the military from the center of Ljubljana. Together with various other groups they attempted to occupy the main military barrack in Ljubljana. Since September 1993 a women's center and a new lesbian group, Kassandra, have been in existence.

19. The role of women in the movements in Eastern Europe that preceded the velvet revolutions was not so different from the role of women in all revolutions. There are two possibilities for women in times of great historical changes: a minority will choose to participate actively in the revolution; most will just "make it through." Revolutions usually bring no advantages or privileges to women. Women's goals in revolution are not very different from men's at the level of discourse about the future system. The East European socialist oppositional groups conformed to this pattern. In Eastern Germany, for example, it was not until the end of communism that women noticed their different perception of democracy and politics. Women-only groups appeared either by accident (as in East Germany, where they struggled more for concrete issues) or, under the influence of Western feminism (via open borders in the case of former Yugoslavia).

20. The belief that women are still less corrupted with public immorality, that they are still closer to the "noble savage" than men, is widespread. How much legitimacy such beliefs have can be shown in women's answers when asked why they do not want to enter politics. They specifically cite corruption and immorality.

21. Four political parties have women's factions: Liberal Democratic Party, Social Democratic Party, Christian Democratic Party, and United List of Social Democracy.

22. In the eighties, Slovene advertising developed some very equalizing gender patterns in advertising household products, showing men washing or cleaning at home. But the entrance of some old Western products brought with it Western producers' old advertisements and views on how housewives in Eastern Europe do, or should, think. So they advertise detergent in the traditional, stupid manner, with a housewife washing for men and children.

BIBLIOGRAPHY

Bahovec, Eva, ed. (1991). *Abortus—pravica do izbire?!* (Abortion—the right to choose?!). Ljubljana: Women for Politics.

Bureau for Women's Politics (1992). Report on the position of women in Slovenia.

Bureau for Women's Politics (1993). Preliminary report on the position of women in Slovenia.

Cigale, Marija et al (1992). *Ko odgrneš sedem tančic* (When you uncover . . .) Ljubljana: Women for Politics.

Delmar, Rosalind (1986). "What is feminism?" In Juliet Mitchell and Ann Oakley, eds., *What is Feminism?* 9-33. Oxford: Basil Blackwell.

Dölling, Irene (1991). "Between hope and hopelessness: Women in the GDR after the 'Turning Point'." *Feminist Review* 39 (Autumn).

Drakulić, Slavenka (1992). *How we survived Communism and even laughed.* New York: Norton.

Einhorn, Barbara (1993). *Cinderella goes to Market. Citizenship, Gender and Women's Movements in East Central Europe.* New York: Verso.

Jalušič, Vlasta (1991). *Dokler se ne vmešajo Ženske . . .* (Until the women meddle . . .). Ljubljana: KRT

Jalušič, Vlasta (1992a). "Letter from Yugoslavia." In Paula Snyder, ed., *The European Women's Almanac,* 387-89. London: Scarlett Press.

Jalušič, Vlasta (1992b). "Zuerick in den Naturzustand?" *Feministische Studien* 2.

Jalušič, Vlasta (1993). "The so-called transition, democracy and women's rights in the East European States." Paper presented at the Conference on Equal Opportunity Politics, Florence, January.

Jalušič, Vlasta & Tonči Kuzmanić (1988). "Rape—The Albanian Way." *Independent Voices from Slovenia.* Ljubljana: Center for peace culture and nonviolence.

Kozmik, Vera (1993). Interview in *Delo,* March 6.

Kveder, Zofka (1990). *Misterij žene* (The Woman's Mystery). Prague.

Molyneux, Maxine (1981). "Women in Socialist Societies." *Feminist Review* (Summer) 1-34.

Muser, Erna (1972). "Slovenke do leta 1941" (Slovenian women until the year 1941). In *Borbeni put Žena Jugoslavije* (Women and the war in Yugoslavia). Beograd.

Muser, Erna (1980). Interview in *Naša Žena* weekly.

Papić, Žarana (1989). *Sociologija i feminizam* (Sociology and Feminism). Beograd.

Rener, Tanja (1983). *Uveljavljanje žensk v delegatskem sistemu* (The Promotion of women in the Delegate System). Ljubljana: Research Institute of the Faculty of Sociology.

Sklevicky, Lydia (1984a). "Žene Hrvatske u NOB-u" (Croatian women in the national liberation struggle). *Povijesni prilozi* 3.

Sklevicky, Lydia (1984b). "Emanzipation und Organisation. Die antifaschistische Frauenfront in den postrevolutionaeren Veraenderungen der Gesellschaft, 1945-53" (Emancipation and organization. The anti-fascist Women's League in the postrevolutionary period, 1945-53). In *Die ungeschriebene geschichte. Historische Frauenforschung* (The unwritten history: history of women's struggles). 5. Historikerinnentreffen, Wien 16-18 April 1984. Bd. 3, 84-101. Vienna: Wiener Fraunverlag.

Sklevicky, Lydia (1987). "Foreword." In *Kultiviranje dijaloga* (Cultivating Dialogue). Zagreb: Žena i Društvo.

Štebi, Alojzija (1926). "Aktivnost slovenske žene" (The activity of Slovene women). In Minka Govekarjeva, ed., *Slovenska Žena* (Slovenian woman), 161-85. Ljubljana.

Tomšič, Vida (1978). *Ženska, delo, družina, družba* (Women, work, family, society). Ljubljana.

Ženske, politika, družina (Women, politics, family) *(1991)* Special issue of *Časopis za kritiko znanosti* 136-37 Ljubljana.

Ženski skup (Women's meeting) (1991). Common Document.

Ženski skup (Women's meeting) (1987). Common Document.

8

Strikes, Trade Unions, and Slovene Independence

Tonči Kuzmanić

In Memory of Vladimir Arzenšek (1930-1989)

BREAKING OUT OF THE OCCULTIST MATRIX

Instead of remaining amidst the empty ideological categories of socialism, postsocialism, and nationalism, this chapter is a fresh attempt to understand the fall of the old regime, proceeding from the greatest lacuna of both left- and right-wing explanations—the role of trade union action.

The stereotypical view of the transition from socialism or communism to postsocialism (meaning capitalism, of course!) is still unchallenged four years after the East and Central European revolutions. The widespread myth that the communist or socialist systems collapsed because of the appearance of nationalist forces still prevails. Communism (socialism)—according to the mass media—was simply replaced, or refreshed, by nationalism.

Ironically, a virtually identical matrix of description dominated both the right-wing and the left-wing interpretations. No matter whether the analysis of nationalism is connected with racism and fascism (left-wing interpretation) or with the final victory of Western liberal and democratic values (right-wing interpretation), a "successful" analysis requires only that one bleats the occultist formula of the transition from socialism to nationalism, the transition from emptiness to nothingness.

Both interpretations of the transition completely omit analysis of class elements, of working people, working class, and, of course, of the trade unions. Starting from the beginning of the eighties with the phenomenon called Solidarity in Poland and finishing with the "Slovene spring" within which various trade union forms of action were central, the (counter)nationalist voodoo matrix cannot explain one iota of the role of trade unions, of their anticommunist action, their struggles to separate themselves from communist parties and regimes and to build up defensible institutions and networks for various independent trade union activities. Independent, of course, from both: from communist and from postcommunist regimes as well! "Independent," furthermore, means free from the age-old perceptions based on the complementarity of socialism and capitalism, and of post-socialism and/or nationalism.

As far as the right wing interpretation is concerned, the analytical absence of the element of workers' struggles could be grasped as a part of a typical, more than century-old system of demonization of the "dangerous workers." This was known in recent decades (especially after the Second World War) as the state-communist danger in which "worker" meant the same as "communist," communism the same as Stalinism, Stalinism the same as Satan. (The word "Muslim" has been similarly demonized today.)

The situation is more complicated when we try to examine the so-called civil society and particularly the new social movement ideologies. These ideas are, at the same time central to the transition in Slovenian circumstances and fundamental to the so-called semi-left-wing interpretation.

The New Social Movements Ideology

The new social movements ideology offered distinctive insights into Slovene reality in the 1980s. The word "new" was quite clearly saying that on the one hand there was a sort of relation between something that was new and something that was "not-new": old. On the other hand, it implied that the content of the new could be deduced from its relationship to the something which was not-new.

There was no serious doubt that the old, or not-new, which served as the essence for the proper self-definition of new social movement in Slovenia, was the "old," "workers'," or "proletarian" movement.[1] The new social movements' destruction of the old social movement was, naturally, a symbolic one, since the real, empirical devastation had already been accomplished by the previous system, the communist rulers themselves. But what was common to all those big and old theories lecturing about hierarchy, mass-movements, *fuehrer-prinzip* of the labor movement, and to the theory of new social movements, was the elongated ideological chain of identification between old working class, social movement and the existing totalitarian system. In other words, implicitly or explicitly, there was agreement. For new and old social movement ideologues alike, the labor movement was the same as the workers' (communist) party, the Party was the same as the party-state, and party-state bore the epithets "political" and "totalitarian." The final designation of "Stalinism" (or totalitarianism) was the proper common name for this chain of reductions (Kuzmanić 1993a, 45-52).

However, one even more important aspect of this problem was situated elsewhere, at the point where these theories were silent. At that precise point lay the problem of social movements (old even in comparison with the workers' movement) that was swept under the rug. The ideology of new social movements was sharply oriented against the labor movement (and this negation was a constituent part of their self-definition),[2] but at the same time totally blind to any other sort of old movements. The labor-communist movement was chosen as the distinctive model in relation to which the paradigm of new social movement was defined, in spite of the fact that—at least from a historical point of view—that movement was actually a very young one. Young in comparison with, for example, the nationalist one.

The next problem is the platform of new social movements, which proved them collectively to be a movement of the people from the margins of the Slovene communist society. In spite of the endeavor to bring to life different marginal groups, and to build up a parallel (civil) society, the field of action and interest for that movement was not at all a marginal one. Social activity, not to mention civil society action, is by definition a phenomenon encompassing literally everything and everyone.

The possible counterargument on this point—that the aim was not to build up any sort of society—is not valid. The very first premise of new social movements and civil society action in Slovenia (elsewhere in eastern Europe, too), was the lack of society as such! In short, the target was not solely marginal groups, or members of new social movements, but, a much larger segment of the population. Moreover, the new movements acted from the standpoint of reformism and antirevolutionism (a commitment to non-violence). It becomes obvious that the "revolutionism" of new social movements was not based on changing or destroying an ancient regime, but, rather, was situated at the "mirror locus": at the point of the production of a new, "parallel society" (Mastnak 1992).

The result of this kind of selective vision in the paradigm of new social movements was (at least at first glance) an incredible oversight: the neglect of the potential of all other forms of already existing elements of civil society within socialism. Probably the most important institutions in civil society in Slovenia were neglected: the institutions that controlled the bulk of the national culture (writers, poets, philosophers acting as the concentrated bearers of nationality in the form of the mother tongue) and the church as the "moral supervisor" of the nation.

THE AGE OF REASON

In the period prior to the 1990 elections, which I would prefer to call "the period mostly influenced by civil society and new social movement action," the main lines of conflict passed between the previous self-managing regime, its institutions and ideologies on the one hand and civil society, new social movements, actions and ideology on the other. During the second stage, leading up to the first democratic elections in which the nationalist bloc won by a small majority, a two-fold conflicting relationship among three outstanding elements or conflicting parties emerged: first, the previous system of self-management (*ancien régime*) together with the sum total of its deep roots within society; second, civil society (the newest ideological paradigm in this part of Europe); and third, the nationalist paradigm, with its over 150-year tradition in Slovenia.

All three forces, strategies, and tendencies had strong influence among trade unions as well. As a matter of fact, they have inspired the trade unions' forms of emergence, their self-understanding and self-organization. Moreover, the very principle of division or of disintegration of the previous system of Slovene self-management runs amid precisely these three forces, tendencies, and—in the last analysis—ideologies. Consequently, the trade union ruptures were simultaneously part of the main processes destroying the self-management system and the result of these processes.

Taking into account the state of the trade unions at the end of the eighties, especially after the 1987 strike in Labin, which represented the structural/symbolic destruction of self-management (Kuzmanić 1988),[3] the events in Slovenia at the end of the 1980s were structured largely around two elements. The main one was self-management itself, as it had functioned within Slovene society for the previous 40 years or so. It comprised the integrated infrastructure of the system, starting from the state institutions in the narrowest sense, traversing the self-managing organization of production (the total cosmos of Basic Organizations of Associated Labor [BOALs] established by the Constitution of 1974 and of the Associated Labor Act of 1976) via the parastatal system of education and health, to the forms of day-to-day life and the existence of the self-managing mass media apparatus.

As far as this "objective" side of the previous system in Slovenia is concerned, it is exceptionally meaningful to stress that even though in the late 1980s everything appeared the same as at the end of the sixties or the seventies, in fact, everything was already radically different. Different in that the profound labor of criticism coming not from the so-called nationalist side of argumentation but from the civil society position (and that was the supreme difference between Slovenia and the rest of the former Yugoslavia) already had changed literally everything! The shift took place within the framework of public work. There was a kind of belated, but enlightened, critique of self-management ideology as well as of the form(s) of day-to-day existence. It was an encouraging, promising critique, opening new possibilities of thinking and living. The critical process lasted for at least five years. Probably the best designation of the period in which civil society was the dominant paradigm would be the "Age of Reason." The most salient element of this period was that enlightened civil society's critique of the *ancien régime* was accepted by the vast majority of the population.

The result of this age of reason was an internal "splitting" of all organizations, institutions, of all (to put it into the language of self-management) sociopolitical lines. Internal (non-violent) political strife was introduced in each segment, section, sphere, domain of the former system. As a consequence, when the formal changes (the elections) came, it was only necessary to perform the very formal substitution of newly elected people. The system itself was already transformed, changed from within. Its internal power, based on individual beliefs and desires for self-management, socialism or anything like that had literally evaporated! Transformation occurred mainly as the result of the rational, enlightened, persistent critique coming from the civil society standpoint, a critique more or less centered around the ideals of the state of law, of pluralism and political equality (women played an important part in the events), of human rights and nonviolence. Change came secondarily by way of democracy grasped as majority rule.

The second "subjective element" operating in the late eighties was the Slovene League of Communists, which already was quite seriously wounded, first by Belgrade, second by Slovene new social movement action, and third by disputes among Slovene hard-liners and liberals within the organization itself. Among the numerous demands addressed to the Slovene League of Communists were emphatic calls for the right to strike and independent trade union organization, demands which have a long tradition in Slovenia.[4]

The Elements of the Past

In the events at the level of the industrial organization, industrial democracy—if it was possible to speak about it at all—went through quite a chaotic stage, both in theory and in practice. As far as theory is concerned we should underline a few elements. As in other east and central European countries, "labor relations" in former Yugoslavia was traditionally regarded as an aspect of legal studies (see Petkov & Thirkell 1991, 1-11). That was the situation in the capital, Belgrade, where the circles around the leading self-management ideologist, Slovene Edvard Kardelj, tried to put into theory different bizarre elements. Other such "theorists" included Jovan Djordjević and Najdan Pašić (International Labor Office [ILO] 1982).

The other side of the coin was the so-called Praxis philosophy in former Yugoslavia. Although the ideas of this school still await full evaluation, it is important to stress that due to the work of this school it was possible to protect at least one part of the "labor paradigm" from the overwhelming destructive influence of the self-management discourse itself. As a result, the position of sociology in general and industrial sociology in particular (sometimes also political science) were different than in other east and central European countries, at least in the seventies and eighties, when it was still possible to teach about and discuss current theoretical problems arising in the West.

During the years 1987-90 former Yugoslavia was among the countries experiencing the highest strike rates in the world. The number of officially recognized strikes ranged from two thousand to four thousand per year. The highest point in Slovenia was reached in a few extremely hot summer days in 1988. A wildcat strike in Maribor, the northeastern industrial center of Slovenia, put the whole town under the command of a few thousand workers for more than a day. The railway station was blocked. Perhaps at this point Slovenia, as a republic of the former Yugoslavia, was closer to a state of emergency than at any other time in the previous ten years.

Independent Trade Unions

The rise of independent trade unions in Slovenia started as a sort of semi-intellectual attempt to develop something new, more liberated and enjoyable than had been possible within the well-mannered self-management system. The emergence of independent trade unions was the result of the thinking mainly of people from Croatia, Vojvodina and Slovenia, as leading theorists from the field of industrial relations tried to promote this organizational form in the former Yugoslavia.[5] It was intriguing that the main organizer of the project was a Slovene worker interested not in intellectual disputes, but in concrete problems of strikes, unemployment, and above all, trade union self-organization. At the end of the eighties Slovenia was an appropriate miniature[6] social and political laboratory in which quite a few ideas and projects found a place for experimentation.

Nevertheless, the dominant form of the emergence of the new, independent trade unions was created from three eternally symbolic elements: first, the workers (from various parts of Slovenia), second, intelligentsia (arguing from the position of the right to strike and right to self-organization) and third, members of self-management structures (around the former League of Socialist Youth of Slovenia), who started to play an important subversive role in the history of Slovenia.

Although as early as the sixties and seventies it was possible to find, at least in some parts of the contemporary literature, the phrase *independent unions,* the first serious, even prestigious usage of the term *independent trade union* came from the northeastern region, from Ptuj (the oldest town in Slovenia) and Maribor (the biggest industrial center of Slovenia). The importance of the concept was not confined to trade unions; in a larger context, the independent trade unions were among the first institutions in Slovenia to begin to create something new, a positive concept rather than merely a negative critique. In that way it was an essential part of the so-called new social movements.[7]

The key significance of the appearance of the independent trade union led by Rastko Plohl and supported by intellectuals and parts of the youth organization (which had already partly separated from the self-management system) was as a symbolic act, a first breach of the overarching principles of self-management in which literally everything under the sun had to be near-at-hand to the sacrosanct system of "workers' rights and duties." The group, as well as the rather petty existence of the union as an organization at the very beginning, did not emphasize negation of the old order. There was no need whatsoever to criticize the old system on the level of ideology, or to produce an extended verbal critique. The idea was to produce a practical and useful network beyond the existing self-managing structures.

The existence of the communist trade unions was not a serious problem for the independent trade unions. The independents just started setting up post-communist unions—the liberalizing nature of Slovene communism and the especially strong pressure of the new social movements supported that approach. The idea that valuable time would be lost by a critique of communist trade unions, which meant that it was necessary to destroy them in order to begin a different form of development, came onto the scene much later—with the appearance of the nationalist trade unions founded mainly on empty and miserable anticommunist ideology. The premise of the independent trade unions was the opposite: solely by setting up the independent trade union net-work the communist regime and its trade unions would come into question. In other words, there were two important elements of the positions held by the independent trade unions proceeding from Plohl's project: maintain an inde-pendent position at any price and do not explicitly attack the existing system. The concept of trade union independence in Slovenia came from precisely this project. And this was the beginning of the Slovene unions' transition from the self-management period to the postsocialist one.

Not-So-Independent Trade Unions

One might expect that the nationalist trade unions had their raison d'etre in attacking the so-called socialist/self-management trade unions. But this was not true. The very first problem for the development of the new nationalist trade unions was the existence of the independent trade unions. Those numer-ous new organizations and unions taking the name of "independent union" not only stood outside the influence of self-management unions and their con-federation of socialist trade unions, but simultaneously produced the main non-nationalist critique of self-management, strongly reinforced by the engagement of the above-mentioned intellectuals. Furthermore, the "real conflicts and conflict itself" at the various levels (in factories, offices, and on the streets) were relatively unimportant to the nationalists at this point of development in Slovenia (approximately 1988-9). The more important problem for the nation-alists was that the name of "independent" was already in use when they came to the stage. The importance of the name was, of course, its influence on pub-lic opinion, which had been consolidating for more than a decade. Every adult in Slovenia knew that the real opposition to the communist self-management trade unions (and to the regime as well) was coming from those under the influence of the ideology of new social movements and civil society. And that included, among others, the independent trade unions, which were not keen on nationalist ideology. On the contrary, they opposed nationalism.

The result was that nationalist trade unions were forced not to attack the communist trade unions, but first to combat the independent trade union itself. In order to inhabit that most desirable place under the Slovene pluralist polit-ical sun, it was necessary to occupy the name and thereby attain the public legitimation that had been the cumulative result of civil society action in Slovenia. Nationalists added their demands to this platform only just before the end of the eighties, and especially before the elections of 1990.

The nationalist trade union, more or less a puppet in the hands of the Slovene social democratic party, started with "soft" action. The aim was to produce a confederation of independent trade unions under its domination. After an unsuccessful meeting with approximately ten trade union representatives, the nationalists declared the establishment of an independent trade union confederation under their command. It was a glaring error. Almost all representatives made protests in the media against this politics of *fait accompli*. The outcome was, in short, a debacle for the nationalists. The new independent trade unions were defended, but the way was opened for a future confederation.

In spite of this setback, the processes of restructuring in Slovenia now took a new course. The appearance of the nationalist trade unions prepared the way for the short period of nationalist rule. The point of departure for this train of events was the important strike at the Litostroj machine-building firm in Ljubljana in 1989. The main demand of the strike committee—the foundation of a new political party, the Social Democratic Party—truly opened a new page in national history. When the Social Democratic Party was established it encouraged the formation of exclusive Slovene nationalist trade unions like the unions appearing at Litostroj.

In this new stage of development, the relationship of two, basically complementary, unions, which tried (fortunately, unsuccessfully) to encompass the whole Slovene trade union space and population, radically changed the political battlefield. The contest between the ideology of new social movements and communists turned into a monologue with communism and nationalism speaking in chorus.

The following list introduces some similarities between the two dominant trade union paradigms (ex self-management and nationalist).

1. Although ideologically defined in very different ways, in both cases the competing unions try to affect one and the same target group: the entire Slovene labor force, employed and unemployed. Both unions strive to play the role of state-oriented, general unions. They are both nationally based unions, founded on nationalist ideology from the end of the eighties when, for the first time in history, Slovenia and Slovenes got their independence. In other words both unions are trying to fit their very different potential membership under the common nationalistically defined roof. If under communism the socialist trade unions (today renamed the Free Alliance of the Trade Unions of Slovenia, led by Dušan Semolič) wanted to unify all unions under the umbrella of socialism, today the so-called Independent Trade Union Confederation of Slovenia, led by France Tomšič, is trying to do the same under the nationalist banner.

2. Both unions are founded on the basis of ideological concepts, or better, projects of the desired future society: socialism versus capitalism. They are

both heavily ideologized unions (which should be distinguished from "political" unions). They find truth outside themselves and within political party positions or oppositions. The position and influence of those unions is in this way very closely connected with political parties they follow.

3. Due to all this, the most crucial element of the highly celebrated "independence" of these trade unions—independence—is missing!

4. As trade unions at the same time targeting the one and "indivisible" entirety of the Slovene nation, each is trying to exclude and even to destroy the other. They automatically transform trade union fights and conflicts into disputes about state, national or even religious aims. Or the other way round, they immediately translate national, religious, and political problems into trade union aims and targets. The main battle cry is still a traditional one: Who is not with us is against us. That was the fundamental reason why—like in all other exclusivist institutions—those two unions helped renew old animosities from the time of the Second World War. Each of these unions is becoming a mirror image of the other. The very logic of their clashes is the logic of an enemy-producing syndrome which always shoots first at the enemy itself (one or another trade union, their own logic and leaders) and not concrete problems (for example, salaries in a specific enterprise, or the terrible weakness of collective bargaining). Animosity between the two has become their dominant source of energy, and mutual self-destruction the most frequent result of their "loving" relationship.

The central difference between nationalist and ex-self-management unions is an a priori one—ideology. Although the differentiation is complex, the question of socialism is still central. Three years after the revolution, they are still discussing the past!

The Free Alliance of the Trade Unions of Slovenia (the former official trade unions of "socialist self-management"), has a membership base in traditional industries (steel works, coal mines, engineering) and in the civil service. Ideologically, it blends together socialist (state) and postsocialist (oppositional) thought, and then mixes in, as non-essential supplements, newer substances, such as liberal ideologies stemming from new social movements: movements that used to single out trade unions as the worst element of society.

The nationalist union, the Independent Trade Union Confederation of Slovenia, attempts to rehabilitate principles of Western trade union organization from the beginning of the century. Among the two "big unions," very often if one tries to defend the "interests of labor," the other tries to defend the "interest of capital." With the change of government they also changed their roles. As pointed out above, the orientation of both unions emanates from the sphere of ideology, from the political parties that they serve. In that sense both trade unions are more or less the puppets of two ideological and political blocs in Slovene society.

It must be emphasized that the nationalist trade union tried in a way to play the very important role of oppositional political party in one important period of its emergence. In this it was structurally similar to Solidarity in Poland, which tried to play a direct political role at a time when direct political (party) engagement was forbidden.

Another important contrast between the two trade unions was seen in their style of behavior. The nationalist unions tried *glasnost,* being extremely loud and politically and publicly omnipresent (especially during the Demos coalition government's rule after the first elections), the old socialist trade unions tried to be quiet and to foster shop floor and company trade unions. Meanwhile the main fight for nationalist unions was the fight for property (not only in the narrow sense of offices, but also in the politics of privatization of extremely large parts of Slovene industry). Last but not least, one should count Slovenia as a Catholic state without—for the time being—Catholic trade unions. However, the nationalist trade unions, at least in part, satisfied that "structural necessity" of Slovene society.

In short, in the postsocialist period the position of the former trade union organization of the self-management era has been both preserved and destroyed. It was deeply eroded by the appearance of the competing trade union, but at the same time it was preserved because the new, competing nationalist trade union continued to work as the mirror image of the previous, self-management union. The appearance of the nationalist trade union actually doubled the previous "trade union monism." The rather bitter result of this promising transition was a blockade of additional processes of pluralization within trade-unionist space in Slovenia. Departures in the direction that were embarked on by the early independent trade unions now became impossible.

Other Trade Union Forms

In light of the fact that the two general trade unions tried to control the "integral national body" with pretensions of being national institutions, it was understandable that new forms of trade unions would come that neglected the principle of national representation intentionally. Trade unions functioning at local and regional levels in Slovenia rejected the political, or more precisely, ideological trade unions. Simultaneously they undertook the important mission of organizing at the shop floor and company levels. As a result of the previous self-management organization of trade unions, in which the regional element was strong, an important battle took place within the self-management trade unions between central headquarters and a few affiliated regional centers. The most important conflict occurred when the coastal regional organization tried to separate from the national. The dispute ended with a "velvet divorce." By the end of the eighties, the coastal organization had become the leading regional trade union force in Slovenia. Exactly this form of trade union activity—regional and local—became the basis for the most important, third trade union institution, Confederation '90, under the leadership of Boris Mazalin.

Beside the very important processes of trade union regionalization and the emergence of the independent trade unions and nationalist ideological trade unions, a few other forms of trade union development could be seen.

An important development was the emergence of small trade unions established at the shop floor or company level. Sometimes they had no more than three or five members. These forms did not emerge in traditional industrial surroundings, but mainly in the industrialized parts of the social services (white-collar workers). The formation of the trade unions at the University of Ljubljana was paradigmatic. Almost every faculty formed its own trade union and joined the common umbrella organization at the level of the university. These trade unions, which attempted to represent the professional interests of specific levels at the university, such as professors, while simultaneously including all employees from the administration to the janitors, were a sort of transitional form between all-encompassing industrial unions and profession-based unions.

Similar organizational forms were found among other professions in Slovenia. The strongest were among teachers and doctors, but these still were not strong enough to set up separate organizations. It may be that without the polarization of serious strikes among these groups, the ties and connections (including official trade union and personal connections) with self-management trade unions remained strong.

Toward Individualization

The nearest to a trade union of professionals was the organization of Slovene journalists. The journalist trade union was not created through a strike, but through the struggle for a collective agreement. Journalists took some examples of collective agreements (primarily from Italy[8]), translated them, and began negotiations, posing as their demand a salary of two thousand deutsche marks (DM) per month. (The average monthly pay in Slovenia has ranged between eight hundred and one thousand DM in recent years.) It was, for those times, rather a revolutionary step. At the same time it was a very peaceful, calm trade union initiative. It took more than a year of bargaining before the first serious results appeared. The peaceful—and what is more important, public—work preceding the collective agreement led, in 1991, to a national trade union of Slovene journalists covering the whole country and almost all communication media. More importantly, the process of developing a journalist trade union was very public, an example from which numerous observers learned and drew inspiration.

An additional interesting point connected with the journalists was the name of the trade union. Because of the inflationary usage of the word *independent*,[9] journalists took the retro name, the Journalists' Trade Union of Slovenia. Last but not least, it is interesting to underline the fact that the journalists' trade union, in contrast to the trade unions of the university, tried to organize itself on a horizontal plane as the union of the profession, on a professional basis. The principle of inclusion for future membership, namely, was the "production of information" and not workplace or company.

From the point of view of the narrowly specialized, professionalized trade unions, the narrowest organizations in that period of development was that of the engine drivers. Their strike in 1988, from which a trade union came forth, was among the most important events in the fight with the old regime. It was a struggle for the rights of self-organization and a powerful continuation of the events coming to Slovenia from Istria. Not only did public opinion resonate with the strike in Labin, but there was also a common administrative railway organization of Slovenia in Istria. A well-organized strike swung public sympathies to the engine drivers, and caused a lot of problems for the government, which tried to resolve the problem in a nonviolent way.[10] The result was a victory for the engine drivers, which had an important moral impact for all future events in Slovenia and all parts of former Yugoslavia.

The engine drivers organized themselves within the old self-management trade union, but—and this was a new experience—without producing a new form of trade union communication, new organization, or new network. They simply changed leaders, or even used the same old people for their new aims, their friends for the new independent trade union purposes. Also, they defended the idea of strong, radically narrow, organized interest of the profession of engine drivers. Furthermore, they behaved in a surprisingly nonideological way. They were simultaneously in collaboration with self-management trade unions and new nationalistic ones, taking support from both, but preserving their independence!

This last characteristic of the engine drivers' trade union was the most important element among all the various trade union activities at the end of the eighties in Slovenia. It was a living monument to the new trade union spirit in this part of Europe, where for trade unions to survive it was (and remains) necessary to pass between the Scylla of socialism and Charybdis of nationalism. But the Slovene unions did survive. In a relatively short period full of chaos and enthusiasm, of high desires and profound fears, the Slovene unions emerged in enormous variety (some 50 different organizations). This period of union formation was simply one of the most interesting and colorful trade union "stage setting" within the central and eastern European region.

THE FORM OF LIBERATION

But this was not all one should emphasize with regard to those furious, chaotic times. Trade union activities were not confined to the narrow meaning of "industrial relations." Activity took on untypical forms such as attempts to renew the role of the city and the spirit of urban life itself. It is important, as well, to stress the outstanding role of trade unions as vehicles for the various activities and concepts connected with recovering, restoring, inventing, and building the new and old civil society institutions in Slovenia. In short, trade unions were the appropriate form of liberation in the largest possible meaning.

Furthermore, from a psychological perspective, this was an period of frenzied trade union growth, when every opportunity for setting up independent institutions was regarded as the last chance of a lifetime. For even the smallest trade union, the feelings of salvation and destiny were carried by the magic word *independence*. (A similar statement could be made about independent business or private enterprises. Every month or so a few thousand private enterprises were started! This process, which fortunately lasted just for one year, perhaps could only be explained as an acute case of gold fever.)

Challenges in Place of "Conclusions"

Today in Slovenia, five relatively strong trade union confederations have developed. From the point of view of numbers as well as other indicators of power and influence, the strongest confederation remains the self-management trade union (Free Trade Unions of Slovenia). Although data concerning membership are still not public (due to problems with recognition), this confederation may have approximately 300,000 to 400,000 members, mainly among traditional blue-collar workers in the biggest industrial centers. According to the same indicators, in second place is the Trade Union Confederation '90, a new organization formed from breakaways from previous socialist trade unions and numerous new trade union organizations, numbering approximately 70,000 to 80,000 members. The members are a mixture of blue- and white-collar workers. In third and fourth place are the nationalist, Independent

Confederation of Slovene Trade Unions, and the Confederation PERGAM (graphic and paper industries trade union) with a few tens of thousands of members. Numerically smaller, but highly important symbolically is the appearance of the first body explicitly self-defined as a white-collar workers' confederation, which has organized the employees from the enterprises formed on the basis of the law of *zavodi* (approximately, civil servants).

In the last few years, the trade union organizations have had much opportunity to test their potential, experiment with their power, examine their own relations. They have already managed to sign the first relatively serious and unemotional national agreement among themselves and have organized some common strike actions. Some of these actions were superbly handled, producing important implications and successes. Meanwhile some other industrial actions (e.g., those of drivers and teachers) manifested inexperienced leadership, problems with proper strike timing, and other weaknesses in the "art of dispute." The confederations and some trade unions outside of the above-mentioned confederations even signed a first national collective agreement with the previous nationalist (Demos) government. Yet the agreement was overturned by the current governing coalition of liberal democrats, Christian democrats, and former communists on the basis of the classical argument that the agreed-upon price of labor was too high!

Nonetheless, from the point of view of the state, the main problem for independent Slovenia is not the trade unions at all. On the contrary. They have already achieved a remarkable degree of self-organization and infrastructure as a result of their struggles in the last five years. The standard they set offers an excellent social basis for a quite solid political democracy as well.

The model that could be extracted from this, however, might contradict the correlation between high levels of unionization in Slovenia, from 80-95 percent, and a strong role for social democratic political parties (observed in Germany, Austria, and the Nordic countries). Additionally, one could emphasize expectations that the role of the Church and the traditionally strong position of the Catholic religion in Slovenia could result in a rupture between Catholic and non-Catholic trade unions similar to that in Italy, France, the Netherlands, or South America.

But this expectation has not been fulfilled. The trade union situation in Slovenia could even be termed "supernormal." At the same time that trade unions are playing a stabilizing role, they are fighting for the preservation of the living standards of inhabitants of the entire state, keeping Slovenia outside of the postsocialist "iron laws of inflation." In other words, the case of Slovenia contradicts the conservative argument that weak or nonexistent trade unions are the main prerequisite for the rapid development, high living standards, and low inflation rates found in the "new models" coming from Japan, Singapore, and Korea. Looking at Slovenia, it could be argued that the stronger the trade union movement, the higher the standard of living.

The leading abnormal element in Slovenia is, similar to all formerly socialist systems, the phenomenon that I would like to term "the missing metaphysical element of capital." While the normal role of the trade unions lies somewhere and somehow "in between," if not beneath, two other structural elements, employers (capital) and the state, the main problem in postsocialist countries is still similar to the problems within previous socialist regimes—namely, the absence of capital. Capital is literally absent at the very basic level, that of the social structure—there are no capitalists.

The outstanding consequence of this structural absence is the establishment of direct relations between state and trade unions without any serious possibility of mediation by capitalists or capital, and vice versa. Any potential conflict between employees and employers cannot be mediated, let alone transcended, with the help of the state, since the state is already involved on the side of so-called capital and by definition cannot be its own mediator. In short, relations exist within which the state is—*nolens volens*—forced to play a double role.

Although historically this "deficiency" could be observed as absence (in comparison with industrially developed Western countries), it looks as if this absence is an important structural element of noncapitalist or non-Western societies that can be transcended or at least limited solely by coercion, perhaps by violent revolution. The unanswered question is: can the societies characterized by absence of capital be capitalized/industrialized by implantation and/or transplantation of capital within a century?

These challenges already overstep the bounds of this article, raising questions concerning de-nationalization, privatization, and similar problems that remain unsettled in Slovenia. The very fact that these problems are still waiting for their resolution provides a subject for future reflection and writing.

ENDNOTES

This paper would have been impossible without the superb help provided by the staff of four libraries: the Instituto Universitario Europeo in Firenze, Ruskin College and the Bodlean Library in Oxford, and the Faculty of Social Science Library in Ljubljana.

1. New social movement and civil society activists in Slovenia actually desperately tried to ignore the many forms of appearance of the "workers' movement" and

trade unions. A solitary attempt to connect both processes (civil society project[s] and, for example, numerous strikes and new trade unions) is Kuzmanić 1988.

2. It is imperative to make a short observation about the metaphysical relation between the Slovene national revolution and work and workers' ethics in Slovenia. Despite the extremely antimarxist, anticommunist, and antisocialist intentions of the Slovene national revolution, its very self-understanding (and self-mythology) starts from a definition of Slovenes as a "nation of proletarians!" This model or icon emanates, paradoxically, from one of the most famous Slovene writers, a social democrat from the turn of the century, Ivan Cankar.

The second element of metaphysical dimension of Slovene self-understanding drew upon the position of Slovenes in the former Yugoslavia. This element was based on the "Slovene Protestant ethic." Naturally, this characterization was made only in comparison with other "lazy" nations (Montenegrins especially, but also Muslims, Macedonians, Serbs, and Croats).

In short, if one part of the modern Slovene mythology of self originated in the socialist (social democratic) way of thinking, another part came from liberal or capitalist perspectives, preaching, in the final analysis, some very Marxist strictures. Namely that the lazy "Southern nations" in former Yugoslavia exploited the Slovenes. This point was the most decisive argument for disintegration of the old state; it was of course impossible to live with someone who exploits you. (A similar argument was developed in Belgrade, but with opposite intentions, of course!)

The next paradox of the postsocialist situation is that when the accomplishment of national revolution took place, both the "nation of proletarians" and "Protestant-nation" images lost their foundations. The problem facing contemporary producers of national mythology is not simply to reinvent the basic mythological picture, but to reinvent it without using the old structure of stereotypes. Perhaps this is why former nationalists who used to warn of the dangers from Croats, Serbs, and Muslims, and the threat to the Slovene language, now are desperately trying to protect the Slovene language from the ruinous English/American influence!

The most important element for the purposes of the text is that the political position of the Slovene state is proceeding from this frustration: it is necessary to suppress workers and their unions because they used to be the cement of the communist system. The problem is how to diminish worker influence (or even "abolish workers") while simultaneously conserving the work ethic in conditions where trade and money have replaced the paradigm of work as organizing concepts. To put it differently: How can the Protestant work ethic be propagated in a country in which Catholics are even stronger than in Italy?

Moreover, the problem is not solely affecting the authorities. It is rather "internal," affecting every Slovene in his or her "innerness." It has become necessary to construct an answer to the following frustrating (or is it modern?) question: how to work and simultaneously be ashamed of working?

3. Proceeding from the experience of self-management, the author argued (Kuzmanić 1988) that the key question about socialism and socialist revolutions was not why Marx's socialism was not realized where he expected it to be realized, in the West, but rather, why was socialism realized in the East? The structure of Eastern societies, in fact, was literally snatching at this kind of

revolutionary theory. The theory came to life as a "dictatorship of work," led by the party of work. The "workocratic" self-management system could be characterized by a chain: work = worker (sexless creature!) = working class = party of work = republic of work (form of state).

Within these coordinates the strike at Labin served as a symbolic incision into the structure of self-management. The miners broke from the chain of work and ceased to feed its stability. They caused the fall of the first two dominoes: work was destroyed by the strike, and workers became negotiators over the terms of sale of their labor. This brought about the destruction of the entire organism of self-management. In this way, the need to build a new basis for legitimation of self-management socialism became apparent, and even the further existence (actual and conceptual) of self-management came under question.

In short, the strike at Labin in 1987 was an extremely important event dividing the history of self-management in two. The most substantial revolutionary event was not the strike, the pains and possible numbers of murdered workers, or other calamities connected with revolution, but rather an influence produced among millions of spectators all over the former Yugoslavia.

Although the strike occurred in Croatian Istria between Croatian management and Muslim miners, its influence was strongest in Slovenia. This was due to previous disputes between the socialist regime and the new social movements, forceful public support by the independent media, nonnationalist interpretations of the strike events, and the perspective available from independent observers. From the point of view of trade unions, Labin was the real beginning of the Slovene Spring at the end of the 1980s, the crucial point of departure in the Slovene transition from communism to postcommunism.

4. Deeply involved in all these undertakings related to strikes and trade unions in Slovenia was Professor Vladimir Arzenšek, an endlessly brave and courageous researcher and public person, who died in 1989. In the darkest times, he advocated and cultivated free thinking and action in Slovenia and in former Yugoslavia. He advocated elementary human rights, struggling for two essential ideas: the right to strike and the idea of independent trade unions.

5. Researchers from all generations as well as from different parts of the former Yugoslavia were engaged. For example, Neca Jovanov from Novi Sad, Josip Županov and Vesna Pusić from Zagreb, Vladimir Arzenšek, Veljko Rus, Lidija Mohar, and Tonči Kuzmanić from Ljubljana, and many others.

6. Slovenia's "pocket size" was endlessly important for the whole development of liberalization in former Yugoslavia. The Slovene Spring was not a reflection of events in Czechoslovakia or Russia whatsoever. Events began at the end of the seventies, when former Eastern Europe could only fantasize about *glasnost,* Gorbachev, or Havel. Slovenia's tiny size was used successfully as an argument to allow liberalization and fend off crackdowns.

7. See also Lundin (1989), Skilling & Wilson (1991), Mastnak (1992), Thompson (1992), and Magaš (1992).

8. Slovenia is surrounded by Croatia, Hungary, Austria, and Italy. Useful trade union and industrial relations experiences could not be gained from Communist-ruled Croatia and Hungary. In addition, Austria's industrial relations model, at least after the Second World War, employed "concertation" (Crouch, 1982)—state direction and state-union cooperation. With frequent strikes under self-

management, and especially in the last five years, Slovenian labor relations were more adversarial. These reasons explain why the "contestative model" from Italy (especially the model of the seventies) had the greatest influence in Slovenia.
9. In those unforgettable heroic days almost everything was "independent" from the state to the champagne. Many people made jokes such as "Today we eat independent salad from independent Macedonia," or "Have you seen how wet that independent rain was this afternoon?"
10. Self-management as a system of production and industrial organization, as a model of development, was not protected by violence at all. The practice of monstrous use of violence took place later as a means of "defending the territories" and, above all, various national/religious/race ideologies. See Kuzmanić 1993a and 1993b.

BIBLIOGRAPHY

Adizes, I. (1971). *Industrial Democracy: Yugoslav Style*. The Free Press.

Arzenšek, V. (1987). "Pravica do stavke in neodvisnega sindikata" (The right to strike and independent unions). *Nova revija* (Ljubljana) 67-68.

Arzenšek, V. (1987). "Marksizem in demokratični socializem" (Marxism and democratic socialism). *Družboslovne razprave* (Ljubljana) no. 5 and *Kulturni radnik* (Zagreb) 6.

Arzenšek, V. (1984). *Struktura i pokret* (Structure and movement). Beograd: Institut drustvenih nauka, Centar za filosofiju.

Arzenšek, V. (1984). "Usoda delavskih svetov" (The fate of the working world). *Nova revija* (Ljubljana) 31-32, and *Sociologija* (Beograd) 1-2.

Banac, I. (1988). *The National Question in Yugoslavia: Origins, History, Politics*. Ithaca: Cornell University Press.

Broekmeyer, M. J., ed. (1970). *Yugoslav Workers' Self-Management*. Dordrecht, Holland: Riedel.

Clissold, S., ed. (1966). *A Short History of Yugoslavia—From Early Times to 1966*. New York: Cambridge University Press.

Comisso, E. T. (1979). *Workers' Control under Plan and Market*. New Haven: Yale University Press.

Comisso, E. T. (1980). "Yugoslavia in the 1970s: Self-Management and Bargaining." *Journal of Comparative Economics*, 4 (2): 192-208.

Crouch, C. (1982). *Trade Unions: The Logic of Collective Action*. London: Fontana Paperbacks.

Crouch, C. (1993). *Industrial Relations and European State Traditions*. London: Basil Blackwell.

Dunn W., and J. Obradović, eds. (1978). *Workers Self-Management and Organizational Power in Yugoslavia*. Pittsburg, PA: University Center for International Studies.

Estrin, S. (1983). *Self-Management: Economic Theory and Yugoslav Practice*. New York: Cambridge University Press.

Ferner, A., and R. Hyman, eds. (1992). *Industrial Relations in the New Europe*. London: Basil Blackwell.

Heath, L., M. Lao, and J. E. M. Thirkell, eds. (1989). *New Collective Forms of Work Organization in Eastern Europe.* Budapest: Institute of Labor Research.

International Labor Office (1962). *Workers' Management in Yugoslavia.* Geneva.

International Labor Office (1985). *The Trade Union Situation and Industrial Relations in Yugoslavia: Report of an ILO Mission.* Geneva.

Jackson-Cox, J., J. McQueeney, and J. E. M. Thirkell (1987). *Strategies, Issues and Events in Industrial Relations.* London: Routledge & Kegan Paul.

Kavčič, B. (1981). "Trade Unions in the System of Workers' Self-Management in Yugoslavia." In K. Sethi et al., eds. *Self-Management and Workers' Participation: Indo-Yugoslav Experiences,* 209-40. New Delhi: Scope Publications.

Keane, J., ed. (1988). *Civil Society and the State: New European Perspectives.* London: Verso.

Kuzmanić, T. (1987). "Streik auf Jugoslawish" (Strikes in Yugoslavia). *Die Zukunft* (Graz) 12.

Kuzmanić, T. (1987). "The Year of Strikes." In *Independent Voices from Slovenia,* Special Edition, Winter. Ljubljana.

Kuzmanić, T. (1988). *The Strike in Labin: The Beginning of the End.* Ljubljana: KRT.

Kuzmanić, T. (1991). "Yugoslavhood and Subnational Conflicts in Yugoslavia." In The Consortium for the Study of European Transition, *New Challenges for Europe After 1989,* 49-60. Budapest: The Center for European Studies.

Kuzmanić, T. (1992a). "Jugoslavia: una guerra di religione?" (Yugoslavia: a religious war?) In *Religioni e Societa,* 14 (luglio-dicembre):107-22.

Kuzmanić, T. (1992b). "La disgregazione della Jugoslavia come disgregazione dello ˇjugoslavismo'" (The disintegration of Yugoslavia as the disintegration of "Yugoslavism"). In *Europa Europe,* 19-36 Cespeco: Fondazione Istituto Gramsci.

Kuzmanić, T. (1993a). "Stalinism as a Problem of Methodology." In T. Kuzmanić and A. Truger, eds., *Yugoslavia, War.* 2nd ed., 45-51. Ljubljana: Schlaining.

Kuzmanić, T. (1993b). "Understanding the War in Former Yugoslavia." In T. Kuzmanić and A. Truger eds. *Yugoslavia, War.* 2nd ed., 183-99. Ljubljana: Schlaining.

Lundin, J. (1989). "Slovenia in 1988: Pluralism and Reaction." *Arbetsrapporter,* 1 (Sept.) (Dept. of Soviet & East-European Studies, Uppsala University).

Lydall, H. (1989). *Yugoslavia in Crisis.* Oxford: Clarendon Press.

Magaš, B. (1993). *The Destruction of Yugoslavia.* London: Verso.

Mastnak, T. (1992). *Vzhodno od raja* (East of eden). Ljubljana: Cankarjeva Založba.

Pašić, N., S. Grozdanić and M. Radević, eds. (1982). *Workers' Management in Yugoslavia—Recent Developments and Trends.* Geneva: International Labor Office.

Pelczynski, Z. A. (1988) "Solidarity and 'The Rebirth of Civil Society' in Poland 1976-81." In Keane, ed., *Civil Society and the State: New European Perspectives,* p. 361. London: Verso, 1988.

Petkov K., and J. E. M. Thirkell (1991). *Labor Relations in Eastern Europe: Organizational Design and Dynamics.* London: Routledge and Kegan Paul.

Pravda, A. (1983). "Trade Unions in East European Communist Systems: Toward Corporatism?" *International Political Science Review* 4 (2): 241-60.

Pravda A., and B. A. Ruble, eds., (1986). *Trade Unions in Communist States.* London: Allen & Unwin.

Radević, M. M. (1981). "The trade union in the self-management society." *Socialist Thought and Practice,* April.

Rawin, S. J. (1970). "Social Values and Managerial Structure: The Case of Yugoslavia and Poland." *Journal of Comparative Administration* 2 (2): 131-60.

Regini, M., ed. (1992). *The Future of Labor Movements.* London: Sage.

Rus, V. (1984). "Yugoslav Self-Management—30 Years Later." In B. Wilpert and A. Sorge, eds. *International Perspectives on Organizational Democracy.* Chichester: Wiley.

Rusinow, D. (1977). *The Yugoslav Experiment 1948-1974.* London: C. Hurst and Company for the Royal Institute of International Affairs.

Singleton, F., and B. Carter (1982). *The Economy of Yugoslavia.* London: Croom Helm.

Skilling G., and H. Wilson, eds. (1991). *Civic Freedom in Central Europe.* London: Macmillan.

Thompson, M. (1992). *A Paper House: The Ending of Yugoslavia.* New York: Vintage.

Trocsanyi, L. (1986). *Fundamental Problems of Labor Relations in the Law of the European Socialist Countries.* Budapest: Akademiai Kiado.

Tronti, M. (1980). *Operai e Capitale.* Torino: Einaudi.

Vidaković, Z. (1970). "The Function of Trade Unions in the Process of Establishing the Structure of the Yugoslav Society on a Basis of Workers Self-Management." In M. Broekmeyer, ed., *Yugoslav Workers Self-Management,* 42-60. Dodrecht: Reidel.

Županov J. (1978). "Two Patterns of Conflict Management in Industry." In J. Obradović and W. Dunn, eds., *Workers Self-Management and Organizational Power in Yugoslavia,* 390-400. Pittsburgh, PA: University Center for International Studies.

SECTION III:

Prospects

■ ■ ■ ■ ■ ■

9

Slovenia's Shift from the Balkans to Central Europe

Dimitrij Rupel

PREPARING THE STAGE: 1986-1990

Theory and History

One of the commonplace assumptions of modern democracy is that plural (multinational, multiethnic, multireligious) societies need specific democratic mechanisms. Otherwise they might break up, experience crisis, or even civil war. The mechanisms foreseen (and practiced in plural societies, such as Belgium and Switzerland) can be subsumed under the category *consensus democracies,* and they differ essentially from so-called majoritarian systems that have worked well in homogeneous societies. I am aware of the problematic character of the categorization, and particularly of the concept of homogeneity. It is true that the majoritarian systems work well in Great Britain, Spain, Italy, and France, but it may not be quite safe to say that these are entirely homogeneous societies.

Yugoslavia used to be—like Austria-Hungary, the Soviet Union, and Czechoslovakia—a plural, multinational, multicultural, and multireligious country. It was first (after 1918) conceived as a unitary state, which, in due time, also because of outside pressure, collapsed. In 1945, Yugoslavia was established as a federation of six republics, but the centralist Communist Party kept their differences and latent conflicts under control. Nevertheless, with the variety of nations, languages, religions, and dissimilar levels of development, Yugoslavia had a built-in explosive device. Once central control exhausted itself—also because of the influence of foreign models and provocations—Yugoslavia followed the example of Austria-Hungary.

In 1974, Tito introduced a new constitution that contained elements of a confederal arrangement of the republics. These elements were downplayed at first and ignored by the self-conscious Party elites, but the confederal ingredients showed themselves interesting and dangerous in the late eighties. In the times of the twilight of the Party's integration potential, a situation of a "relaxed" central authority, which the last prime minister of the Socialist Federative Republic of Yugoslavia (SFRY), Ante Marković, tried to restore in an inadequate manner, ensued. The Serbian political elites, led by Slobodan Milošević, stepped in, and brought down the system completely. The first republics to dissociate themselves from the Serbian-controlled Yugoslav government were Slovenia and Croatia. They proclaimed independence in June 1991. Milošević understood this volatile situation as an opportunity to expand the borders of the Republic of Serbia to the limits of the Serbian ethnic space and beyond.

Constitutional Debates

After Tito's death in 1980, Yugoslav political life was slowly drifting toward the patterns it knew in prewar times. Tito's successors in the federal presidency, in the federal organs of the League of Communists, and in the Yugoslav People's Army invested a great deal of their energies to stop this drift. In October 1986, the Presidency of the SFRY and the Presidency of the Central Committee of League of Communists of Yugoslavia (LCY) produced a document called "Information on Fundamental Characteristics of the Ideological-Political Situation in Society and in the LCY, and on the Penetration of the Bourgeois Right and other Antisocialist Forces." Its primary function was to list and incriminate various phenomena and groups of dissenters ("counter-revolutionaries," "the bourgeois right-wingers") throughout the federation. In February 1987, the Party prepared constitutional amendments (to the 1974 "confederalist" constitution) that would inaugurate a stronger centralist grip on anti-Party and eventual secessionist tendencies.

This development aroused, but also integrated large segments of the Slovene population. It was widely discussed and publicized.[1] Although, at the beginning, the Slovene leadership approved the initiative, it later expressed strong reservations, as it became clear that the constitutional amendments would restrict many fundamental rights of the republic, and abridge cultural rights through centralization of education and of the media. The leadership was, therefore, under pressure from several cultural organizations, professional associations, and from the more and more vocal opposition of the general public. The slightly modified official version of the amendments entered the stage of formal public discussion in December 1987, but the amendments were—at least in Slovenia—publicly debated also in their earlier variations. The first to organize a critical debate was Društvo slovenskih pisateljev (Slovene Writers' Association) and it was followed by sociologists, ecologists, philosophers, and others. The writers were the most resolute among those who rejected the project. In April 1988, the Writers' Association brought together a group of lawyers, sociologists, philosophers, and their own members who produced an alternative constitution. This is a more or less hypothetical document which consists of various introductory theoretical articles and of "Theses for a Constitution of the Republic of Slovenia" (Društvo slovenskih pisateljev 1988). The group started out from the idea that each of the Yugoslav nations/republics should first formulate its own constitutional text which would serve as a basis for "international" negotiations that would eventually produce a common (federal) constitutional document.

The Slovene intelligentsia perceived the constitutional amendments as an attempt to combine the centralist Yugoslav and the Great Serbian policies, which would certainly endanger the autonomy of the republics. Without Tito's charisma this indicated an outright Party and Army dictatorship.

Critical Years: 1986 and 1987

The end of 1986 and the beginning of 1987 were important for two more reasons. In 1986, the Serbian Academy of Arts and Sciences produced—under the leadership of Dobrica Ćosić (who was to became the president of the new Federal Republic of Yugoslavia consisting of Serbia and Montenegro in 1992—a memorandum which complained about the unjust position of Serbia within the federation. Two changes were demanded: the Serbs should be given more rights, and Yugoslavia should be reformed to become a unitary state (Rupel 1987). Also, in 1986, a group of Slovene oppositional intelligentsia gathered around the monthly cultural journal *Nova revija*. They prepared, and in January 1987 published, their "Contributions for the Slovene National Program" (the well-known issue Number 57). The official Party reaction was in both cases negative. The interesting development was that the dividing line between the Great Serbian position and the official Yugoslav-Communist position slowly disappeared, and two variants of Serbian-inspired policy emerged: one was a Serbian-dominated Yugoslavia (we called it Serboslavia), the other was Greater Serbia, which presupposed that all ethnic Serbs should live in one state.

Slovene Cultural Syndrome

To compensate for the lack of statehood, Slovenes have produced a formidable quantity of cultural institutions throughout their modern history (Rupel 1976). In the post–World War II era, Slovenia was not so much deprived of statehood, as it was deprived of democratic institutions. Again, culture and, especially, literary publications were used as a substitute—this time as a substitute for political opposition. A very important role, in this respect, was played by cultural journals. The authorities allowed their establishment, but also often prohibited their publication. Dissident ideas flourished in the liberal periods (e.g., the late sixties and the eighties), but they were severely criticized and incriminated in the hard-line periods, such as the seventies, not to mention the forties and fifties. One of the most important cultural journals, *Nova revija,* was established in 1982. Its course is an interesting documentation of the evolution of the last liberal period in Slovene political life. Three main fields of endeavor were characteristic for the journal: cultural modernization (information and debates on recent developments in Western philosophy, sociology and art), establishment of Western-style democracy, and formation of an independent national state.[2] *Nova revija* criticized the Slovene cultural and political establishment, and analyzed the Yugoslav crisis. It managed to attract a relatively numerous group of Western-oriented, well-read and outspoken intellectuals who designed a coherent program of political transformation for Slovenia. After the program's publication, the Central Committee of the League of Communists of Slovenia (LCS), headed by Milan Kučan, issued (in February 1987) a strong statement which said that the authors should not be prosecuted, but that their ideas would never be permitted to be implemented in real life. In the typical political campaign that followed, the main message of the LCS was that the people around *Nova revija* were dangerous fanatics who did not take into account the fact that Slovenia was not able to survive without Yugoslavia. An independent Slovenia would lose much of its territory and its vital markets in the south, and would destabilize the region. The movement for independence was characterized as "ahistorical."

Democratic Changes in Slovenia

Kučan's position—that *Nova revija* and other dissident groups should not be prosecuted, but "just" politically rejected—was, at the time, a progressive and welcome position. Kučan skillfully maneuvered between the hard-liners and the liberals within the Party, and slowly prepared for the break with Belgrade.

Nova revija understood that the fate of Tito's Yugoslavia was more or less sealed. It analyzed the historical circumstances and concluded that Slovenia should prepare for democracy and independent life as a European rather than a Balkan national state. An interesting chain of events led to the formation of anticommunist parties, to the first Slovene free elections after decades of one-party rule, to a democratic government, and to the dissolution of Yugoslavia.

As far as *Nova revija* was concerned, the Yugoslav and Slovene political authorities were most upset by statements about the lack of Slovene sovereignty, about the illegitimacy of the Communist government, and by the rehabilitation of the ethnic/national concept of state. Especially offended were the Macedonian officials who "misunderstood" one author's recommendation that Macedonia stop relying on the federal funds for economic assistance (and on the "solidarity" of the supranational working class) and instead establish itself as a sovereign nation responsible for its economic situation. The federal public prosecutor asked his Slovene colleague (as prescribed by the constitution and the law—a prescription abolished in the proposed constitutional amendments!) to start legal proceedings against *Nova revija*. The Slovene prosecutor, however, after consultation with the Slovene leadership, rejected the Belgrade initiative. The Slovene leadership opted for a policy of "renovation" (a Slovene version of the Soviet *perestroika*) and openness; they only organized an "all-Slovene" critical discussion of *Nova revija* and fired the two responsible editors.

The crucial Slovene cultural-political controversy was of a military nature. In May and June 1988, the Ljubljana police arrested Janez Janša and David Tasić, two young and outspoken journalists of the increasingly popular countercultural magazine *Mladina* (Youth). At the same time, the military police arrested an employee of the Ljubljana Military Command, the army officer, Ivan Borstner. All three were arrested for allegedly revealing a military secret. The city police almost immediately handed Janša, who held a bachelor's degree in defense studies[3], and Tasić over to the military authorities who had, according to popular belief, directed the whole thing from the very beginning. The three arrests and the ensuing indictment of four people (the fourth man being *Mladina's* "responsible editor," Franci Zavrl) by the military prosecutor provoked a strong emotional, but extremely disciplined reaction from the media, many prominent Slovene intellectuals, and many others in the urban population. The defendants were kept in isolation and denied, in a rigid but correct interpretation of the law, civilian defenders. The opposition to the military trial organized themselves as the Committee for the Defense of Human Rights which started issuing daily bulletins, but also managed to penetrate the leading media. The committee was a loose organization with open membership, led by a group of left-leaning intellectuals who had in the past identified themselves as representatives of an "alternative culture."[4] At first, the committee's words were met with a reserved and cautious response, but eventually the Slovene authorities, lending a sympathetic ear, produced quite a number of diplomatic statements in favor of a fair trial. Toward the end of the trial, these statements became less and less diplomatic, until they grew into straight-out protests. The committee qualified the whole procedure as illegitimate, but the politicians were particularly upset by the use of the Serbo-Croatian language in a court located on Slovene territory, a practice that was in contradiction with the Slovene constitution, although it was a matter of routine to the military. Nobody could deny that there was a conflict of civilian and military interests, a test of Slovene "civil society." On July 27, 1988, Milan Kučan gave a strong speech accusing the military of several improprieties and reassuring the Party and general audience that he stood for national, as well as class interests (*Delo* 1988).

The Army Steps In

The arrests, and later the trial, at the court of the Ljubljansko armadno območje (Ljubljana Military Command), have a controversial history. They were preceded by a series of propagandistic gestures by the military authorities, which culminated in a secret session of the Military Council (a mixed party and army body) in Belgrade. As was later disclosed by Milan Kučan himself, the council discussed the possibility of military intervention in Slovenia. Such an intervention should take place if local police were unable to control the situation, which seemed (to the military) on the verge of civil unrest and where (again, according to the military) "a special war" was developing under the leadership of dissident young journalists and academics, a situation that the legal Slovene leadership was suspected of tolerating, if not inciting. As the civilian authorities swore to the uneasy Slovene public, the problem was that no civilian (Yugoslav or Slovene) state organ authorized the activities of the Military Council that, in Kučan's words, was trying to establish itself as a new center of political power. At the meeting in Belgrade, Kučan criticized the document's implied message of a widespread prosecution of dissidents. The minutes of this meeting appeared in Ljubljana, and the police, seconded by army counterintelligence agents, arrested the four people presumed responsible for the dissemination.

Still, the young journalists and their military companion (who the military prosecutor believed was the original offender) were kept in isolation for a month and a half, and tried in the absence of the public, without civilian defenders, and in Serbo-Croatian, for betraying a military secret which many believed was a plan for military intervention in Slovenia. Even if it was not, there was still the problem of Slovene national sovereignty and of the juris-diction of military courts over civilian offenders.

New Parties and Elections in Slovenia

The military trial led to a series of popular antigovernment and anti-Yugoslav manifestations and mass rallies, to a vocal human and civil rights movement and, in 1988 and 1989, to the formation of various anticommunist parties. The Slovene Farmers' Union, Slovene Democratic Union, Social Democratic Union of Slovenia, the Greens of Slovenia, Slovene Christian Democrats, and Liberal Party formed an anticommunist coalition that was victorious in the elections of 1990. The coalition, which called itself Demos, promised two reforms: a proper parliamentary system supported by a modern democratic Slovene constitution and an independent national state.

The Slovene Communist Party of Milan Kučan had an important role in the transition. In January 1990, they walked out of the Yugoslav Party congress and qualified themselves as an independent (Slovene) party. By changing their name a few months before the elections to Party of Democratic Renewal (PDR), they attempted to present themselves as a democratic party and shed their Communist heritage. Many of those who elected Kučan president of the five-member Presidency, and voted for the PDR candidates believed them. They voted for a smooth transition from socialism to democracy, but they did not know for sure whether this also meant a transition from Yugoslavia to an independent Slovenia.

After the inauguration of the new Slovene government in May 1990, but before the formation of the Croatian one, the Yugoslav People's Army (whose officer corps was 70-80 percent Serb and Montenegrin) began confiscating arms owned and separately stored by the republican organizations of the Territorial Defense, an alternative, decentralized, and subsidiary defense sys-tem introduced throughout Yugoslavia in the late sixties. Slovenia prevented this from happening on its territory, while Croatia could not.

Relations between the new Slovene government and the federal institutions were uneasy from the very beginning. Slovenia started to introduce confed-eral legislation, and to get total control of its own economic and financial resources. Throughout the year 1990, Slovenia (together with Croatia) advo-cated confederal solutions. Still in 1991, after the plebiscite which authorized them to move to independence, the Slovene representatives took part in the Yugoslav consultations regarding the future coexistence of the republics. Slovenia and Croatia proposed the dissolution of Yugoslavia; Macedonia and Bosnia wanted confederation; and Serbia and Montenegro opposed all of them with the idea of preserving Yugoslavia in its original form.

New Legislation

During the spring of 1991, Slovenia prepared itself for independent life. The production of legislation and defense activities were hectic. A special group of ministers was chosen to supervise the legislative work and the operational preparations for independence.[5] We needed and prepared new laws in the fields of foreign affairs and foreign trade, citizenship, customs, defense, banking, and fiscal and monetary reform. Since a completely new constitution was not yet ready, we needed a constitutional charter which would sketch the outlines of our policy toward Yugoslavia and the rest of the world. Since 1974, Slovenia had independent legislation and jurisdiction in areas such as education, science, culture, and the environment. In spring 1991, we decided that in certain cases we would simply amend Yugoslav legislation. But in some cases, especially strategic ones, legislation had to be new. One of the most pressing issues was finance. Since Serbia used the National Bank of Yugoslavia in Belgrade almost as a supermarket, "borrowing" more than $1 billion in December 1990, we decided that we would sever the ties with the Yugoslav banking and monetary system. For this purpose, we ordered the printing of new banknotes.

Naturally, the central government was watching these developments with great preoccupation. Marković visited Ljubljana on several occasions. We knew that he enjoyed the support of several foreign governments, primarily the Americans. On June 21, James Baker flew to Belgrade, and warned Kučan and myself against any one-sided moves.

On June 25, one day before the officially declared date, the Slovene parliament proclaimed independence, and the next day the Yugoslav army attacked the Slovene border posts and several key traffic points such as the Ljubljana airport.

THE DISINTEGRATION OF YUGOSLAVIA
Diplomatic Activity

After Slovenia had been advocating a peaceful settlement and proposing a rational approach to the problem of secession for more than a year, the beginning of the dissolution of Yugoslavia indeed began to happen in June 1991. For months, we had been telling our foreign friends (particularly the Austrians, the Germans, the Italians, and also the Americans) that we intended to declare independence and that life inside Yugoslavia was unbearable to us. The Serbs had, at the end of 1990, practically robbed the Yugoslav National Bank and used its foreign currency reserves according to their tastes and needs. We had been opening foreign missions and contacting foreign governments from the moment we came to office. I remember numerous letters I wrote to foreign governments and international forums before the invasion of the Yugoslav People's Army (JNA), seeking support for Slovene independence.

Italy and its foreign minister Gianni De Michelis were really hard to persuade. Together with the Americans, they were our severest critics. In May 1991, I visited Rome, where I saw two key figures of the Italian Christian Democrats, Fanfani and Forlani. They listened to me, and promised to organize further meetings. On May 15, at the meeting of the "Pentagonale" countries (Italy, Austria, Hungary, Czechoslovakia, and Yugoslavia) the Yugoslav foreign minister, Budimir Lončar was energetically contradicted by the Austrian foreign minister Alois Mock, who announced the reversal of their previous policy, which supported the integrity of Yugoslavia. I traveled to Scandinavia where I lectured in the foreign policy institutes of Denmark, Sweden, and Norway. The Danish (Liberal) foreign minister Uffe Elleman-Jensen was the most sympathetic to the idea of Slovene independence. In June, the president, the prime minister and I traveled to Rome for official meetings. After those I flew to Berlin, to the Conference on Security and Cooperation in Europe (CSCE) conference. There, the Austrians opened some doors to us. I did not attend the conference as a member of the Yugoslav delegation, but as a guest of the Austrian one.

The "prewar" days were full of travel. We flew to Vienna and Budapest, we drove to Zagreb, where we coordinated our plans with the Croats. On June 21, the American secretary of state tried to dissuade us in Belgrade (see Rupel 1992). After the declaration of independence on June 25, I wrote more than one hundred letters to all the foreign ministers. In the name of my government, I asked them to recognize independent Slovenia. I added that we are still ready to "negotiate with the Yugoslav sovereign republics about all questions of common interest."

The Conversations with the Troika

The invasion took place on June 26, 1991. The government of Slovenia, immediately after the invasion, contacted the European Community (EC) presidency, and asked for mediation. On June 27, I wrote a letter to Helmut Liedermann, who headed the Vienna office of the CSCE. I also wrote to the governments of the CSCE. In these letters, I explained that the newly independent Slovenia had been a victim of military aggression. I quoted the menacing statements of the JNA generals, and revealed their plan to capture the Ljubljana airport, so they could fly in reinforcements. I complained about the breach of the CSCE norms by the Yugoslav army, and defined their action as illegal. We produced and sent out a document signed by President Kučan with the title "Slovenia in a State of War." Ljubljana was full of foreign correspondents who immediately informed the main TV stations about the events.

The European mediation took place at the end of June and in the beginning of July: twice in Zagreb and once on Brioni. Our partners were the three ministers of the EC: Jacques Poos, Hans Van den Broek, and Gianni De Michelis. It was this famous "troika" which helped us to arrange the cease-fire and the withdrawal of the Yugoslav troops. They first (in Zagreb, on June 28) asked us to reverse the independence process. Poos was more precise. He proposed that we "freeze" the implementation of the declaration of independence for the period of three months. The EC also wanted the Croatian member of the Yugoslav Presidency, Stipe Mesić, to assume the presidential powers which were denied to him by the Serbs. There was a lot of discussion of whether the Slovene side had committed an illegal act by declaring independence, but at the end they accepted our statement that we were willing to negotiate with Marković and that we could not agree to anything else without prior consultation with the Slovene parliament. For us, the Slovene decision about independence was irreversible. The Slovene parliament agreed to our mission, and approved Kučan's and my behavior. Before the second Zagreb meeting, we received Marković. He was worried because of our blockade of the JNA barracks in Ljubljana. He threatened us with "full" operation of the army. Returning to Zagreb, we heard a changed version of the EC conditions: establishment of the status quo ante. Then, the Belgrade government would reconsider its options. De Michelis told me in private, "You wait for three months, then you are free! But the Croats are in a different position!"

The next day, I discussed the situation over the phone with a few foreign ministers: De Michelis, Van den Broek, Mock, Genscher, and Hurd. I informed them about the movement of troops. Our side decided to continue with the blockade of the barracks, since this was a warranty against further attacks from the outside. In the middle of bombing and border fights Kučan and I met with Hans Dietrich Genscher in Klagenfurt. We informed him about the situation, and he promised to talk to his colleagues. I believe his contribution was vital.

The Brioni Declaration

At the decisive July 7 meeting on Brioni, the EC and the parties involved in the Yugoslav crisis arrived at the following agreements:

1. The control of the border passages will be in the hands of the Slovene police, who will work in accordance with federal norms.

2. Customs will be collected by Slovene customs officials, but they will be put in a separate account controlled by federal and republican ministers of finance plus foreign controllers.
3. Air traffic control will be under federal control.
4. The organization of border security will gradually develop according to European norms (i.e., no army on the borders).
5. The cease-fire will be accompanied by removal of the blockades around the barracks, the JNA will return to their barracks, all roads will be freed of barricades, the Territorial Defense will be deactivated, and the weapons returned to their original owners.
6. The prisoners will be released.

The chief negotiator, Dutch minister Van den Broek, ruled in such a way that neither side would feel satisfied. One of the key elements of the agreement was the arrival of European monitors who would supervise the agreement's implementation. Slovenia was no longer alone in its conflicts with the Yugoslav army; in a way, it was protected by the EC.

Slovenia agreed to stop further implementation of the declaration of independence for three months, and the Yugoslav side promised to stop the hostilities. After the Brioni agreement, when all Slovene and also many other recruits abandoned their units, the JNA started to withdraw from Slovenia. In October this process was completed, and Slovenia introduced its own currency, the *tolar*. The fulfillment of this agreement between Slovenia and the EC was the basis for further talks and for the international recognition that took place on January 15, 1992.

At Brioni, the Slovene delegation (Kučan, Peterle, Bučar, Drnovšek, Rupel) did not know when and how we would get rid of the Yugoslav army. During the Brioni talks, the Slovene member of the Federal Presidency, Janez Drnovšek, had an initial conversation regarding this issue with the Serbian representative Borisav Jović. The Serbian reaction regarding Slovene independence was basically positive. Their only problem was how to allow the army to save face. The Serbian politicians were one step ahead of the Serbian generals. The main reason for the withdrawal of the Yugoslav troops, of course, was the confusion created by "ethnic purification" in the barracks throughout Slovenia: practically all Slovene and the majority of Croatian recruits had simply fled, and many officers had deserted the Yugoslav camp to join the Slovene and the Croatian ones.

After persistent and tiresome lobbying with the European and other governments, Slovenia managed to project the image of a peaceful and cooperative country, distinct from the rest of former Yugoslav republics. We managed to attract a positive response from the United States and the United Nations.

We were recognized by the United States on April 7, and we joined the UN on May 22, 1992. Slovenia was active in the CSCE and in the Višegrad group of former communist Central European countries, as well as a series of bilateral arrangements.

In my prerecognition conversations with foreign politicians, I continually heard the excuse that nobody ever objected to the independence of Slovenia, but its recognition did not solve the main problem, which was Yugoslavia. I realize that Slovenia and Croatia together were already a considerable portion of the Yugoslav problem, but the negotiators—especially the Americans—wanted to find a solution for everybody. A simultaneous recognition of Slovenia, Croatia, Macedonia, and Bosnia-Hercegovina would be the ideal solution—so I heard from American Secretary of State Lawrence Eagleburger. Greek objections about Macedonia spoiled this solution. Otherwise, the Americans relied on Europe which, under the pressure of Germany (and also Italy), finally recognized Slovenia and Croatia. Genscher, the Austrians, and the Hungarians told us that individual recognitions by the friendly countries would not be a good solution, so they pressed for unanimity in the EC. Everybody recognized that Slovenia was the only ethnically homogeneous republic, and everybody knew that problems intensified when one moved to the south.

Ljubljana became a frequent and useful stopover station on the journey to the Balkans for many foreign officials. Slovenia wanted to portray itself as a country out of war and out of the Balkan tinderbox, and we cultivated our relations with the Central European nations, but we were still able to provide dependable information on the Croatian and the Bosnian situation.

Why Croatia and Slovenia Are Not Siamese Twins

Already at the meeting in Zagreb before the declaration of independence, the Slovenian side came to the conclusion that Croatian President Franjo Tudjman was not as resolutely autonomist as we expected from his public statements. Croatia was not at all prepared for independence in June 1991. One could speculate that they had not completely abandoned the Yugoslav option. After the tragedies of Dubrovnik and Vukovar, Slovenia, of course, could not but support the Croats, who rather directly attached themselves to our diplomatic initiatives. In due time, we realized that we were regarded by international public opinion as co-responsible for the Croatian moves. One of Croatia's mistakes, even before their separation from Yugoslavia, was an inadequate policy toward the Serbs in the Croatian Krajina region. We did not approve of the Croatian policies restricting the autonomy of the media, and, most of all, we did not want to be pulled into the Balkan "powder keg." Therefore we began a policy of distancing ourselves from certain radical Croatian political positions. We would certainly not go as far as comparing or identifying Serbian and Croatian policies in general. For Slovenia, the Serbs were the evident aggressor. In my conversations with my foreign colleagues, I would argue that Slovenia and Croatia were allies but not Siamese twins.

Objectively, Croatia has always been in a position different from the Slovene one. The Croatian complication is the Serbian minority which is around 15 percent of the population. For their separation from Yugoslavia, the Croatian politicians used the Slovene blueprint, which did not suit exactly the Croatian circumstances. On the other hand, Croatia developed a military policy that soon affected its civilian and economic life to an extent that is unimaginable in Slovenia. The differences between Slovenia and Croatia, which are evident from such a simple indicator as the stability of the currency (the exchange rate in October 1991 was 1:1, in July 1993 it was 1:30), led to complications in the relations between the countries. Croatia has not yet[6] signed the agreements that Slovenia has signed with all other neighboring countries. Cooperation and friendly relations between the two new states will have to be established because Croatia can only reach the West through the territory of Slovenia. Slovenia, conversely, will be able to develop its maritime potential only with the cooperation of Croatia.

Bosnia-Hercegovina

Bosnia-Hercegovina used to be one of the republics of the multinational system called Yugoslavia, but it was itself a multinational system. Population figures from the 1961 census and 1992 sources are respectively: Serbs, 42 and 31 percent; Muslims, 24 and 45 percent, and Croats, 21 and 17 percent. Once Bosnia-Hercegovina became independent, the virus of destruction that had infected Yugoslavia proceeded to this republic called the tinderbox of the Balkans. Throughout the Yugoslav crisis, practically all federal arms remained under Serbian control. Even if the army was called the Yugoslav People's Army, and even if all the republics, especially the solvent ones, had contributed to its budget, it was 80 percent Serbian controlled—even before the crisis. At the beginning in Croatia, and later in Bosnia-Hercegovina, the Serbs had the upper hand militarily, because they had unimpeded access to the enormous stocks of Yugoslav weaponry.

At the beginning, the international community tried to resolve the Yugoslav crisis by keeping the multinational state in one piece. For a long time, even as late as the spring of 1991, the most important international forums were advocating the principles of unity and integrity of Yugoslavia. Only a few countries (Germany, Austria, and some Scandinavian countries) and only some foreign political parties supported the idea of dissolution.

The international community tried through the Vance-Owen plan to resolve the crisis in BiH by forming ethnically homogeneous territories, a patchwork of cantons. The problem with BiH is that its ethnic groups do not live in separate places, but—except in a few locations like the Croatian Hercegovina and the Serbian region of Banja Luka—in a mixed and scattered way throughout the country. A "Swiss" (or some similar modern multiethnic) solution based on the coexistence of the three ethnic groups would not be impossible, but would take a lot of political and organizational imagination. This is something that the Bosnian Serbs have tried to prevent by sheer force. Their leader, Radovan Karadžić, has, in one of his interviews, admitted that they would not be satisfied with the territories Vance and Owen assigned to them, because they do not include the rich parts. The Serbs do not want a just proportion of the Bosnian land, they want the best parts of it. Such a "policy" is the background for ethnic cleansing.

Slovenia has directed its strategic orientation toward central Europe, but it is still very much interested in keeping good relations with the partners to the southeast. One of the reasons is peace. Without peace in the neighborhood, Slovenia is just the last station before wilderness and a *cordon sanitaire*. Then, there are economic interests. Slovenia knows the territories, the markets, the culture, and the people. Once the war has stopped, interesting trade could be developed with the Balkan countries.

THE END OF THE BIPOLAR WORLD
After Bipolarity

We have seen, since the dissolution of Austria-Hungary, that the national/ ethnic principle has prevailed over historical rule. The intellectual elites in Austria-Hungary, the Soviet Union, Yugoslavia, and Czechoslovakia lost interest in advocating and preserving the unity of their respective countries. After the failure of the central authorities, the principle of multinational co-existence in these countries lost its physical power, but, what is even more important, it lost appeal and justification. The intellectual elites, under the spell of the European liberal tradition, all advocated the natural rights of their nations to self-determination.

It is true, and it has been argued, that the recent nationalist movements and democratic developments have filled the void left by the collapse of the bipolar ideological and defense systems (Rupel 1993). If there is no socialist and no capitalist, no Left and no Right, no authoritarian and no liberal, no progressive and no conservative policy left to defend and to inspire, many values, institutions, parties, doctrines, schools, and jobs will get lost as well. In the moment of uncertainty, during this difficult period of transition, many new identifications and prophecies have developed; one of them is national, another, religious distinction. With the evaporation of the old East-West, socialist-capitalist division of Europe, new divisions are entering the political stage.

The idea of international coexistence, the idea of cooperation between different national and religious groups—even within a transnational quasi-state called a federation, a confederation, or a community—is not dead at all. The unbearable difficulty that we have experienced in Yugoslavia, and which other European nations have experienced, or may be experiencing in various multinational systems, is not the difficulty of coexistence as such. The difficulties are domination and lack of an appropriate democratic system.

Homogeneous and Plural Societies

Democracy in a culturally homogeneous society (whereby I presuppose a modern democratic society) tends to be a majoritarian democracy[7]: the majority, which must be subjected to, and must be aware of, the risk of becoming a minority, shall rule. The size of a country should, in principle, correspond to the possibility of introduction of the majoritarian rule. The ideal setting for majoritarian democracy is a nation-state. As the process of national fulfillment is accomplished, Europe is becoming a highly fragmented, patchworklike structure, too fragmented to withstand the competition of superpowers like the United States, Russia, Japan, and China. Confronted with this challenge, European visionaries have developed the idea of the "European Union." This will become a confederation, maybe a federation of European nations. Our generation will have to find a proper way to accommodate the European nations and to reconstruct European unity. Many politicians have discussed the problem, and many interesting concepts have been developed: from the concept of a deepened European Community of the twelve current members (after the Maastricht treaty called the European Union), or the widened "European community of the fifteen," to the concept of an Europe of various concentric circles or the concept of a common "European home."

In the past, the membership of the EC grew according to economic and political criteria, the main criterion being adherence to Western democratic values. Now, this story has been complicated by the emergence of new democracies in the East, for example, Hungary, Poland, the Czech Republic, Slovakia, Slovenia, Croatia, Romania, Bulgaria, Lithuania, Latvia, Estonia, and others. Many of them have developed strong democratic institutions, and some of them are economically as sound as some of the EC members, for example, Greece or Portugal. The East-West and the socialist-capitalist division is gone; what will be the excuse for nonadmittance?

Respect for Universal Rules

What does admittance to the European Community require? What does its membership mean today? And what does it mean for Slovenia or any aspiring country? It no longer means siding with the West, but it means adherence to a system of internationally, universally valid rules of behavior. As the issue of the Serbian war and the UN sanctions against it show us—in an, alas, too conservative and ambiguous way—we are confronted with the ultimate criterion of modern political division: respect versus disregard of a universally adopted and sanctioned set of rules. Serbia has broken these rules, and is, albeit too slowly, becoming an outcast. The division is between those who respect the rules, and those who do not. This division will align with divisions between north and south, between the developed and the backward, the center and the periphery, but it can also be called the distinction between the "in" and the "out." It resembles the difference between the law-abiding citizens and the criminals. Today, for example, Italy is being divided into north and south, the north protesting against the Italian sort of "Balkanization," against corruption, against the Mafia and the traditional party establishment. This reminds me of a conversation I had with a Serbian friend some time ago, when Yugoslavia was still a united country. "Yugoslavia," he told me in confidence, "could, of course, be divided in a 50/50 manner, as was suggested by the cold warriors Churchill and Stalin, i.e., into its western and its eastern parts. But it could also be divided into its northern and its southern parts." A quick glance at the map will show that my Serbian friend meant a division which is today becoming a reality. The Serbian conquests have marked a (north-south) border that touches Slavonia in the north and the Adriatic in the south. Unfortunately, it cuts Croatia into two parts, but it leaves all of Slovenia in the northern part.

The question that one might ask oneself at this point is whether the international community really has the means and the will to punish those who break the universal rules. The Balkan situation is the most serious challenge in this respect. If Serbia is allowed to keep the territories conquered by force, the universal (UN and CSCE) system built with patience in the past decades will be greatly damaged. So, the Balkan conflict may become the catalyst for further elaboration of the system—or its end.

THE PROSPECTS FOR SLOVENIA

Zbigniew Brzezinski once[8] described a division of Europe into three categories: Europe I (EC and European Free Trade Area), Europe II (Hungary, the Czech Republic, Poland, and Slovenia), and Europe III (the rest of eastern Europe). I would add a category: Europe Out for the countries that do not respect the conventions and resolutions of the UN or the rules of the CSCE and other international bodies.

Several analyses and "special reports"[9] have included Slovenia in a group of "fast movers," namely, Poland, the Czech Republic, Hungary, Estonia, and Slovenia. Fast movement means "radical economic transformation at a rapid pace through the combination of government commitment and a sufficient measure both of parliamentary and public support. Progress in liberalization, stabilization, and privatization comprises the yardstick." (Kusin 1993, 1). In the future, Slovenia will undoubtedly associate itself with the fast moving countries of former eastern and central Europe. One of the aesthetic irregularities of the Slovene case is a rather strong presence or persistence of former Communists (now called the United List of Social Democrats) in the government and other high offices. This is the price Slovenia is paying for its soft transition from communism to democracy.

Slovenia did not become an independent country because it wanted to become an island out of Europe. Slovenia realizes that a partnership with, or a membership in, the European Union is a threat to the sovereignty of the state. But sovereignty is a universal problem, and universal solutions are being investigated to cope with it. As a transnational system, the European Union could not become a unitary state dominated by one or the other nation. It will never become a nation of states (like the United States), but, maybe, a state of nations. This multinational system will be challenged by the same difficulties that plagued Austria-Hungary, the Soviet Union, and Yugoslavia. The mistakes committed in these countries should not be repeated, but remembered. The democratic system operating in the future Europe should certainly not become a fully majoritarian one, but a system built on consensus and on the preservation of all the democratic rights, including the identity of all the European nations.

ENDNOTES

1. A rather exhausting critical discussion of the project has been published in *Nova revija* 6, (November-December 1987): 1717-1878.

2. The author of this chapter was one of the six founders and the "responsible" (i.e. political) editor of *Nova revija*. In 1987, after the scandal that broke out because of issue no. 57, he was removed from his editorial post.

3. Janez Janša served as defense minister in three consecutive governments of Slovenia, starting in 1990.

4. As a matter of fact, the military threat somehow reconciled two previously opposing groups: the "inside-party alternative" and the "outside-party alternative." *Mladina* used to oscillate between the two positions; *Nova revija* was more "outside-party" oriented.

5. The group consisted of Prime Minister Peterle, Vice-Prime Minister Mencinger, Defense Minister Janša, Interior Minister Bavčar, and myself as the Minister for Foreign Affairs. In its final stage, the group was led by Mr. Bavčar. It seems that Peterle was more interested in the "privatization" issues than in independence itself.

6. Croatia has even reversed its decision to sign an agreement on economic cooperation. Slovenia has proposed around 30 drafts of agreements (also concerning the border-commission) that Croatia—as of this writing in July 1993—has ignored.

7. For a discussion of these problems see Lijphart (1989).

8. At a meeting of Aspen in Bologna, spring 1992.

9. One of them is by a special adviser for central and eastern European affairs for NATO (Kusin 1993).

BIBLIOGRAPHY

Delo (1988). "Ni mogoče zahtevati zaščite ali arbitraže, ko gre za pravico in suverenost naroda" (It is impossible to demand protection or arbitration when the right and the sovereignty of a nation are at stake). July 28, p. 4.

Društvo slovenskih pisateljev (Slovene writers' association) and Delovna skupina za ustavni razvoj pri slovenskem sociološkem društvu (Working group of the Slovene sociological society for constitutional development) (1988). "Gradivo za slovensko ustavo" (Materials for the Slovene Constitution). *Časopis za kritiko znanosti*, Ljubljana, April.

Kusin, Vladimir V. (1993). "Fast Movers' Politics." May. NATO: Photocopy.

Lijphart, Arend (1989). *Democracies, Patterns of Majoritarian and Consensus Government in Twenty-One Countries*. New Haven: Yale University Press.

Rupel, Dimitrij (1976). "Slovene Literature as an Instrument of National Emancipation." Ph.D. diss., Brandeis University. University Microfilms International, Ann Arbor, Michigan.

Rupel, Dimitrij (1987). "Imperij zla vrača udarec" (The evil empire strikes back). *Nova revija* 58-60.

Rupel, Dimitrij (1992). *Državna skrivnost* (State secret). Ljubljana.

Rupel, Dimitrij (1993). "Slovenia in Post-Modern Europe." In Henry R. Huttenbach and Peter Vodopivec, eds., *Nationalities Papers* (Special Issue), "Voices from the Slovene Nation, 1990-1992," 21 (1): 51-60.

On Its Own: The Economy
of Independent Slovenia

Evan Kraft, Milan Vodopivec, and Milan Cvikl

conomics certainly played a role in the fall of communism in Slovenia. A wave of strikes, beginning in 1986 and lasting through 1990, drama- tized the impact of falling living standards and exposed the reality behind the fine words "worker self-management," putting the Communist government on the defensive.[1] And aspirations for a "European" standard of living moti- vated much of Slovenes' enthusiasm for joining into "Europe 1992."

However, before 1989, the only aspect of Slovenia's economic problems that explicitly called its relationship with the rest of Yugoslavia into question was the much complained about aid to less developed regions.[2] Slovenes—not without some justice—contended that their hard-earned money was being wasted in the less-developed regions of Yugoslavia by politicians who were not accountable to the donors for the use of the aid.

Conceivably, this wastefulness could have been overcome without Slovene independence. For example, some economists proposed turning the Federal Fund for the Crediting of the Development of the Insufficiently Developed Republics and Autonomous Provinces into a development bank qualified to compare alternative projects, pick ones having the greatest economic impact, and monitor project performance.

In fact, Slovenes only embraced the idea of independence when it became apparent that powerful forces in the rest of Yugoslavia opposed the goals of Western-style political democracy and market economy. Above all, Slovenes embraced independence when it became clear that the political orientation and practices of the Serbian leadership were making Yugoslav inclusion in European integration impossible (because of Serbia's imposition of a state of emergency in Kosova and its refusal to acknowledge human rights violations there) and also were making Serbian domination of the Yugoslav federation an immediate threat.[3]

Economics, therefore, played a powerful role in generating dissatisfaction with communism and giving rise to the social movements of the Slovene spring (as well as Milošević's "antibureaucratic revolution"). Nonetheless, it is doubtful whether economic causes can fully explain Slovene independence.

Taking the argument a step further, Slovene independence may not have been a rational economic choice. The short-run costs of separation from Yugoslavia, especially the costs resulting from the imposition of trade barriers between Slovenia and its (hitherto) best markets in the rest of Yugoslavia, were certainly high. But, given the Serbian boycott of Slovene goods (begun in 1989), human rights violations in Kosova and the impasse reached in attempts to reform the Yugoslav federation, Slovenia faced little choice.

But even if Slovene independence was not the result of a rational economic calculation, it remains relevant to ask, What were its economic consequences? Is Slovenia a viable country? Will Slovenes live better, materially, after independence? This chapter attempts to answer these questions. Complicating the issue is the fact that Slovenia is undergoing what Jože Mencinger calls a double transition: from part of Yugoslavia to independent country, and from communist to market economy. Both sets of issues will be addressed here.

THE YUGOSLAV ECONOMIC SYSTEM AND ITS WEAKNESSES

To a great extent, Slovenia's economic problems under communism stemmed from the weaknesses of the Yugoslav economic system. In this section, we examine these systemic weaknesses; in the next section, we turn to problems stemming from Slovenia's relationship to the rest of Yugoslavia.

State Paternalism and the Micro Causes of Low Productivity

The continual efforts to change Yugoslavia's economic system provide an excellent indicator of the gravity of Yugoslavia's many economic and political problems. After the break with Stalin in 1948, Yugoslavia gradually abandoned centralized, Soviet-style institutions, and instituted a newly conceptualized system of self-management. After its introduction in the early

1950s, the self-management system underwent frequent changes. The most significant ones were the so-called liberalization reforms of the mid-1960s, and, as a reaction to them, the negotiated planning reforms of the mid-1970s.

Throughout all this institutional innovation, the feature of the Yugoslav system that can be singled out as the most important cause of its failure is *state paternalism,* that is, a single-party political system coupled with ill-defined property rights.[4] That system was characterized by massive, pervasive redistribution through a soft budget constraint, a system whereby profitable firms were discretionally taxed and the proceeds were used to bail out unprofitable firms. State paternalism created an environment in which poor economic performance could persist. By keeping everyone in the game, state paternalism allowed less productive enterprises to endure, and dulled the motivation of more productive enterprises and their workers to improve their performance.

An important special feature of Yugoslav state paternalism was the role of self-management. The Yugoslav system made the workers at an enterprise, organized into a Workers' Council, the final decision makers. The Workers' Council had the right to elect managers (in partnership with local government before 1965, alone thereafter). It had final say on all strategic decisions within the firm. Day-to-day decisions naturally devolved upon management. Self-management held great potential for increased identification with the firm, greater participation and greater productivity (Vanek 1970; Blinder 1990). But while there is some evidence of such positive effects in Yugoslavia (Vodopivec 1989; Kraft 1989), Yugoslavia's overall experience with self-management was disappointing. Sociological studies consistently showed that managers and party officials wielded dominant influence in Yugoslav firms (see Arzenšek 1984, for a review of the literature). Dismissal of unpopular managers often proved impossible, especially after the early 1970s, as the Party tightened its grip on personnel decisions. Finally, self-management created a situation in which there were multiple groups deciding on important matters, none of which took ultimate responsibility for bad decisions. No one was ever responsible for mistakes, or so it often seemed.

Macroeconomic Instability

State paternalism underlay macroeconomic imbalances in Yugoslavia as well. The government redistributed significant portions of GNP through ad hoc taxation or subsidization of firms, and misuse of the financial system. Unprofitable firms got subsidies (such as straight subsidies, concessionary crediting, and tax waivers) that were in turn converted into components of demand. But this massive redistribution of income was typically only partly financed by fiscal revenues. Yugoslavia traditionally relied heavily on monetary expansion to finance government interventions—with unavoidable inflationary implications.

In addition, the self-managed form of Yugoslav enterprises meant that workers got to determine their own wages (called "personal income" in Yugoslav parlance). With no actor in the firm to represent "capital," and facing soft budget constraints, Yugoslav enterprises consistently chose to raise wages. This gave rise to strong cost-push inflationary pressures.

These systemic weakness were manifested in growing inflation beginning in the 1970s. However, inflation only really took off in the 1980s, when it climbed from 30 percent in 1980 to 1,356 percent in 1989—a true hyperinflation. At the same time, economic growth and employment stagnated. The cost of fighting inflation and servicing Yugoslavia's near $20 billion debt was slow growth, rising unemployment, and falling personal incomes. Social product[5] in 1988 was only 4 percent above its 1980 level, unemployment had risen from 11.9 percent in 1980 to 14.9 percent in 1989, and personal incomes in 1988 were a stunning 27 percent below their 1980 level (Savezni Zavod za Statistiku 1991).

These figures provide the economic backdrop to the Slovene spring. Clearly, the Yugoslav system was no longer able to "deliver the goods." But what was Slovenia's place in the Yugoslav system?

SLOVENIA'S RELATIONSHIP WITH THE REST OF YUGOSLAVIA
Perpetuation of Economic Differences Across Regions

Accommodating its vast ethnic, religious, and cultural differences, Yugoslavia became a federation of six republics. (Later, two autonomous provinces, Kosova and Vojvodina, were created as separate administrative units within the republic of Serbia). The federation, it was thought, would resolve the burning national question, unresolved in interwar Yugoslavia, bring prosperity for all ethnic groups, and decrease regional disparities.

Yugoslavia did not succeed in diminishing, let alone eliminating, regional differences. The social product per capita of Slovenia rose from 176 percent to 203 percent of the Yugoslav average between 1954 and 1988, while the social product per capita of Kosova fell from 43 percent to 27 percent in the same years (Savezni Zavod za Statistiku 1991, 407, 411). Indeed, of the less-developed regions, Kosova, Montenegro, and Bosnia-Hercegovina all saw their GSP per capita decline relative to the Yugoslav average, with only Macedonia showing improvement.

The strengths of Slovenia can be further illustrated by examining GSP and export shares. Slovenia's share of Yugoslav exports consistently exceeded its share of Yugoslav GSP, thanks to the superior competitiveness of Slovenia's economy. Furthermore, Slovenia's share of Yugoslav exports grew from 1973 to 1989, while that of all the less-developed regions (LDRs) except Bosnia-Hercegovina fell slightly. Clearly, the gap between Slovenia and the LDRs widened over the years. This was true despite the LDRs' growing share of Yugoslavia's fixed assets, and in the decline of Slovenia's, from 20.1 to 16.9 percent (Savezni Zavod za Statistiku 1991, 412).

Interregional Redistribution

Besides hampering work incentives and contributing to an unstable macro-economic environment, the paternalistic redistribution described above included significant interregional redistribution of income from more-developed to less-developed regions of Yugoslavia. According to calculations by Kraft and Vodopivec (1992), and Kraft (1993b), based on the final accounts of all Yugoslav industrial enterprises in 1974 and 1986, the LDRs of Yugoslavia (Bosnia-Hercegovina, Macedonia, Montenegro, and Kosova) were the main beneficiaries of redistribution.

The main source of redistribution was subsidized credits. Aided by trans-fers from the federal fund, LDRs were also able to levy much lighter taxes on their enterprises than the more-developed regions (MDRs). Net of redistrib-ution, LDR manufacturing received subsidies amounting to a stunning 57 per-cent of LDR income from manufacturing in 1986; and net subsidies for Montenegro's and Kosova's manufacturing considerably exceeded the two regions' income from manufacturing (123 percent and 145 percent respec-tively)! The enterprises of only one region, Slovenia, were net payers, with a rate of 11 percent (Kraft and Vodopivec 1992).

More-developed regions have always looked upon development transfers as a burden, so it is surprising that actual redistribution exceeded mandated levels. There are two reasons for this. First, such subsidies are the outcome of the federation yielding to the LDRs' pressures to put out the fire—that is, to make up for both enterprises' losses and local governments' deficits. Second, Yugoslavia's development plan for LDRs has historically favored capital-intensive industries. That plan was backed with concessionary credits and direct investments by firms from MDRs in LDRs.

Yugoslav observers have noted that price distortions favored the MDRs. According to estimates by Kraft (1992b), price distortions were far smaller than the redistributive flows described above. In fact, price distortions appear to have been smaller than direct Federal Fund credits, and these credits seem to be far smaller than "hidden" forms of redistribution.

What is the significance of all these calculations? First, they suggest that Slovene enterprises—and indeed Slovene taxpayers—did pay significant sums to aid less-developed regions. This conclusion implies that an independent Slovenia will save by ending such aid. Second, these figures suggest that the less-developed regions may have been even more dependent on outside help than was recognized by foreign observers, a troubling prospect now that the LDRs are independent countries. Third, the magnitude of redistributive flows raises questions about the effectiveness of Yugoslav regional development policy. While the advances made by the LDRs were undeniable, these calculations suggest how high the price of LDR development was. (See Kraft 1992b and Pleština 1992 for more on Yugoslav policy toward the LDRs.)

Regional Production Structure and Disintegrative Tendencies

While the above calculations bring out the importance of interregional transfers in Yugoslavia, in other ways Yugoslav efforts to create a unified economy faltered. The liberalization reforms of the mid-1960s and institutional changes in the 1970s triggered the creation of regional barriers which prevented the creation of a genuine national market. This hindered interregional trade within Yugoslavia and, at the same time, pushed regions into external trading. These tendencies produced a production structure much less geared to a Yugoslav market than the one that would have evolved either under central planning or under a genuine economic union. The cloud may have a silver lining: the newly created independent parts of former Yugoslavia now find themselves able to reorient production to markets outside Yugoslavia.

Levels of interregional migration were also low in Yugoslavia. Certain types of migration were fairly common, such as Bosnian migration to Slovenia, but the overall levels were not large. Migration in Yugoslavia averaged 0.25 percent in 1989, and the highest regional figure was 0.5 percent from Bosnia-Hercegovina. By contrast, migration was 1.1 percent in Germany, 2.6 percent in Japan, 2.8 percent in the United States and 3.9 percent in Sweden. (Yugoslav data comes from internal material of the Statistical Office of Yugoslavia; the other figures come from the Organization for Economic Cooperation and Development [OECD] Employment Outlook, Paris, July 1990, and correspond to 1987 data.)

Finally, the system of foreign trade stimulated balanced foreign trade by each region. Regions were explicitly encouraged to look at their own comparative advantage vis-à-vis the rest of the world. Specialization within Yugoslavia was de-emphasized, and the effects of decisions on Yugoslavia's balance of payments was subordinate to the effect on republics' balance of payments. This added a final element to Yugoslavia's economic disintegration.

THE AFTERMATH OF INDEPENDENCE: STABILIZING THE ECONOMY

Slovenia's exit from Yugoslavia has allowed it to manage its own economic affairs. In the first two-plus years, the record is impressive: Slovenia has successfully introduced a new currency, the *tolar*. It has brought inflation from a monthly rate of 21.5 percent in October 1991 to an annual rate of 20.8 percent in 1993. It accumulated some $1.47 billion of foreign reserves by the end of 1993, and created the basic institutions and instruments for effective macro-economic policy. It seems doubtful that such accomplishments would have been possible in a unified Yugoslavia, even without the war.

TABLE 10.1
The Slovene Economy, 1990-93

	1990	1991	1992	1993
Inflation[a]	549.7	117.7	201.3	20.8
Real GDP growth rate	-4.7	-9.3	-6.0	1.0
Unemployment rate[b]	4.7	8.2	11.6	14.5
Real wage index[c]	100.0	89.1	81.1	93.3
Current account[d]	526.2	190.4	764.3	5.0

[a] Percentage change of retail prices.
[b] Registered unemployment. Survey data shows significantly lower unemployment; for example, a survey in May 1993 showed only 9.1 percent unemployment, compared to 14.0 percent registered unemployment.
[c] 1990=100.
[d] million US dollars.
Sources: Bank of Slovenia 1993a and 1993b.

Table 10.1 gives the basic facts on the Slovene economy's performance since 1989. Graph 10.1 shows how inflation was tamed. The success of the anti-inflation struggle and Slovenia's attempts to achieve current account surpluses are clearly seen, as well as the high costs of economic and political instability in terms of output and employment. The following sections provide more detail on Slovenia's stabilization efforts.

Gaining Economic Control: The Introduction of the Tolar

To assert its economic self-determination, independent Slovenia needed to gain control of fiscal and monetary policy. Fiscal control proved easier, because, like other regions in former Yugoslavia, the fiscal system and policy had been for the most part under the control of Slovenian authorities since the constitutional reform of 1974.[6] To gain full control, Slovenia simply stopped paying taxes to the federal government and took over customs.

INFLATION IN SLOVENIA
Monthly change in retail prices

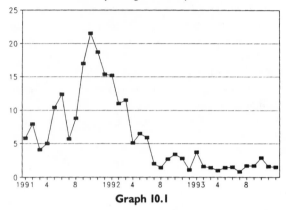

Graph 10.1

Slovenia began its push for monetary control by drafting or redrafting laws regulating the financial system in the fall of 1990. These included the Bank of Slovenia law, the Banking Law, and laws regulating bank supervision, bank liquidation, deposit insurance, international credit relations, and customs. With the exception of the Banking Law, the financial laws are similar in instrument design and institutional setup to the old federal Yugoslav financial laws as amended on the federal level in the late 1980s.[7] However, based on experience with the expansionary monetary policies of the Yugoslav central bank (NBY), the central bank law gave the Bank of Slovenia (BoS) full independence in conducting monetary policy. This proved crucial in implementing macroeconomic stabilization policies after October 1991.

These financial laws were passed in June 1991, together with the declaration of Slovenian independence. Their implementation was temporarily suspended due to the outbreak of the war and the subsequent Brioni Accord that froze further moves toward independence for three months. The introduction of a new currency became an imperative, however, once the NBY's monetary policy became totally subservient to Serbia's war finance needs. The main impetus for implementing currency reform was, thus, to prevent the republic from being sucked into the inflationary spiral of the dinar.

The currency reform was undertaken immediately after the expiration of the Brioni Accord moratorium in October 1991. The new currency, named the tolar (SIT), was well received by the public. Its introduction proceeded remarkably smoothly.[8] Some 8.6 billion Yugoslav dinars, equivalent to about $75 per person, were exchanged. Bank deposits were automatically converted into tolars. Financial contracts were left untouched by the conversion, since

Slovenian law stipulates that contracts can be written in any currency. External payments with former Yugoslav regions required some new arrangements, which were concluded in the ensuing months.

Successful Macroeconomic Stabilization

In contrast to the unsuccessful stabilization attempts of the federal Yugoslav authorities, Slovenia by and large had brought inflation under control and stabilized its international economic position by the fall of 1992. One key was the tight monetary policy of the Bank of Slovenia, which was the exact opposite of NBY redistributive and expansionary monetary policies.[9] Monetary policy was supported by a market-determined exchange rate policy, which resulted in the buildup of Slovenia's international reserves. Fiscal policy, including a wage freeze in the government sector, also played an important role. Finally, the restraint of wages in the rest of the economy played a role as well.

A crucial factor enabling restrictive monetary policy was central bank independence, established by the law on the Bank of Slovenia. The law mandates the BoS alone to execute monetary policy, free from political interference. Price stability and smoothly functioning domestic and international payments are its only objectives. The governor and the members of the board cannot be connected with the government or any organization controlled by the BoS. The BoS is legally allowed to extend only short-term loans to the government for bridging cash-flow problems. The stock of these loans cannot exceed 5 percent of the current budget, or 20 percent of the total budget deficit. The BoS Law totally excludes the use of selective credits, a key mechanism for redistribution and monetary expansion in socialist Yugoslavia.

Slovene exchange rate policy reinforced macroeconomic stabilization and promoted economic integration with the West. When the new currency was introduced, Slovenia was not a member of international organizations and was not in line to receive any financial support. Because the country's level of net international reserves was low—at the end of September 1991 reserves in the banking system only amounted to $204 million, and the BoS had literally no reserves—a floating exchange rate was introduced, with some exchange restrictions imposed to protect reserves.[10]

Fiscal policy also contributed to the stabilization effort. Tight fiscal policy helped rein in inflation and kept imports in check. Public expenditure was reduced sharply in 1991, with most of the reduction coming from elimination of Slovenia's contribution to the Yugoslav federal budget and a government wage freeze. Despite dramatic decreases in tax revenues due to inflation and late payments by enterprises hurt by the collapse of trade with the rest of former Yugoslavia, the government achieved a substantial surplus of 2.6 percent of GDP in 1991 and a surplus of 0.3 percent of GDP in 1992 (Bank of Slovenia 1993b, 53).

Finally, through restrictive income policy, wage increases were kept below the rate of inflation. Real wages, which had fallen to 86.7 percent of their 1990 level by June 1991, plummeted all the way to 67.9 percent of the 1990 level by February 1992 (Bank of Slovenia 1993b, 52). Although such low wages were unsustainable (and probably undesirable), wage restraint in the months after independence played a part in the successful stabilization both of inflation and of the current account.

PRIVATIZATION AND RESTRUCTURING: CREATING A MARKET ECONOMY

The transition from socialism to capitalism poses a host of issues. New social relations and institutions have to be created out of old ones: social ownership has to be replaced by more clearly defined forms, such as individual ownership, joint-stock companies, or worker-owned cooperatives. At the same time, much of the existing capital stock, and much of the preexisting economic activity, simply has to be replaced. Production of obsolete, environmentally harmful or simply unsalable products has to end, and this means that the machines and buildings so employed must be scrapped or remodeled to serve more useful ends. Naturally, this also means that labor must be reassigned and retrained as well.

Although Slovenia has been a pathbreaker in its rapid and successful accomplishment of currency reform and stabilization of inflation in its first two years of independence, it has made less progress on restructuring issues. In particular, ownership change was slow, financial sector restructuring was limited, and labor-market institutions are only beginning to be changed. The sections below explore these experiences in more detail.

Privatization Legislation

Slovenia has privatized slowly. Whereas other ex-communist states moved rapidly to privatize small enterprises, Slovenia decided not to privatize small enterprises separately. As a result, most of the growth of the private sector has occurred through the startup of new enterprises. The number of registered commercial companies roughly tripled between 1989 and 1991. Private sector employment increased by 4 percent, and self-employment by 8.1 percent in 1991 (Pleskovič and Sachs 1994; see also Kraft 1993a for information on the growth of the private sector in prewar Slovenia).

No fewer than three privatization bills were considered by the Parliament of Slovenia. The two failed bills represented diverging approaches: one favored internal privatization through worker-manager buyouts, and the other favored external privatization through distribution of shares to citizens and pension funds, coupled with the establishment of mutual funds. The latter approach is similar to methods used in Czechoslovakia, Russia, and Poland.

Internal privatization was denounced by Harvard professor Jeffrey Sachs, who was called in by Prime Minister Lojze Peterle. Sachs argued that the plan unfairly benefitted existing managers, was open to speculation since accurate evaluation without functioning capital markets is impossible, and failed to fit the circumstances of large, capital-intensive and expensive enterprises (Pleskovič and Sachs 1994).

Defenders of internal privatization argued that Slovene managers are not typical of managers in communist countries. Many are highly capable, and quite familiar with management in a market milieu. Furthermore, Slovene workers may have taken advantage of self-management structures to achieve a degree of participation in management. Insider privatization therefore makes sense in Slovenia, they argue, as a way of utilizing workers' and managers' firm-specific knowledge and of nurturing the efficiency advantages of worker participation (Štiblar 1992).

A compromise bill was finally passed in November 1992, combining internal and external approaches. The bill permits sale of the whole enterprise, employee purchase, or transfer of shares. The latter approach requires 10 percent of the book value of social capital to be distributed as shares to the Slovenian Pension and Invalid Fund, 10 percent to the Compensation Fund, 20 percent to authorized investment companies, 20 percent to employees, and 40 percent to the population at large.

The method of privatization is chosen by the individual company, subject to the approval of the Agency for Privatization of the Republic of Slovenia. It is hoped that this framework will prove flexible enough yet simple enough to facilitate rapid privatization in the near future.[11]

A unique feature of the Slovene law is that workers must choose between getting a share of their own company and getting vouchers good to buy any company. This approach has been praised by Bogetić (1993), who argues that it is a good way to preserve the benefits of workers' participation under self-management.

Privatization Accomplishments

Despite the slow progress of legislation on privatization, a significant amount of social property has been converted into other forms. In some cases, this has occurred as a conversion from social ownership to limited-liability or joint-stock companies. The latter two are not necessarily private, since socially owned companies may be the main stockholders. Nonetheless, these two forms have significant advantages: it is now clear who owns the company and who is responsible for decisionmaking. Anecdotal evidence suggests that such companies are more focused on excelling in their business, and less focused on lobbying for favors from a paternalistic state, than their socially owned predecessors. Data reported by Vodopivec and Korže (1993) show that between 1989 and 1992 social ownership fell from 96.4 to 76.1 percent of the total in manufacturing.

In the absence of a mandatory privatization program, enterprises have found ingenious ways to effectively privatize themselves. In some cases, spontaneous privatization has given ownership to managers; in others, to managers and workers. An illustration of how this transfer is done is the "asset drop": the socially owned enterprise creates a holding company, and transfers its assets, workers and operations to a subsidiary. It then sells the subsidiary—perhaps at a major discount—to the employees (Vodopivec and Korže 1993, 4).

Finally, joint ventures with foreign companies represent a significant element in Slovenia's restructuring. Joint ventures actually have a long history in socialist Yugoslavia. They were first legalized in 1967. But, with the passage of legislation in 1989 that allows 100 percent foreign ownership of enterprises, the ownership share of foreigners in joint ventures in Slovenia has risen from 14.7 percent in 1985 to 40.1 percent in 1990. The 162.5 million deutsche marks of foreign capital that arrived in Slovenia in 1989 dwarfed the previous high of 31.4 million; and in 1990 and 1991 the figures swelled to 499.8 and 598.7 million (*Delo* June 14, 1993, 4).

Among the most significant foreign investments were several in the auto industry, involving TAM in Maribor, Cimos in Koper, and the REVOZ in Novo Mesto with Fiat, Citroen, and Renault respectively; auto equipment makers TAM Motor and Saturnus with German partners Kloeckner, Humboldt Deutz, and Reinhold Poersch; Tobačna Ljubljana, a tobacco producer, 76 percent owned by Reemstsma of Germany and Seita of France; Belinka Perkemija, Ljubljana, in partnership with Laporte Chemicals and Solvay ET; Black and Decker Grosuplje, 60 percent owned by U.S. toolmaker Black and Decker; and papermakers, Papirnica Količevo with Saffa (Italy), Papirnica Vevče with Brigl and Bergmeister (Austria), and Goričane with Maschinenfabrik (Austria).

Another significant aspect of privatization was the privatization of the housing stock undertaken in late 1991. Tenants in state, municipality, or firm-owned apartments—altogether about 33 percent of the total housing stock in Slovenia (Stanovnik 1992)—were given the opportunity to buy their flats. The price of the apartment was based on book value, not market value; the book value took into account various attributes of the apartment but, amazingly enough, did not take into account location. As a result, book values were well below market values: Stanovnik cites cases in central Ljubljana where the book value was only 10 percent of market value. On top of this, a 60 percent discount on book value was offered for cash payment.

While the housing privatization did put a significant portion of the housing stock into private hands, and raised some revenue for the government, it exhibited several glaring weaknesses. First, the prices were clearly too low; the government missed out on a significant chunk of revenue (Mencinger 1991). Second, buyers did not take the opportunity to use their foreign currency accounts to pay for their new houses. Instead, they brought out money from "under the mattress" or foreign bank accounts, expanding the money supply and complicating stabilization efforts. Third, privatization led to massive windfall gains for those lucky enough to have apartments in favorable locations, cementing much of the pattern of housing inequality of the old regime. Fourth, housing privatization did not help poorer tenants, who remained unable to buy and now faced the prospect of even worse maintenance of their flats.

Rehabilitating the Financial System

Financial system rehabilitation has been recognized as a key to the transition to market economy. Functioning capital markets play a crucial role in the allocation and mobilization of resources.

The main weaknesses of the Slovenian banking system were inherited from the old Yugoslavia. One bank, the Ljubljanska Banka, played a dominant role. Also, Slovene banks were owned by social enterprises, which have their representatives sitting on bank boards. But, at the same time, these enterprises are the bank's major debtors. Experience from all over the globe shows the dangers of such a situation. In addition, Slovenian banks had a very high proportion of nonperforming loans in their portfolios even before independence. The loss of traditional markets in the rest of Yugoslavia led to further loan delinquency in 1992 and 1993. Banks bore much of the brunt of the collapse of the Yugoslav market.

With urgent tasks such as introducing a new currency and taming hyperinflation at hand, Slovenia could not solve the banking crisis immediately. In 1991, banks were audited and a Bank Restructuring Agency was established. In late 1992 the rehabilitation of Ljubljanska Banka was announced. The agency exchanged 30-year bonds, denominated in deutsche marks and yielding 8 percent interest, for most of Ljubljanska Banka's bad assets. These included not only loans to Slovene enterprises, but also loans and guarantees to banks in ex-Yugoslavia, and claims on the National Bank of Yugoslavia.

Similar operations were undertaken at two other banks in early 1993. Unfortunately, the exchange of bonds for bad assets is only the beginning of rehabilitation, for it leaves the banks without adequate liquidity. In addition, a certain amount of bad loans were left on the banks' books, due to lack of funds. The process of rehabilitating and privatizing Slovene banks will last for a minimum of two to three years more, and the initial cost of 2.2 billion deutsche marks can only rise.

The preliminary results of the bank rehabilitation process seem to be positive. Interest rates fell through 1993, indicating that banks were lowering their costs and that borrowers were returning to the market. Further decreases in interest rates, along with the consolidation of the more than 30 banks in Slovenia into 4 or 5 strong banks, are anticipated.

A stock exchange was set up in Ljubljana in 1990. By 1993, the exchange had grown considerably. It was still dominated by trading in government paper (both Republic of Slovenia and city of Ljubljana bonds), along with bonds issued by the likes of drug firm Lek Ljubljana, the Slovene Postal Service, and the appliance manufacturer Gorenje, and paper issued by the Bank of Slovenia. Shares of only seven companies traded on the market as of summer 1993. Officials of the exchange, aware of the unfamiliarity of the public with investing, felt obliged to warn investors that stocks could go down as well as up. It remains to be seen whether the stock market will prove an important secondary market for corporate equities once privatization gathers momentum, or whether it will continue to play a minor role in mobilizing capital.

The Labor Market

As a part of the comprehensive economic transformation toward a market economy, the Slovene labor market underwent major changes after 1990. Above all, workers can be laid off. Unemployment, which had been a mere 1.6 percent in 1987, rose to 4.7 percent in 1990, 8.2 percent in 1991, 11.6 percent in 1992, and reached 15.4 percent by the end of 1993 (Bank of Slovenia 1993b, 52). Plant closings, once unheard of, were now a reality. Companies also used the cover of bankruptcy to reorganize and shed labor. The job security of the socialist period ended with a vengeance.

Few would dispute that Slovene firms were overstaffed under self-management. Very likely, firms will need to shed more labor in the future. The problem that must be addressed is how to create new jobs that can provide decent wages and at the same time allow Slovenia to gain its place in world markets. Two improvements that may be part of the solution are more flexible hiring legislation, and the replacement of the rigid system of wage determination that prevailed under self-management by collective bargaining.[12]

Unfortunately, Slovenia made two moves that have hurt the economy in the longer run. In July 1991, following the June aggression and the pending loss of the Yugoslav market, Parliament halted new initiations of bankruptcy procedures, and the Ministry of Labor began providing employment subsidies for those enterprises unable to meet wage payments—no doubt, a bad industrial policy.

Moreover, there has been a lack of trust and coordination between the two major institutional players in collective bargaining (the government and the trade unions), resulting in the suspension of incomes policy in February 1992. By August 1992, the total wage bill had increased 40.2 percent in real terms (Ministry of Planning of Slovenia), seriously threatening to fuel inflation. In February 1993 the government imposed new controls on indexation methods, which had practically the same effect as a wage freeze. This measure helped ease inflationary pressures, but it did little to establish trust. Strikes of teachers, metal workers, and farmers during 1993 indicated the difficulties of keeping wages (and farm prices under government regulation) under control. Establishment of a more harmonious labor-management atmosphere will be one of the most important imperatives for future governments.

PROSPECTS FOR THE FUTURE

Slovenia has undertaken a two-fold transition: from Yugoslav republic to independent country, and from socialism to capitalism. Each of these raises specific problems. We will deal first with the costs and benefits of independence[13] and then touch briefly on the results of the transition to a market economy.

Costs of Independence

While Slovenia may well benefit in the long run from its separation from Yugoslavia, in the short run there are obvious and significant costs.[14, 15] These include the cost of reorienting trade, heightened perception of political risk in Slovenia due to the war, and spillovers from war-torn republics, such as the refugee problem.

The *cost of reorienting trade* has already proven significant. In 1987, 35.7 percent of Slovenia's deliveries went to the rest of Yugoslavia. By 1993, this had fallen to 15.9 percent (Bank of Slovenia 1993b, 41). In addition to the obstacles created by armed conflict, ex-Yugoslav states have erected trade barriers with each other, and most have nonconvertible currencies. Even Slovenia and Croatia now levy tariffs on each others' goods, making trade diversion a problem. Therefore, in the near future, much of Slovenia's trade with the old Yugoslavia will have to be reoriented.

The costs of reorientation go well beyond the costs of finding new customers. Slovene producers had many advantages within the old Yugoslavia: familiarity with the market, customers' familiarity with Slovene goods, and superior productivity and quality relative to other Yugoslav producers. The international market is far more difficult to penetrate and profit margins are probably lower than on the old Yugoslav market.

Finally, the loss of the Yugoslav market and of many of the assets Slovene firms possessed in other Yugoslav republics has greatly increased the firms' liquidity problems, and thereby the problems of Slovene banks. A particularly difficult problem here is the loss of Slovenian claims on the National Bank of Yugoslavia. The rehabilitation of the banking system would not have been nearly such a big problem if Yugoslavia had not broken up.

Bole (1992) estimates that the collapse of the Yugoslav market has caused Slovene GDP to shrink by 6 percent. In light of the 38 percent decline in Slovene industrial production between June 1989 and June 1992, the collapse of the Yugoslav market appears not to have played the decisive role. Rather, it seems to be one cause of problems, alongside with hyperinflation, the demand shock involved in the stabilization attempt of 1990 and the stabilization of 1991-92, the collapse of the Council for Mutual Economic Assistance (CMEA) market, and the recession in western Europe.

The small size of the Slovene market also detracts from Slovenia's attractiveness as a location for foreign investors. Motives for foreign investment such as a desire to cooperate with Slovene partners who possess outstanding knowledge or skills, or strategic considerations such as a company's share of production in the central and eastern European region will bring foreign investment to Slovenia, not the Slovene market.

These problems are somewhat alleviated by the high degree of autarky within former Yugoslavia. As noted above, Yugoslav regions tended to view their balance of trade as distinct from the federation as a whole, and had a good deal of freedom to find their own pattern of comparative advantage. Slovenia's initial degree of competitiveness was fairly good. As early as 1989, it sold 60.8 percent of its exports to EC and European Free Trade Area (EFTA) nations (Bank of Slovenia 1993a, 21). While reorienting trade will not be easy, Slovenia's initial conditions are not nearly as unfavorable as those of less-developed former Yugoslav republics.

Slovenia's proximity (both physical and political) to ex-Yugoslavia has resulted in its sharing much of the *political risk* that foreign investors associate with Yugoslavia. This political risk is, of course, not the result of independence per se, but of the wars in ex-Yugoslavia. It took Slovenia more than a year after independence to gain admission to the International Monetary Fund (IMF), and its relationship to the European Community, although good, has been far slower in developing than other central European nations'. A related strain on the Slovenia economy is the *refugee problem*. While the refugee situation in Slovenia is not nearly so bad as in Croatia, an estimated 75,000 refugees (3 percent of Slovenia's population) arrived between July 1991 and October 1992.

A key question is whether these costs will continue to affect Slovenia over the next five to ten years. Trade reorientation costs are essentially one-time costs incurred during the transition from one trade pattern to another. The other costs have a longer duration. Trade diversion will continue as long as trade with other ex-Yugoslav republics is disrupted, and even after that if tariff or non-tariff barriers remain in place. Political risk, and the refugee problem, too, may linger for a considerable period of time. Hence, we may conclude that the costs of separation are not only felt in the short run, but will probably continue to accumulate through the end of the decade.

Benefits of Separation

The overarching benefit of separation for Slovenia has been political: exit from the chaos of ex-Yugoslavia. Following the end of the one-week war between Slovenian forces and the Yugoslav People's Army in late June-early July 1991, Slovenia has been able to separate itself from the brutality and violence of the Yugoslav war.

In the eyes of the Slovene people, this political benefit justifies any short-run economic sacrifices. Nonetheless, a case can be made for the proposition that Slovenia will experience medium- and long-term economic benefits. These fall under three headings: enhanced macroeconomic stability through Slovene sovereignty and control over monetary and fiscal policy; enhanced capital accumulation through the dismantling of the old system of redistribution; and faster access to the European Union (EU) and its benefits.

Enhanced macroeconomic stability is the fruit of political sovereignty. The old Yugoslavia did not possess adequate federal mechanisms for managing the macroeconomy. The formal balance of the federal budget hid a significant but unmeasured deficit. The difficulties in achieving approval by all the federal units in parliament for compromises on federal allocations made fiscal policy response sluggish. Disagreements over taxation policy also made it difficult to achieve a coherent federal policy in this area.[16]

Similarly, federal monetary policy was hampered by the political setup and power balance in the National Bank of Yugoslavia. With its governors chosen by republican parliaments, the central bank lacked any substantial degree of independence. Controlled by a coalition favoring redistribution and easy money, it chose to put out the fires that started at the regional level. For Slovenia, which practiced greater fiscal discipline than other federal units, this meant an unexpected and unwanted inflationary impulse without corresponding benefits.

Slovenia's assumption of fiscal and monetary independence must be understood in this context. The introduction of the Slovenian tolar, in particular, has proved an invaluable instrument in protecting Slovenia from the hyperinflation of the dinar in late 1991 and 1992. In this sense, independent Slovenia might prove to be an optimal currency area, for it has turned out to be an area within which coherent monetary policy has been politically feasible.

The point here is that Yugoslav regions—in an ethnically heterogeneous society with large differences in economic development—functioned as distributional coalitions (Olson 1982) that prevented coherent fiscal and monetary policies. In fact, fiscal and monetary policy became vehicles of redistribution, and efficiency was relegated to subordinate status. Hence, the potential advantages of participation in a larger entity were not realized, and separation from the larger entity provided an improvement in this area.

Another aspect of macroeconomic stability could derive from Slovenia's new-found flexibility to create labor market institutions appropriate to its own circumstances. With a small economy and a fairly ethnically homogeneous work force, Slovenia is a candidate for all-encompassing corporatist bargaining between labor and management. Similar institutions have proved highly successful in small, open European economies like Sweden and Austria. They provide a way to keep the overall level of wage increases within the bounds necessary to ensure macroeconomic stability. Also, they facilitate the achievement of macroeconomic targets established for exchange rates, relative unit labor costs, and employment (Layard 1990). However, it should be stressed that Slovenia has not succeeded in creating well-functioning labor market institutions at the time of writing.

Enhanced capital accumulation is the second benefit expected from Slovenian separation. Interregional subsidization was ended immediately upon separation from Yugoslavia. But thanks to the economic collapse engendered by the war, Slovenia has been unable to end all subsidies. Reported losses in 1991 reached 31.4 billion tolars (8.7 percent of GDP; Pleskovič and Sachs 1994), with two-thirds of the losses concentrated among the largest 100 industrial enterprises. Wage subsidies have been employed to keep insolvent enterprises afloat.

The key question is whether Slovenia will be in a better position to end such cross-subsidization as an independent nation than it would have been within Yugoslavia. The passage of privatization legislation suggests that the answer may well be yes. Slovenia's political system still must find a way to carry out bankruptcy proceedings and rehabilitate the financial system. Nonetheless, Slovenia's progress so far compares favorably with what Yugoslavia achieved in 1990, when the Marković government's privatization and restructuring program became hopelessly mired in regional conflict.

If the process of restructuring the enterprise and financial sectors is successful, capital accumulation should improve.[17] The old pattern of subsidization effectively taxed more successful enterprises while subsidizing the less successful ones. Estimates by Vodopivec (1989) suggest that this policy had a negative effect on productivity. Similarly, Kraft (1992a) has found that soft budget finance allowed loss-making enterprises to maintain their level of investment despite continued losses.

Another factor contributing to faster capital accumulation and higher living standards will be Slovenia's ability to fashion its own tariff policies. The less-developed regions of Yugoslavia stoutly resisted lowering tariff barriers. Slovenia, with its greater competitiveness, should be able to lower tariff barriers much further than Yugoslavia as a whole. Indeed, as a small economy, Slovenia is forced to be open, and must have lower tariff barriers. This creates some dangers: whether it can thrive in a competitive international environment remains to be seen.[18]

A third benefit is *faster access to the European Union.* Yugoslavia's aspirations to enter the EC were frustrated by its inability to meet EC human rights and political democracy conditions. A major impetus for Slovene independence was the assessment that the Milošević leadership in Serbia was unwilling to resolve the Kosova situation in a way satisfactory to the EC (as well as the rest of the international community). Naturally, the wars in ex-Yugoslavia have only reinforced this assessment.

Slovenian independence appears to have unblocked the way to Europe. Close cooperation with EFTA and the EU have already begun, including the signing of an economic agreement building on the old EC-Yugoslavia agreement in April 1993. Also, Slovenia has fashioned a good relationship with the Višegrad group, and is negotiating free trade agreements with some of its members. While the continuation of the war renders Slovenia's situation somewhat uncertain, it appears that Slovenia is on a much faster track to Europe than any of the other ex-Yugoslav republics.

What will closer association with Europe mean for Slovenia? First, it will mean a stamp of approval for foreign investment in Slovenia. Second, it will mean guaranteed access to European markets. Third, membership in the EU would also allow Slovenes to work anywhere in Europe without special permission, and likewise would allow EU citizens to work in Slovenia. Fourth, should Slovenia accede to the EU, it would probably be eligible for funds from the EU's regional programs. These funds from the European Regional Development Fund (ERDF) and the European Social Fund (ESF) have proved a major enticement to membership for the poorer EU members (Ireland, Portugal, and Greece especially).

Of course, it is far from inevitable that Slovenia will become a full member of the EU. Such a development is hard to foresee within the current decade. But closer association seems highly realistic, with ties growing stronger rather rapidly.

Transition Prospects

The results of Slovene independence are clearer than the results of Slovenia's transition to a market economy. A few general comments seem in order, however.

Slovenia started its life as the richest postcommunist state, with a GDP per capita over $6,000. Perhaps even more important, Slovene managers had considerable experience operating in a market milieu, and many Slovene firms had success selling their goods on Western markets.

This experience gives Slovenia some advantages in its quest to create a market economy. The setbacks Slovenia has received from the wars in ex-Yugoslavia have certainly hurt. Nonetheless, Slovenia's prospects for becoming a "normal" European state by the year 2000 seem relatively good.

Key variables in the equation include attracting foreign investment and encouraging Slovene citizens and Slovene nationals living overseas to put their money in the country; handling privatization in a way that is perceived as fair, brings effective managers into responsible roles, and builds on the advantages of worker participation; creating an effective system of labor-management relations, perhaps by comprehensive bargaining; handling the inevitable bankruptcy and exit of large numbers of firms without excessive dislocation; building effective capital markets and nurturing healthy banks; and creating an adequate feeling of social well-being and security. Many of these are political issues; all are politically sensitive. Hence it is clear that Slovenia's success in transition relies heavily on political outcomes.

Slovenia's problems are in many ways typical of the problems of all the postcommunist states of eastern Europe. One can only hope that Slovenian politicians will have the required will, sensitivity, and dedication to the interest of their people and that Slovene citizens will continue to show the patience and perseverance needed to accomplish these difficult tasks.

ENDNOTES

1. For detail on strikes and the Slovene Spring, see chapter 8 of this volume.
2. Yugoslavia's republics and autonomous provinces are referred to as "regions" for convenience.
3. The Serbian leadership was not necessarily an opponent of market economics. Serbian leaders showed some attraction to a marriage of market economics and authoritarianism in the Korean or Chilean style.
4. See the discussion of this and an opposing view—attributing the failure to workers' control of enterprises—in Vodopivec (1992).
5. Social product differs from national product in that "non-productive" activities (in the Marxist sense) are excluded.
6. This puts Slovenia at a great advantage compared to the states of the former Soviet Union. Even the Czech and Slovak republics had to revamp the whole budget process, converting subsidies and direct appropriation of enterprise revenues into the state budget, just before their separation.
7. Indeed, the organizational structure of the central banking system of former Yugoslavia provided the basic institutional setup for the currency reform. In Yugoslavia the regional National Banks executed commonly agreed-upon monetary policy on the regions' territories. This institutional heritage gave Slovenia a big advantage over the ex-Soviet republics.
8. The first step toward introducing a new currency was the printing of coupons in summer 1990. This was seen as an emergency measure, taken in light of the increasing danger of a new hyperinflationary cycle following the failure of the second phase of the Marković program. It proved extremely important in facilitating a smooth currency exchange.
9. Kranjec (1992) and Bank of Slovenia (1992) give thorough discussions of monetary policy.
10. An excellent discussion of the motivation for the choice of a floating exchange rate is found in Mencinger (1993).
11. For a discussion of the politics of privatization and prospects for the future, see chapter 11 in this volume.
12. For a discussion of recent trends, legislation, and major issues concerning the labor market, see Vodopivec and Hribar-Milić (1992).
13. The following section is a slightly condensed and updated version of the argument in Cvikl, Kraft, and Vodopivec (1993).
14. Even before the civil war, Aleksander Bajt, perhaps Slovenia's most eminent economist, warned that the drive for independence could not be justified on economic grounds (Bajt 1991).
15. Independence was a political necessity. The purpose of the cost-benefit analysis in the text, therefore, is not to provide ex ante analysis of an open choice, but to underline the expected effects of Slovene independence.

16. An old but nonetheless relevant diagnosis of Yugoslavia's institutional inability to conduct fiscal policy is found in Horvat et al (1973).
17. As was noted above, this improvement is beginning to be seen. Right after independence, stabilization and the initial steps toward financial-sector restructuring led to extremely high interest rates and cautious lending practices, as banks tried to build their reserves and capital.
18. Boris Majcen (1992) argues that, since 1989, Yugoslav and Slovene legislation may have lowered tariffs too fast. He points out that the old system of quantitative restriction, export licenses and special measures was not replaced by an equivalent tariff, and provides evidence that Slovenia's effective rate of protection may be below the EU average.

BIBLIOGRAPHY

Arzenšek, Vladimir (1984). *Struktura i pokret* (Structure and movement). Belgrade: Institut Društvenih Nauka.
Bajt, Aleksander (1991). "Visoka cena samostalnosti" (The high price of independence). *Danas* (February 19).
Bank of Slovenia (1992). *Annual Report.* Ljubljana.
Bank of Slovenia (1993a and b). *Monthly Bulletin* (January and December).
Blinder, Alan (1990). *Paying for Productivity.* Washington, D.C.: Brookings.
Bogetić, Željko (1993). "The Role of Employee Ownership in Privatization of State Enterprises in Eastern and Central Europe." *Europe-Asia* 3.
Bole, Velimir (1992). "Slovensko gospodarstvo v splošnem 'neravnotezju'" (The Slovenian economy in general disequilibrium). *Gospodarska Gibanja* 230 (August) 23-36.
Cvikl, Milan (1990). "Denarna politika osemdesetih let v Jugoslaviji," (Yugoslav monetary policy in the 1980s). M.S. thesis, University of Ljubljana.
Cvikl, Milan, Evan Kraft, and Milan Vodopivec (1993). "Costs and Benefits of Independence: Slovenia." *Communist Economies and Economic Transformation* 5 (3): 295-315.
Gray, Cheryl, and Franjo Štiblar (1992). "The Evolving Legal Framework for Private Sector Activity in Slovenia." World Bank Policy Research Working Papers, WPS 893 (April).
Jenko, Miha (1993). *Tuje naložbe pri nas: Botri razprodaje premoženja smo lahko le sami, ne tujci* (Foreign investment in Slovenia: Only we, not foreigners, can be the godparents of sale) *Delo* June 13.
Horvat, Branko, Hasan Hadžiomerac, and Boris Gluščević (1973). "The Economic Functions of the Federation." *East European Economics* 2: 3-46.
Kraft, Evan (1989). "Capital Allocation, Industrial Structure and State Investment Policy in Yugoslavia, 1966-82." Ph.D. diss., New School for Social Research.
Kraft, Evan (1992a). "Soft-Budget Subsidies and Investment Finance in Yugoslavia: A Model with Estimates for 1986-7." Salisbury State University, Salisbury, MD, photocopy.
Kraft, Evan (1992b). "Regional Policy in Yugoslavia, 1966-90: Measurement of Flows and Evaluation of Effectiveness." *Comparative Economic Studies,* 4 (Winter).

Kraft, Evan (1993a). "The Growth of Small Enterprise and the Private Sector in Yugoslavia." In Perry L. Patterson, ed., *Capitalist Goals, Socialist Past: The Rise of the Private Sector in Command Economies.* Boulder, CO: Westview.

Kraft, Evan (1993b). "The History of the Soft Budget Constraint in Yugoslavia: A Note." Salisbury State University, Salisbury, MD, photocopy.

Kraft, Evan, and Milan Vodopivec (1992). "How Soft Is the Budget Constraint on Yugoslav Firms?" *Journal of Comparative Economics* 16 (September): 432-55.

Kranjec, Marko (1992). "Monetary Policy of the Bank of Slovenia Since Independence." In Marjan Senjur, ed., *Slovenia—A Small Country in the Global Economy,* 203-14. Ljubljana: Center for International Cooperation and Development.

Layard, R. (1990). "Wage Bargaining, Incomes Policy and Inflation: Possible Lessons for Eastern Europe." World Bank Seminar on Managing Inflation in Socialist Economies, March. Vienna, photocopy.

Majcen, Boris (1992). "Protection of the Slovene Economy and Slovenia's Approach to the European Community." In Marjan Senjur, ed., *Slovenia—A Small Country in the Global Economy,* 107-26. Ljubljana: Center for International Cooperation and Development.

Mencinger, Jože (1991). "Ekonomika privatizacije stanovanja" (The economics of housing privatization). *Gospodarska Gibanja* 222 (November).

Mencinger, Jože (1993). "Rojstvo in otrostvo tolarja" (Birth and childhood of the tolar). *Slovenska ekonomska revija* 44 (1-2): 24-47.

Ministry of Finance (1992). Republic of Slovenia, "Sponsorship Statement." Reprinted in *Euromoney (*September) 190-93.

Olson, Mancur (1982). *The Rise and Decline of Nations. Economic Growth, Stagflation, and Social Rigidities.* New Haven: Yale University Press.

Pleskovič, Boris, and Jeffrey Sachs (1994). "Political Independence and Economic Reform in Slovenia." In Olivier Blanchard, Kenneth Froot, and Jeffrey Sachs, eds., *Transition in Eastern Europe.* Chicago: University of Chicago Press.

Pleština, Dijana (1992). *Regional Development in Communist Yugoslavia.* Boulder, CO: Westview.

Savezni Zavod Za Statistiku (1991). *Statistički godišnjak Jugoslavije 1990.* (Statistical yearbook of Yugoslavia). Belgrade: Savezni Zavod Za Statistiku.

Stanovnik, Tine (1992). "The Sale of the Social Housing Stock in Slovenia: What Happened and Why." Inštitut za Ekonomska Raziskovanja (Ljubljana), photocopy.

Štiblar, Franjo (1992). "Privatization in Slovenia." In Marjan Senjur, ed., *Slovenia— A Small Country in the Global Economy* Ljubljana: Center for International Cooperation and Development, 181-190.

Vanek, Jaroslav (1970). *The General Theory of Labor-Managed Economies.* Ithaca, NY: Cornell University Press.

Vodopivec, Milan (1989) "Productivity Effects of Redistribution in Yugoslavia." Ph.D. diss., University of Maryland.

Vodopivec, Milan (1992). "State Paternalism and the Yugoslav Failure." In Arye Hillman and Branko Milanović, eds., *The Transition from Socialism in Eastern Europe: Domestic Restructuring and Foreign Trade,* 159-78. Washington, D. C.: World Bank.

Vodopivec, Milan, and Samo Hribar-Milič (1992). "The Slovenian Labor Market in Transition." World Bank, photocopy.

Vodopivec, Milan, and Uroš Korže (1993) "The Incidence and Effects of Spontaneous Privatization: Slovenia." World Bank, photocopy.

11

Quasi Privatization: From Class Struggle to a Scuffle of Small Particularisms

ANDREJ RUS

The political transition in eastern Europe was so unexpectedly peaceful and smooth that it inspired hopes of even smoother economic transition from central planning to a market economy. Everyone knew that the economies of the East were devastated and that it would take enormous amounts of money and effort to help them adjust to the standards of competitive capitalism. But optimism prevailed; with the overnight collapse of authoritarian regimes, everything seemed possible.

The new elites in the region eagerly embraced the ideas of international institutions and private consultants who charted the economic transition. The guiding idea was that economic recovery could only be successful if the role of the state were strictly limited. Paternalistic state economic intervention was the first target of reforms. Privatization of state or socially owned enterprise was ubiquitously offered as the remedy for state control, with promises that it would engender entrepreneurship and economic growth. Reformers also targeted the allegedly over-generous welfare state which, according to neo-liberal arguments, excessively taxed the economy and inhibited economic growth. Privatization of social services would limit the state's claim on national resources and improve the notoriously low efficiency of the welfare sector, resulting in substantial savings and productivity gains.[1]

When transition programs were first implemented, the tremendous magnitude of the social costs became clear. Massive unemployment, and plans to dramatically curtail social services in general and unemployment benefits in particular, led toward a very tense and explosive social situation. Adam Przeworski (1992) explained the situation with his concept of a *compatibility dilemma*. He argued that transformation of East European democracies will incur huge transition costs. The population, however, might be unwilling to absorb these costs and use newly-constructed democratic institutions to put painful reforms on hold. Such a response, however, might erode democracy itself and lead back to some sort of authoritarianism. Are economic transformation and democracy, therefore, compatible? Przeworski did his best to argue for the affirmative answer, but there were others, such as Arato (1990), who thought otherwise.[2]

The debate was important because it scaled down the high expectations about economic transition by showing that the reform process was inevitably enmeshed with social and political realities. Researchers showed that structural conditions like the maturity of state-society relations (Stark 1992; Bruszt 1992), combined with a particular balance of power (Stark 1990), preshaped the spectrum of socially acceptable policy options.[3] The main merit of this research was that it forcefully demonstrated the interdependence between economic reforms and social and political realities. Those who thought that economic transition could be an orderly, well-planned, externally monitored, centrally dictated, and perfectly implemented process were suddenly presented with a body of research which argued otherwise, depicting a process which is contingent, chaotic, and swaying between opposite extremes.

In this chapter, I would like to go a step further than previous research by arguing that seemingly chaotic patterns of change are to a large extent the result of a single structural feature, namely, the unstructured competition among new political parties. This leads to a paradoxical result in which reform efforts aimed at reducing the role of the state end up granting the political parties and the state an even larger role than they had before.

Political transition preceded economic reforms, creating a structural problem: new political actors, mainly parties, engaged in a fierce competition without any firm institutional base to structure this competition by providing basic rules of behavior. In the absence of such rules, the parties stretch the fronts of engagement over an increasing number of issues, making the political game increasingly complex and hard to master. In order to monitor each other better, the parties bring issues into parliament where the rules give every party an equal chance. The effect is the increase rather than decrease of the role of the state, resulting in a quasi privatization.

To make this argument I first analyze the sources of the uncertainty in which the reforms are taking place and then turn to the analysis of two case studies in which the thesis is fully examined in an empirical context. The chapter concludes with a discussion of the conditions under which the argument might be generalized across the countries undergoing economic transformation.

THE SOURCES OF UNCERTAINTY

The main structural condition generating uncertainty in eastern Europe is a particular sequence of events in which the political transition preceded economic transformation. Why? Social scientists have long argued that stable institutional arrangements usually emerge out of well-established practices in everyday life. Tilly (1988), for example, showed how nineteenth-century capitalism was preceded by innumerable local adaptations in the ways in which people organized their work. Social change, which we now consider revolutionary, was basically a culmination of the proto-industrialization of previous centuries. This gave industrialization a stable, permanent foundation. Both are lacking when political change precedes economic and social change. The new political arrangements are left with a formidable task—to create new economic, social, and cultural patterns exactly at the time when political arrangements need the maximum economic, social and cultural support.

The most important consequence arising from structural disembedding of political institutions from societal structures was the urgency and haste with which the changes were sought in all areas of social life. Pressed with the need to swiftly conclude the transition, the reformers emphasized speedy changes to stabilize their new regimes. Paradoxically, in their search for stability they emphasized speed and favored often uninformed imitation, rupturing the existing networks of exchange and support and creating instability. The four points discussed below are meant to summarize the major consequences of the reversed pattern of development: speed[4], rupture, imitation, and instability.

Speed

Political institutions cannot last long without immediate changes in the economy and supporting social system. The pressure to implement changes overnight is tremendous. This pressure is felt not only on the institutional level but also on the level of day-to-day life. The need for rapid transition of the society creates an hysterical situation in which the old ways of getting things done are delegitimated and labeled as remnants of "old thinking." Those who cannot emulate the yet-unwritten rules of the new age are considered the biggest obstacles to speedy transition. The pressure is exacerbated by both foreign and domestic observers who keep telling "horror stories" about the persistence of old thinking and mentality, antiquated values, old ways of going about daily business, old corrupt attitudes toward social justice, rights, and obligations, improper habits, and mass misunderstanding about the new era, all of which are in their eyes major obstacles to change.

Rupture

One of the most important consequences of the emphasis on speed in transition is the rupture of networks through which things were done under the previous regime. This result can be found on all levels of society. In the economy, supplier networks fell apart after the opening to world markets pushed numerous companies into bankruptcy, forcing survivors to scramble for replacement sources of inputs. In the political arena, a flurry of new parties crowded a newly established political scene. Political competition lacked a clear structure of responsibility, making it virtually impossible to either predict the political situation or to acquire important information or support for more or less trivial undertakings. And in the culture at large, because of the pressure to replace daily routines with new patterns of political, work, and consumer behavior, people perceive the changes as forced, destructive, and overwhelming. The reshuffling of networks creates uncertainty about how to solve routine problems, whom to ask for support, and what to expect from those who provided the goods and services before the change. It makes it hard to decide what is a legitimate way of doing things, and what might be the sanctions against breaking rules that hardly anyone knows. People suddenly lose the skills required to deal with the situation, and feel helpless and resentful. These feelings grow with the seriousness of the rupture of the social networks.

Imitation

A widespread solution to the problem of rapid change is imitation. This saves time, since the new patterns do not have to evolve but are instead transplanted from other contexts. But imitated forms may be difficult to integrate into existing social and political structures. Imitation has been most obvious in the institutional sphere. The East European parliaments passed laws that were almost literal translations of Western examples without much consideration of local conditions. As a result, laws once passed unanimously were later vigorously debated and revised on a monthly basis, exacerbating the already high level of uncertainty. Imitation is also strongly present in the economy, especially among managers. Too many try to impose restructuring on their firms by assuming the image of tough bosses, an approach that usually provokes resistance and paralyzes the firm. And in the culture at large, the transition to a nonegalitarian society creates moral uncertainty about how the newly differentiated groups should relate to one another. How can the nouveaux riches, for example, establish a claim to distinction? Their answer is usually blind imitation of pretentious lifestyles, and a silly adoption of extravagant consumer behavior. Slovene economists complain that private enterprise is having only marginal effect on economic prospects because most of the gains are not reinvested but are spent for conspicuous consumption. They tend to mistakenly attribute this behavior, however, to some sort of rational deficiency, rather than the moral uncertainty of actors.

Instability

As in Russia, political instability is not only expressed in violent clashes between reformists and conservatives, but more often takes the form of sudden shifts in political alliances, splitting of political parties, radical changes in crucial legislation, and abrupt changes in agendas pursued by national parliaments.

Political transition preceded social and economic change, creating profound systemic instability, uncertainty, and fluidity, which are often underestimated. In most countries of the region any reversal back to totalitarian rule is hard to imagine. But the fluid nature of the environment is deeply engraved in the path of social, economic, and political change. Uncertainty, for entrepreneurial actors, equals opportunity to exploit the lack of rules, precedents, tradition, and routines that might provide sanctions and limits to their dealings. In an unstructured opportunity space, social actors struggle for power and control, trying to limit and block actions of others while striving to cement temporary advantages into structured inequalities and permanent privileges (White 1992). As a result, outcomes are highly contingent and unpredictable.

Slovenia, together with the other eastern European societies today, has all the properties of such a fluid system, making an orderly transition from communism to capitalism look like another utopian idea. When external observers complain about the slow and puzzling path of development in eastern Europe, they usually cite government vacillation between moderate and radical alternatives, unpredictable outcomes of parliamentary sessions, and sudden shifts in national policies. They usually attribute the pace to the reformers' lack of commitment, or they simply blame it on the public. Their criticism is logical but misdirected, since it assumes the system is well ordered and well controlled. This assumption is obviously wrong. Eastern Europe is going through an unsettled period in which ground rules are lacking and the entire bag of cultural tools needs to be reinvented (Swidler 1986).

In such an environment alliances are short-lived, loyalties can turn suddenly in most unexpected directions, and affinities to ideals and ideologies become questions of time not principle.[5] National policies of privatization and liberalization of markets fully reflect the volatile social conditions in which they take place: they are always a contingent outcome of a history of political struggles for control, clashes of vested interests, competition among various lobbies, and incessant plotting.

The next two sections present two case studies of the political process of the reforms with contrasting outcomes. The first one looks at the political history of privatization legislation. The second looks at the reform of the welfare state. The analysis of these two cases will show that when there were high levels of uncertainty the parties quickly turned the reforms into a scuffle of small interests. The initial goals of the reforms were quickly displaced as the parties tried to use privatization as a means of expanding party control over the economy and the welfare state to improve or maintain their political significance in the future.

PRIVATIZATION OF THE ECONOMY

Slovenia was the only country in which a privatization program was installed by the communists before the turmoil and dismantled by their successors right after it. The first privatization legislation in Yugoslavia, of which Slovenia was an integral part, was introduced in the late 80s by the Communist leadership. It was a result of agonizing reforms during the whole decade, in which once sacred notions of social ownership gradually lost their aura. By 1989, privatization of economy was viewed as a natural solution to persistent problems of economic inefficiency and declining competitiveness.

The Communists' rationale for privatization was both economic and political. As the economic situation deteriorated it became clear that economic conflicts had to be uncoupled from growing political tensions. Failing enterprises pressed for government money, using the threat of social unrest that would grow out of the closing of the inefficient plants as a goad. While draining the treasury, these enterprises blamed governmental policies for their lack of success.

Privatization of the economy seemed a perfect way to both get rid of economic inefficiency and strengthen the rulers' shaky legitimacy. The enterprises would get owners who would take responsibility for the operation of their business and leave government to concentrate on other problems.

The Pretransition Roots of Privatization

The Company Act of 1989 and its subsequent amendments passed under the Communist government allowed the employees to buy out their companies at 30 percent discounts. The idea behind this law was an intention to make the transition from social to private ownership organic, smooth, and highly legitimate. The fact that for 30 years the system of self-management had empowered employees to take part in the management of their enterprises created an atmosphere in which the employees came to regard their companies as property to which they had acquired certain rights. In such a context the translation of acquired rights into property rights seemed like a natural, organic development.

The amendment of the Company Act in August 1990 triggered the first privatizations among Slovenian companies. The companies were given two options. The first one was to buy out the assets, the other was to invest private capital into their own firm. The assets were valued at book value. The discounts ran around 30 percent, varying with the years of employment of individual employees. The buyout option required employees to pay cash for the desired shares to the Agency of Privatization. The second alternative was to invest the money into their own company and then use the discounts to write off equal amounts of the socially owned capital. The latter option was obviously more attractive because a company could determine the investment level at which the discounts would essentially wipe out socially owned capital while keeping all the cash paid by the employees within the firm as investments.

Most of the Slovene companies that took advantage of this law chose the investment option. Of course, these were companies with strong cash flow and relatively low book value of assets—typically, service industry companies. There was, however, a problem that the lawmakers did not foresee: public reaction to this kind of privatization was extremely negative. It was based on the impression that a privileged few got a lot for nothing. Had the privatization cases been more balanced including companies that were less prominent and less well-to-do, the negative reaction would not have been provoked at all. But the law was not in place long enough to allow the less well-to-do firms to study their options. Responding to public pressure[6] the newly elected Parliament passed a constitutional law in October 1990 that, for all practical purposes, dismantled the privatization program only three months after its enactment. During that short period, only 17 companies managed to complete privatization while many more were caught by surprise in the midst of their plans. A contentious relationship arose between the economic actors and the new political elite, which affected the subsequent events.

The Politicization of Privatization

It was hoped that a new Slovenian version of privatization would be available in a matter of a few months. Indeed, a draft was ready by the spring 1991. It was built around a decentralized privatization strategy in which the government would determine the ground rules and leave it to the companies to self-administer privatization. The law offered a choice of four types of ownership restructuring in an attempt to account for the differences among companies in terms of size of assets and economic viability. Buyout of existing equity would appeal mostly to the small firms. Raising additional equity capital was particularly convenient for firms with either ample cash flow or a strategic foreign partner willing to enter a joint venture. Transfer of equity capital to the state was an option for firms heading into bankruptcy. And finally, debt-equity swaps would accommodate the cases in which creditors found interest in such a transaction. The draft law left it to the companies to devise their own mixture of the four models (Mencinger 1992).

In June 1991 when the vote was taken in the Parliament, it became clear that the economic rationale for privatization had been displaced by purely political considerations. The Parliament rejected the draft in a bizarre episode that announced increasing politicization of privatization. The draft, written by the deputy prime minister, a respected economist, was submitted to the Parliament as a proposal of the government. The draft generated only limited discussion, and was so favorably received that the deputy prime minister felt he could miss the parliamentary session and attend instead a meeting outside the country. In the Parliament, however, the prime minister unexpectedly attacked the draft legislation of his own government. He brought in Harvard professor Jeffrey Sachs, whose authority was instrumental in killing the proposed privatization law. Before anyone could do anything, the deputy prime minister was forced to resign and the whole affair ended up in a shakeup of the government and the breakup of the governing coalition. Eventually it led to the fall of the government itself, but not before it unsuccessfully submitted an entirely different version of privatization law.

The course of events and ensuing accusations made it clear that the opposition to the draft by the prime minister and his Christian Democratic Party was based on one single consideration, namely, political control of the economy. What troubled them most was the fact that most of the managers of socially owned enterprises were appointed under the rule of Communists—they were automatically suspect. The privatization law would have given the firms, their managers, and their employees full discretion in ownership restructuring. It would, from the Christian Democrats' perspective, only serve to perpetuate the power of the Communist economic elite. The proposed law interfered with their plans to place their own party cadre in the successful firms, to thus open channels of influence over the economy and to build up their own resource base. In their zeal, they openly argued that the change in political power should be paralleled by a change in economic power. They sought a mandate to purge the companies of all the "communist cadre."

The motives behind this affair were transparent. In the elections, the former communists proved that they would remain a significant political force and that the Left, in general, was far from discredited. To constrain their political competitors, the Christian Democrats wanted strategic positions in the economic elite in order to provide their party with a network of patronage that would assure them a steady source of cash in the present and political dominance in the future.

The incident had long-term consequences for the structure of the Slovenian polity and for the way the reforms were conducted. It marked a break with the public commitment of newly elected parties to keep politics and economy separate. As petty political interests and appetites multiplied it became obvious that the privatization legislation would be reduced to a struggle for control over the economy.

After ridding the government of dissenters, the prime minister launched a new privatization law. It was built around Jeffrey Sachs's ideas of a centralized, two-stage privatization strategy. In the first stage 80-90 percent of the shares of all socially owned enterprises would be transferred to the state development fund and the difference distributed among the employees free of charge. In the second phase the fund would distribute 60 percent of its shares among pension, compensation, and investment funds and sell the remaining 40 percent. A distinctive feature of the plan was that privatization of the economy would be achieved overnight. With one single act the state would become the majority stake holder in 2,277 companies that in 1991 employed 613,666 people (94 percent of the entire labor force), realized $35.7 billion in revenues (89 percent of national figure), and represented 93 percent of all assets valued at a book value of $39.4 billion (Služba Družbenega Knjigovodstva 1991).[7]

The crucial question was, of course, what would the government do between the first and the second phase of privatization when the assets would be under its control? One of the first priorities of the government was to assert its ownership rights and purge most of the "red directors." Moreover, the government's leading role in selling large amounts of equity would give it control over the formation of the new economic elite.

By the time the draft legislation reached Parliament the formula of anticommunism no longer worked. Bickering for their share of the pie, the other parties were uneasy with the idea of letting the Christian Democrats have it all. Most important, the managerial elite became an active constituency in the debate against the legislation, a constituency that was impossible to neglect. The draft was rejected again and the government failed to withstand the vote of confidence. The protracted period of legal void was extended again, until November 1992, when a compromise draft proposed by the interim government was finally passed.

The Crippling Compromise

Current privatization law bears all the characteristics of the compromise: it contains bits of everything proposed in earlier drafts. The decentralized strategy of self-executed privatization is combined with centralized management of state funds and free distribution of vouchers. The privatization law allocates 40 percent of the shares of each company to the pension, compensation, and development funds while leaving the remaining 60 percent to self-privatization by the companies. Companies are offered the same variety of privatization models as in the first draft. But the 50 percent employee discount on the face value of shares and the possibility of trading in the vouchers for the company's shares makes an internal buy-out strategy the most attractive option.

Nonetheless, privatization will take a long time to implement. The privatization law fell victim to its own history. Due to the contested nature of its creation, the law suffers from overregulation. The parties in the compromise tried to defend themselves against each others' potential abuse by taking all possible contingencies into account in a series of complementary laws and regulations. Before the privatization law can be implemented at all, 14 laws and 11 regulations have to be passed. In September 1993 there were still 6 laws and 3 regulations left to be passed by Parliament and the government respectively.

Some of these laws will inevitably create a lot of heat. A good example is the law on allocation of the proceeds from privatization. Political parties are scrambling to get the largest share of the proceeds for their own purposes. By law the list of potential beneficiaries includes areas as diverse as economy, technology, ecology, demography, preservation, and compensation for political injustices. The irony of this scuffle over the share of the proceeds is that their estimated annual value is only $85 million a year over the next four years (*Government Session 38* 1993). The tragedy behind this distributive enthusiasm lies in the fact that the proceeds coming from an already battered economy will be drained in petty projects instead of being reinvested in the economy.

The legal effort to bring the economy under the control of political parties will continue under the present law. At stake is the 40 percent of equity to be allocated to the state funds. Legislation regulating these funds is still in the making but the emerging contours are telling. All parties seem to agree that these funds should become private investment funds. But they also converge on the point that no limits should be placed on the maximum amount of shares of a single company one fund is permitted to hold. The consensus on these two issues is not surprising when the appetite of political parties for the economy is taken into account. On the one hand, private investment funds escape direct control of the state bureaucracy and allow the parties to become shadow partners controlling the funds. On the other hand, the lack of limits would allow these investment funds to fill their portfolios with shares of a handful of selected companies, and to strive for a controlling stake in them. Although the legislation is only being drafted, it is already possible to hear various scenarios about how this system could elegantly return control of the economy to the political parties, which would probably divide the economy among themselves based on the election results.

Much worse than delays and uncertainty about legislation is the negative atmosphere arising from the attempts of political parties to prosecute those managers who restructured their companies during the three years of legal void and replace them with their party favorites. The race for control of the economy continues without respite. The rightist parties initiated a campaign to audit all the firms that have restructured prior to the compromise law and to apply it retroactively. This triggered an avalanche of audits by the Služba Družbenega Knjigovodstva (Social Accounting Service); it has about one thousand companies under its review. Most of those companies underwent capital and organizational restructuring in order to adapt to the changes in their business environment. The irregularities that are found based on the retroactive application of the law have a dubious legal status. But they are instrumental in political plots meant to delegitimize the management in a particular firm and possibly force it to resign.

The result of this overregulation and political pressure is a general slowdown in privatization activity. From November 1992 to October 10, 1993 the agency of privatization received a total of 42 privatization programs, out of which only 14 have been approved, insignificant not only in numbers but also in their economic relevance: most of them were small service firms; three were beauty salons (*Delo* October 9 1993).

Concern over political intrusion in the economy is omnipresent. A recent survey showed that 78 percent of the companies are considering internal buyout as their privatization strategy. This strategy will give a majority stake to the employees and management at a price that many of the firms will, in the end, find prohibitive or disastrous. This figure therefore indicates that a vast majority of the firms are willing to trade their financial health for autonomy and independence from the political interference.

Privatization of the economy in Slovenia is a case which clearly illustrates how political competition emerges and escalates in an unstructured political space. At the beginning, the problem of privatization was still a problem of making the changes acceptable to the citizens. But the parties soon realized that privatization holds a potentially invaluable prize. The resulting political competition destroyed not only two draft laws but also the opportunity for a speedy transition. This was possible because of the lack of any external constraint on the political parties involved in the scuffle over who will get control over what. On the one hand the political transition delegitimated the state apparatus, whose weakened position did not allow it to confront the political parties. On the other hand, the public was still living under a false sense of security, believing that democracy is in itself a sufficient vaccine against political abuse of power.

If in this vacuum the channels of political influence on the economy multiply and at the same time drift from the domain of the state into the hands of political parties, the system can turn into an elaborate network of political patronage. Compared to a universalistic paternalism exercised by a modern state, the patronage system means a return to the past through a revival of clientalism and the hegemony of petty party interests.

One of the major reasons why Slovenia did not drift entirely into this option was the emergence of an independent managerial constituency opposed to political interference in the economy in general and in companies in particular. No matter what its ideological convictions, the managerial constituency brought the alternative criterion of managerial autonomy to the debate, forcing the parties to abandon primitive muscle flexing and to address the concerns of this constituency.

In the next section I turn to a different case, privatization of the welfare state, in which a constituency for autonomy was not mobilized, leading to a very different outcome.

THE REFORM OF THE WELFARE STATE

In spite of the overall consensus to limit the role of the allegedly paternalistic state, reforms of the social service sector developed in exactly the opposite direction. In fact, the reforms reinstated the dominant role of the state in this sector and created the conditions for the politicization of the welfare state. This section is about how and why this happened.

The Slovenian Welfare State in International Comparison

Before the transition the social service sector had two distinctive features. First, it provided free services for all, irrespective of their contribution. Among these services were free education, free health care, subsidized child care, and the like. Second, due to the attempts of previous elites to extend self-management to this sphere, its organizational structure was conceived as a decentralized system of management and provision of services. Self-management ideology intended to democratize the social service sector by transferring responsibility for the planning and provision of social services from the state to direct providers and users. Local communities and enterprises negotiated on behalf of their members with the providers of the social services for the amount, quality, and cost of the services. Locally negotiated quantities were then pooled on the national level (i.e., republic) and presented to the state (i.e., republic) as a budgetary demand. The state responded by revising the demands, setting the targets, and prescribing contribution rates for each of the dedicated social service funds (e.g., education, health care, pension fund etc.), which were paid by firms and employees directly to the funds. For their part, the services had to revise their programs to match the spending limits provided by the projected aggregate funding. This mechanism allowed the state to effectively withdraw from the day-to-day management of the whole sector, while retaining financial control over aggregate social service spending.

Decentralization went so far as to institute separate Self-Managing Communities of Interest (SCIs) for each social service. This policy produced competition among rather than within social services; it effectively limited costs, but at the expense of segmentation of social policy. A major weakness of this system was the rapid growth of bureaucracy in the network of SCIs. A powerful alliance between bureaucrats and providers effectively eliminated the influence of the users, resulting in the dominance of supply side interests over those of the demand side. A strong professional lobby for the maintenance of the quality of social services gradually emerged, putting lasting constraint on the government (Rus 1993a; Svetlik 1990).

In spite of its weaknesses, the system established a solid performance record. Comparative national statistics indicate that, contrary to its critics' allegations, Yugoslavia's social expenditures were not excessive. Costs were effectively contained by the state spending caps. Table 11.1 provides a comparison of the social expenditures of the former Yugoslavia and Slovenia with selected industrial countries. The selection of the first three is based on the typology suggested by Esping-Anderson (1990), who distinguishes between liberal, conservative, and social democratic models of the welfare state and takes the United States, Germany, and Sweden as typical examples of each of the respective types. The figures suggest that in 1980 the social expenditures in Yugoslavia and Slovenia were well below the average for the Organization for Economic Cooperation and Development (OECD), barely surpassing the level of those in the United States. During the 1980s, as the economic situation deteriorated, social expenditures even declined. The comparison with the four less-developed countries of the European Union is incomplete, but it nevertheless suggests that social expenditures in Slovenia and Yugoslavia were of the same order of magnitude as in these countries.[8] Contrary to reformers' allegations of an overly generous welfare state and lavish benefits that led to the curtailment of health care, pensions, and unemployment compensation benefits, the statistical record shows that social service spending did not run out of hand.

TABLE 11.1
Government Social Expenditures as a Proportion of GDP

	1960	1975	1980	1985
Slovenia	n.a.	18.7	19.0	16.9
Yugoslavia[a]	10.5	17.7[b]	19.7	17.5
OECD average[c]	12.3	21.9	23.3	24.6
Contrasting welfare state regimes:				
Sweden	15.6	27.4	33.2	32.0[d]
West Germany	17.1	27.8	26.6	25.8
United States	9.9	18.7	18.0	18.2
Europe's less-developed four:				
Greece	n.a.	10.0	12.6	19.5
Ireland	11.3	22.0	23.8	25.6
Portugal	n.a.	n.a.	17.3	n.a.
Spain	n.a.	n.a.	15.6	n.a.

[a] The data for 1960 and 1970 are taken from Pusić (1987), those for 1980 and 1985 are calculated from Statistički Godišnjak Jugoslavije.

[b] 1970

[c] The OECD average figures are the unweighted averages excluding Portugal and Spain for all years and Belgium and Greece for 1960.

[d] 1984

Sources: OECD (1988), Pusić (1987), Savezni Zavod za Statistiku (1990) and Zavod Republike Slovenije za Statistiko (1990).

Note: The data in this table refer only to public expenditures and do not include private expenditures. Differences among countries with respect to private expenditures can be significant. In Slovenia and Yugoslavia the public expenditures approximate total expenditures. In the United States, for example, private expenditures contribute a significant portion of GDP to the total.

These numbers do not address the issue of the quality of the services. But they do say that the system managed to provide a relatively generous package of social rights of the Swedish type at a cost comparable to that of the most restrictive welfare model, the United States.

The organizational structure of the Yugoslav social service sector was a matter of intense interest among Western observers in the late seventies because it addressed issues that were also emerging in their own countries: decentralization of the social service system as a whole, democratization in the sense of giving users of services a voice, and the relative autonomy of service-providing agencies. Decentralization, for example, is the key issue in the German health system. Universal coverage is mandated by law. Employers arrange for insurance through one of 1,200 *Krankenkassen,* nonprofit funds that protect patients' interests and negotiate with providers, following government guidelines. The result of this system is that Germany has the lowest average cost per day of hospital stay, the second lowest annual expenditure per capita (less than one-half of the United States's), and the highest average annual physician contacts per capita among itself, the United States, Canada, France, and Switzerland (*Business Week* 1992).

Decentralization and autonomization is also the goal of reforms in the Netherlands. During the Grand Efficiency Program, most governmental agencies have been transformed into QUANGOs (quasi-autonomous nongovernmental organizations), which had to renounce the security of state budgeting for a more market-oriented approach in which the agencies sell their services to the government and other users. Autonomization was one of the steps in the Next Steps Program in the United Kingdom, laying groundwork for privatization and the establishment of semi-independent executive agencies. The notion that reorganization along these lines might help to enhance the quality of public services and improve utilization of state resources is also found in a number of Scandinavian countries, notably in the Norwegian Renewal Program.

The Reform of the Social Service Sector

After the turnaround elections, the welfare system became a target of reforms. The justifications for its reform were largely ideological. Cost conscious critics who argued that a country in transition cannot afford the luxury of such an expensive welfare state were the most vocal. Others joined them with an argument that any system not subject to market mechanisms is immanently irrational in resource allocation and unresponsive to the needs of the users. There were also morally inspired critics who argued that the social safety net "spoils" people by extending a hand instead of letting them take care of themselves.

The spirit of the reforms was summarized in the parliamentary bulletin which stated that the social services needed to be curtailed in order to make the people aware of their own moral responsibilities for their well-being (Poročevalec 1991, 4-6). The analysis presented in the same document showed that moral education rather than cost reduction was indeed the leading motive of the reform. Health care costs were reported to have remained stable throughout the eighties at 6.7 percent of the GNP, with public expenditures for health care decreasing from 5 percent of GNP in 1980 to 4.7 percent in 1989. The growing difference between total and public expenditure was due to the increasing obligations of employers and private expenditures for services because of deductibles. The transformation of the national health care system into a health care insurance system was expected to save only 2 percent of costs at a proportional reduction of benefits.

What seemed to have initiated the reforms of the social service sector was a mixture of fuzzy ideologies and revolutionary fervor seeking to overturn every single aspect of the previous system. But after the reforms entered the political arena they became part of the political contest.

The Law on Institutions passed in March 1991, covering education, health care, social insurance, child care, science, culture, sport, and national television, reshaped the social services. Subsequent laws went in the direction of curtailed benefits, especially in the area of health care, pensions and unemployment insurance (UI). The law simply ignored the ideals of market competition and privatization and went the opposite direction. The Law on Institutions centralized the entire system under direct state control, bringing once quasi autonomous agencies under state authority. The state gained the right to appoint agency managers and to interfere with budgets. Social service sector employees became state employees, swelling state employees' ranks to 130,000 people, or 16 percent of the total labor force, and creating a new administrative problem. Social services were incorporated into the state budget, with the exception of health care and pension funds, which were to be replenished through direct payments of the employers and employees at fixed rates. The three funds (i.e., health care, pensions, and UI), however, were brought under much tighter state control.

While the state was taking over the public sector it was withdrawing from the private one. The law envisioned strict division between public and private agencies. No privatization or gradual mixing of private and public services was envisioned by the law. Private services were to be privately funded and managed. The only bridge between the two were concessions, the role and significance of which were detailed by subsequent laws for each separate social service area (Rus 1993b).

A Paradox of Transition

To understand why the reform of the social service sector turned to centralization and away from those legacies of the old system that coincided with trends in western Europe, we need to examine the political context. In a highly contested arena with the rules of the game still in the making, little things can trigger important consequences. The political community, keenly aware of this fact, had strong incentives to look for solutions that would make it hard if not impossible for anyone to exploit opportunities for expanding his/her domain of political influence. By bringing the social service sector under the direct control of the state, the parties actually addressed their own problems and not the problems of health care or any other social service.

In early 1991 the political identities of non-Communist parties were only emerging and their constituencies were only vaguely defined. Having been brought to power by a wave of anticommunist sentiment, the anticommunist coalition was keenly aware that they were sharing a pool of voters that would eventually undergo differentiation and identification with one or another of the parties. This made coalition members eager to monitor each other's moves so as to prevent any single competitor from gaining any political advantage that might later translate into a big electoral gain. The parties searched for monitoring mechanisms that would enable all the parties to learn through them and react on time (Sabel 1993). They did this by bringing the social service sector into the parliament where the rules of the game were highly institutionalized. The state, it was thought, would provide the procedural rules for allocation and flow of resources, formulation of policies, and distribution of appointments. Since all important decisions would have to be approved by the Parliament, all parties would be granted equal opportunity to register and respond to their competitors' initiatives.

Once the parties found themselves at the helm of the vast machinery of the welfare state they encountered a weak and disintegrated "coalition for bureaucratic autonomy" (Shefter 1977). This type of coalition usually consists of groups that defend the autonomy of bureaucracy from politicians either by virtue of their own position as bureaucrats or because they benefit from a universalistic system in which public benefits and burdens are distributed according to a set of general rules and procedures. In Slovenia, like everywhere else in the region, the bureaucracy lost power and prestige during the transition because it was considered a remnant of the old system. Constant calls for purges based on allegations of complicity in contrived "communist crimes" eroded its claim to legitimacy, rendering it powerless to stand up to politicians. Other potential candidates for this coalition, professional societies, and other actors in the civil society, were isolated, locked into their own factional battles and simply too weak compared to the mobilization potential of political parties. With the resources of the welfare state at their disposal, the parties suddenly found a convenient ground for the expansion of their power and pursuit of political goals that could not be realized within the political arena. The reform of the social service sector has created favorable conditions for the development of a system in which political patronage could develop into a major political *modus operandi*.

Political patronage in Slovenia is not just a logical possibility but an emerging fact. One of the most telling signs is the absence of any explicit social policy in Slovenia which would commit the parties to a specific set of consistently applied measures. For the system of patronage to work it is important to leave access to resources open and unconstrained. That means that parties should not be locked into an explicitly stated social policy or committed to autonomous public or private institutions which would distribute resources according to producer interests and customer demand. Such opportunistic social policy has been characteristic of all the parties in power, from the conservative government dominated by the Christian Democrats to the incumbent Liberal Democrats. And not surprisingly, there is little pressure in Parliament to come up with a general document on social issues.

Another telling tendency is the pressure of the government on the professional organizations and unions, the very social actors that have organizational capacities to effectively oppose the political parties' raid on their territories. The breakup of the medical association in the course of the abortion debate was among the most significant events in this respect. Another example is the recent failure of the teachers' union to realize their demands for full salaries. In blatant disregard of collective contract, the government has kept teachers' salaries low while raising those of the new political class. No less important was the successful infiltration of political parties into the student organization. Once a significant institution of civil society, it was effectively colonized by the parties and turned into another influence zone.

But the most explicit attempts to weaken the actors capable of resisting political intrusion are the repeated calls to purge the bureaucracy. This usually serves as a pretext for the redistribution of executive jobs in the service-providing agencies. The first draft of the law on institutions even provided for the wholesale dismissal of some two thousand agency directors, a proposal that was later withdrawn under pressure from the professional and academic community. But this could not prevent the parties from trying to push out the incumbents and replace them with their own candidates at every opportunity. As a result, the administrative integrity of the social service sector has been profoundly shaken, weakening its role in the process of implementation.

The Future of Reforms

It is hard to predict how far patronage will extend beyond the early attempts. Since not all parties are equally interested in and capable of engaging in client-patron networks, further developments will depend on future governing coalitions. In theory, whether or not a party is inclined toward patronage depends on how a party initially mobilizes its constituency (Shefter 1977). Those parties that initially broke into the national political arena through conflict are less prone to resort to patronage because they had to mobilize their followers through ideologies rather than through the distribution of divisible benefits. On the other hand, parties that enter the national political arena without conflict do not need revolutionary ideologies to mobilize a mass electorate and are more likely to use patronage.

Among the four parties that define the matrix of Slovenian political differentiation, the two that are least likely to resort to patronage are the Democrats of Slovenia and the United List of Social Democrats (the former communists). Both parties' identities were established during their long-standing conflict as the major antagonists prior to the transition. The Democrats, who were the center of the opposition movement against the Communists in Slovenia, were able to endure a long and risky standoff with the Party by rallying their constituency around a democratically inspired ideology of civil confrontation and reforms. Their opponents, the Communists, responded not with the repressive apparatus they controlled, but with the call to orderly transition. As they did once before in this century, they mobilized their support around an ideological vision of the future, only now they switched from revolutionary to social democratic rhetoric. As the conflict wore on, both sides became increasingly dependent on constituencies concerned more with ideals than with tangible benefits.

The situation was quite different for the Liberal Democrats and the Christian Democrats. They entered the political arena only after the stage was already set for multiparty politics. The Christian Democrats were formed late in the transition, when the political differentiation of the opposition was well under way. Most of the risks involved with early confrontation were eliminated, but their tardiness created a problem of identity. For election purposes, they allied themselves with more exposed parties. Only after establishing themselves as a coalition partner did they start to differentiate themselves from others.

The Liberals emerged from the Alliance of Socialist Youth, an institution which was an integral part of the previous regime, but managed to cast themselves as youthful reformers. They too, avoided all risks by renaming their organization into a party only after the emergence of a multiparty polity. In addition, they also had an existing organizational structure and politically integrated party elite that allowed them to avoid coalitions.

Because both parties could simply walk into the political arena, their major problem was not to mobilize for struggle but to mobilize for elections. In solving the problem of building an electoral base these parties were in a position to resort to patronage. The future therefore depends on the composition of the governing coalition. Currently the improbable coalition that joins the Liberals, Christian Democrats, and former communists is keeping the government divided and in check. But if the conservative parties succeed in forging an alliance among themselves the left bloc will be forced out. Under a conservative-liberal coalition we can expect the growth of patronage; the parties will encounter little resistance while having a strong incentive to boost the limited ranks of their dedicated supporters with new voters. If the coalition government remains dependent on the left bloc, not only will mutual controls stay in place but the need for patronage will fade out in the face of a growing significance of coordination, cooperation, and compromise.

CONCLUSIONS

The transformation in eastern Europe today is a result of the interaction between two different processes. On the one hand, there is a political process of ongoing competition among political parties in search of resources, constituencies, and power. On the other, there is a process of economic and social reforms which contain their own dynamics generated by massive redistribution of economic power, resources, and social rights. The two processes inevitably interact with one another, since all the reforms have to be enacted by political actors; but no reform can be implemented without active participation of actors in economy and society. The result is a complex system of action in which every change in one process disrupts the consolidation of the other. When we interpret the trajectories of change in eastern Europe we cannot afford to assume that they resulted from the will or preferences of any set of identifiable actors. Instead, we need to account for the contingent, unstable nature of the process, whose outcomes might be unintended, unexpected, and perhaps unwanted by any of the actors.

The argument and cases studied above help to explain why east European elites who profess their market orientation actually end up expanding the role of the state. When asked why, they always point to their opponents, charging, "They made us do it, it was the only way to tame their greed for power and reintroduce fair play." Slovenia just recently furnished a perfect example. On November 12, 1993, the Slovenian Parliament nationalized all casinos in the country with the simple explanation that they generate so much cash that they cannot be allowed to be privatized. It was the culmination of a long history of party struggles for control over the casino industry.

Wild competition among political parties and their search for an authoritative binding source of order creates a paradox of transition. The very elites that are trying to diminish the role of the state through privatization are finding, much to their surprise, that the state is the only source of order and authority that can effectively tame competition among themselves. Whether or not the state will expand its authority depends largely on the social context within which the competition takes place. The more organized the constituencies, the less successful the monopolization of power by the political parties. Political scientists have developed a systematic argument demonstrating that strong societies can counter attempts at reforms by weak states (Migdal 1988). And sociologists have shown the importance of preexisting organizational structures for the capacity of society to mobilize against the state (Tilly 1990). In the context of eastern Europe the reforms affect everyone, but they affect some constituencies in particular. To what extent the political parties will be able to bring various areas of reform under direct state control will largely depend on how organized are the constituencies most affected by reforms. In other words, the future of privatization will depend on organized resistance to political action of party politics.

To illustrate this argument we refer to the case studies above. In the case of privatization of the economy, parties encountered strong resistance from economic actors. Thirty years of self-management built a strong, relatively independent managerial class which had cultivated an alliance with the workers (Granick 1975). Firms became active participants in the process. While the parties fought over legislation, about 35 percent of all firms underwent major restructuring, thus prejudging the steps of privatization (Rus 1994). The attempt by the parties to revise all the restructuring was met with anger but also with ridicule, because it would take years for the government to reestablish the initial state of affairs.

The social service sector was a different case. The strongest constituencies there were the professionals and the supporting bureaucracy, who both lost power and legitimacy after political transition. The political parties met no serious resistance on their way to monopolizing this sphere. But it remains to be seen what the reforms can achieve with only the passive participation of service providers. Due to the domination of politics, the change will be much slower and more exposed to patronage. A few areas of activity that started to thrive on the legal fringes of the system have been either reintegrated into the state system or—in the case of private ventures in child care and care of the elderly—segregated from the public sector. In sum, due to the relative strength of economic actors and relative weakness of the actors in the social services, the processes of the reforms in each sector have gone in separate directions and carry different chances of success.

While the future remains highly unpredictable, it is possible to see the contours of coming conflicts. In Slovenia, they will erupt most violently in response to the curtailing of social rights in the social service sector, while the conflicts in the economic sphere will remain infrequent. The prediction is perhaps surprising. But it derives from the nature of the recent reforms. The decentralized nature of privatization of the economy will create a myriad of local solutions that will allow compromise and adaptation. In contrast, the state monopoly over the increasingly restrictive welfare state provides a readily available target for popular dissatisfaction, especially in times of economic hardships and growing dependence on the welfare state. How constructive this wave of discontent will be in practice will depend on the potential for self-organization of society. Only a strong society can use conflicts to keep the power of the parties in check and avoid the breakout of chaos.

When Vaclav Havel addressed the Slovenian parliament in 1993, he warned against political parties' establishing their hegemony over the state and society. His remarks could not be more to the point. As this chapter has tried to show, Slovenian parties have exploited the transition that demolished the state and weakened the society. In order to counter the incipient trend, we need a strong society and a strong state. Only the balance can keep particularisms of party interests in check and make sure the reforms will have at least a chance to succeed.

ENDNOTES

1. For a review of these arguments, see Rus (1990).
2. Arato was skeptical about compatibility between democracy and radical reforms. Probably thinking about the Latin American experience he argued that east European countries need some kind of enlightened dictatorship which would push through the needed reforms, thus establishing the basis for a democratic regime.
3. The east European countries differed widely with respect to the tolerance of their constituencies for change. In those countries like Czechoslovakia in which extrication was swift the reforms proceeded without much organized resistance due to the lack of organizational capacity of the civil society. Poland experienced much slower and less radical reforms because of the Solidarity movement which strengthened civil society in the eighties. After the fall of communism, Polish civil society had the capacity to resist the reformers.

4. The question of speed has been widely discussed among both scholars and practitioners. The most famous commentary was probably the insistence of Jeffrey Sachs on rapid privatization and shock therapy (Lipton and Sachs 1991). The compatibility debate broke with the illusion of planned and speedy transition and offered a vision of protracted messy transformation (Stark 1992; Bruszt 1992; Bartlett 1992).
5. In Slovenia, for example, the conservative Christian Democrats, who were at one time allied with the progressive Democrats against the former communists and the Liberal Democrats, found themselves only a year later allied with the left block and the Liberals against the Democrats. Wild shifts of this sort are an ordinary thing, making the political process of reforms highly unpredictable.
6. As elsewhere in eastern Europe, political parties were formed in Slovenia in the fall of 1989 and the first free elections were held in April 1990. Riding a wave of anticommunist feelings, the Demos alliance of parties ranging from the nationalist right to the liberal left was elected to power. The new political elite obviously felt that it had to prove its democratic provenance by accommodating the public sentiment. This concern was exacerbated by the conflicts within Yugoslavia which were getting to the point where a breakup became an increasingly viable option. Under these circumstances anything related to Yugoslavia—even privatization legislation—was perceived as increasingly illegitimate.
7. These figures represent all the companies in social and private ownership active in industry and commercial services. Excluded are social services and all other noneconomic organizations.
8. It is worth noting that social expenditures are not related to the economic strength of a country but rather to the institutional arrangements of a particular country.

BIBLIOGRAPHY

Arato, Andrew (1990). *Revolution, Civil Society and Democracy.* New School for Social Research, NY, photocopy.

Bartlett, David (1992). "The Political Economy of Privatization: Property Reform and Democratization in Hungary." *East European Politics and Societies* 6 (1).

Bruszt, Laslo (1992). "Transformative Politics: Social Costs and Social Peace in East Central Europe." *East European Politics and Society* 6 (1).

Business Week (1992) "Can Europe Help Cure America's Health Care Mess?" March 9.

Esping-Andersen, Gosta (1990). *The Three Worlds of Welfare Capitalism.* Cambridge, UK: Polity Press.

Government Session 38 (1993). Ljubljana, July 29. Ljubljana: Government Information Office.

Granick, David (1975). *Enterprise Guidance in Eastern Europe: A Comparison of Four Socialist Economies.* Princeton, NJ: Princeton University Press.

Lipton, David, and Jeffrey Sachs (1990) "Creating a Market Economy in Eastern Europe: The Case of Poland." *Brookings Papers on Economic Activity* 1.

Mencinger, Jože (1992). "Decentralized Versus Centralized Privatization: The Case of Slovenia." paper presented at the International Symposium on Privatization, February 6-9, Bled.

Migdal, Joel S. (1988). *Strong Societies and Weak States: State-Society Relations and State Capabilities in the Third World.* Princeton, NJ: Princeton University Press.

Ministry for Economic Relations and Development (1993). *Poročilo o izvajanju zakona o lastninskem preoblikovanju podjetij,* Government Session 38, Ljubljana, July 29.

Organization for Economic Cooperation and Development (OECD) (1988). *The Future of Social Protection.* Paris: OECD.

Poročevelec (1991). *Poročevelec Skupščine Republike Slovenije in Skupščine SFR Jugoslavije* (Gazette of the parliament of Slovenia and the Socialist Federal Republic of Yugoslavia) 17 (16). Ljubljana: Skupščina Republike Slovenije in Skupščina SFRJ.

Przeworski, Adam (1991). *Democracy and the Market: Political and Economic Reforms in Eastern Europe and Latin America.* Cambridge: Cambridge University Press.

Pusić, Eugen (1987). "The Development of Welfare State in Yugoslavia." In *Modern Welfare States: A Comparative View of Trends and Prospects.* Brighton, UK: Harvester Wheatsheaf Books Ltd.

Rus, Andrej (1994). "Managerial Networks and Strategies of Privatization in Eastern Europe: The Case of Slovenia." Paper presented at the Fourteenth International Sunbelt Social Networks Conference, New Orleans, February 17-20, 1994.

Rus, Veljko (1990). *Socialna Država in Družba Blaginje* (The Welfare State and Social Welfare). Ljubljana: Institute for Sociology.

Rus, Veljko (1993a). "Možnosti in meje privatizacije na področju družbenih dejavnosti." (Possibilities and limits of privatization of social services). In *Privatizacija na Slovenskem, 1990-1992 (Zbornik)* (Privatization in Slovenia, 1990-1992, [an anthology]) Ljubljana: Državna Založba Slovenije in Slovenski Inštitut za Management.

Rus, Veljko (1993b). "Privatizacija kot most med socialno državo in družbo blaginje." (Privatization as a bridge between the social state and welfare society) In Miha Kovač, ed., *Privatizacija na področju družbenih dejavnosti: možnosti in omejitve* (Privatization of social services: possibilities and limits). Ljubljana: Državna Založba Slovenije.

Sabel, Charles (1993). "Learning by Monitoring." Massachusetts Institute of Technology, photocopy.

Shefter, Martin (1977). "Party and Patronage: Germany, England, and Italy." *Politics and Society,* 7: 404-51.

Služba Družbenega Knjigovodstva (1991). *Informacija o poslovnem izidu podjetij s področja gospodarstva Republike Slovenije* (Information on the business transformation of economic enterprises in Slovenia) March. Ljubljana: Služba Družbenega Knjigovodstva.

Stark, David (1990). "Privatization in Hungary: From Plan to Market or From Plan to Clan?" *East European Politics and Societies* 3: 351-92.

Stark, David (1992). "Path Dependence and Privatization Strategies in East-Central Europe." *East European Politics and Societies* 6 (1).

Savezni Zavod za Statistiku (1990). *Statistički Godišnjak Jugoslavije* (Statistical Yearbook of Yugoslavia). Beograd: Savezni Zavod za Statistiku.

Svetlik, Ivan (1990). "From One-Dimensional to Multi-Dimensional Welfare System." In Bob Deacon and Julia Szalai, eds., *Social Policy in the New Eastern Europe*. Aldershot, UK: Avebury.

Swidler, Ann (1986). "Culture in Action: Symbols and Strategies." *American Sociological Review* 51: 273-86.

Tilly, Charles (1988). "Misreading, then Rereading, Nineteenth-Century Social Change." In Barry Wellman and S. D. Berkowitz, eds., *Social Structures: A Network Approach*. Cambridge: Cambridge University Press.

Tilly, Charles (1990). *Coercion, Capital, and European States, AD 990-1990*. Cambridge, MA: Blackwell.

White, Harrison C. (1992). *Identity and Control: A Structural Theory of Social Action*. Princeton, NJ: Princeton University Press.

Zavod Republike Slovenije za Statistiko (1990). *Statistični Letopis Republike Slovenije* (Statistical Yearbook of Slovenia). Ljubljana: Zavod Republike Slovenije za Statistiko.

▪Notes on Contributors▪

JILL BENDERLY is an independent scholar, writer, and organizer whose work focuses on social movements in the former Yugoslav republics. She received an A.B. from Princeton University and an M.A. in Women's Studies and East European Studies from George Washington University. She has been a participant/observer and documenter of feminist, peace, and civil society movements in ex-Yugoslavia for ten years, having lived in Ljubljana, Zagreb, and Belgrade. She has published in a wide variety of journals, newspapers, and anthologies.

MILAN CVIKL received his M.A. at the University of Ljubljana in 1990. His masters thesis concerned Yugoslav monetary policy in the 1980s. He was deputy director of the Research Department in the Bank of Slovenia until 1991, working on monetary independence issues. He is now an economist in the Central Europe Department of the World Bank.

ERVIN DOLENC studied history and philosophy at the Faculty of Arts of the University of Ljubljana and graduated in 1985. He received his Ph.D. from the same faculty in 1992. His dissertation concerned Slovene cultural policy in the Kingdom of Serbs, Croats, and Slovenes between 1918 and 1929. Since 1986, he has been a research associate for cultural history between the two world wars at the Inštitut za novejšo zgodovino (Institute for Contemporary History) in Ljubljana.

VLASTA JALUŠIČ received her M.A. (Women and Revolution) from the Department of Sociology, Faculty of Arts, University of Ljubljana. She is currently working on her doctoral thesis, "Violence and the Political in the Theory of Hannah Arendt" at Vienna University. Jalušič is a director of the Peace Institute in Ljubljana. She is author of *Dokler se ne vmešajo Ženske* . . . (Until the Women meddle . . .).

EVAN KRAFT is assistant professor of economics at Salisbury State University, Salisbury, Maryland. He received his Ph.D. from the New School for Social Research. His publications on ex-Yugoslavia deal with soft-budget redistribution, regional policy and problems, financial sector reform, and Slovene independence. He was the recipient of an International Research and Exchanges Board grant for Zagreb in 1990, and a Committee for the International Exchange of Scholars Fulbright scholarship for Ljubljana in 1993.

TONČI KUZMANIĆ is a political scientist and researcher at the Faculty of Social Sciences in Ljubljana. His research centers on conflicts and political thought, especially strikes, wars, and theories regarding political space and antipolitics. His recent publications include *The Strike in Labin, the Beginning of the End,* and "La disgregazione della Jugoslavia come disgregazione dello 'jugoslavismo,' (The disintegration of Yugoslavia as the disintegration of "Yugoslavism").

ŽARKO LAZAREVIČ received his Ph.D. in 1992 from the Faculty of Arts at the University of Ljubljana. His dissertation concerned peasant indebtedness in Slovenia. He is research associate for the economic history of Slovenia at the Inštitut za novejšo zgodovino (Institute for Contemporary History) in Ljubljana.

TOMAŽ MASTNAK is a senior fellow at the Institute of Philosophy in the Center for Scientific Research of the Slovene Academy of Sciences and Arts in Ljubljana. His book, *Vzhodno od raja: civilna družba pod komunimom in po njen* (East of Eden: Civil Society under and after Communism) appeared in 1992. He is currently working on the history of European ideas of peace and Western views of Islam.

CAROLE ROGEL, born in Cleveland, Ohio, is of Slovene descent. Her M.A. (1961) and Ph.D. (1966) are both from Columbia University, where she also earned a Certificate from the Institute on East Central Europe (1962). Until 1990 she taught European history, with an emphasis on east central and southeastern Europe, at Ohio State University. Since 1990 she has been an Emeritus associate professor. From 1984 to 1989 she was president of the Society for Slovene Studies. Her book, *The Slovenes and Yugoslavism, 1890–1914* was published in 1977.

DIMITRIJ RUPEL studied history and philosophy at the University of Ljubljana and received his doctorate in 1976 from Brandeis University. The author of numerous books and articles, he is professor of sociology at the University of Ljubljana. He was a founding member of the journal *Nova Revija* and in 1989 became the first president of the Slovene Democratic Alliance. He was minister of foreign affairs of the Republic of Slovenia from April 1990 to January 1993 and is currently a member of Parliament.

ANDREJ RUS is a Ph.D. candidate in sociology at Columbia University in New York. He is writing a thesis on managerial aspects of economic transformation in eastern Europe and Slovenia. He obtained his undergraduate degree at the Faculty of Sociology, Political Sciences and Journalism at the University of Ljubljana, Slovenia.

GREGOR TOMC is a researcher at the Institute of Sociology at the University of Ljubljana. He is also head of research at the Peace Institute. He has published two books of sociology, *From Poland to Pol Pot* (1984), a critique of socialism, and *The Other Slovenia,* on Slovenian youth subcultures. His third book, *The Profane—Culture in the Modern World,* is forthcoming. Gregor Tomc also publishes in professional journals at home and abroad. His main field of interest is the sociology of culture.

MILAN VODOPIVEC received his M.A. from the University of Ljubljana, and his Ph.D. in 1989 from the University of Maryland at College Park. Since 1989, he has been an economist at the World Bank, focusing on transitional economies. He is the author of papers on topics such as soft-budget redistribution, productivity, and earnings in Slovenia, and labor markets in Slovenia and other economies in transition.

PETER VODOPIVEC was born in Belgrade to Slovene parents. He completed his dissertation in Ljubljana in 1978 on "Middle Class Social and Economic Ideas in Inner Austria in the Pre-March Period." He did post-doctoral research in social history in France (Paris 1978–79), and later pursued research in France, Austria, and the United States. He is the author of numerous articles and publications on Slovene, Austrian, French, and central European history of the eighteenth and nineteenth centuries. He is a professor of Modern European and American History, Department of History, Ljubljana University.

▪Index▪

A

abortion 105, 135–7, 149
agriculture 10, 50–1, 31, 55–7, 62–4
Alexander, King 17
Arzenšek, Vladimir 176n
Austria-Hungary
    see Habsburg Empire
Austro-Marxism 13, 43, 78

B

Baker, James 108, 190
Bank of Slovenia (BoS) 208–9
banking and finance 49–50, 53–4, 57, 190, 208–9, 213–4
Baučer, Martin 70
Bavčar, Igor 124–5, 129, 131, 200n
Bavdek, Boris 129
Bismarck, Otto von 10
Bleiweis, Janez 7, 73
Bohorič, Adam 5
Borstner, Ivan 187
Bosnia-Hercegovina 28, 106–8, 195–6
Brioni agreement 192–3, 208
Broken Jug, The 23
Bučar, France 193

C

Cankar, Ivan 14, 24–5, 29
Cankar, Izidor 81
Catholic church 69, 73–4, 79, 82, 96, 162
    see also clericals
Christian Democratic Party 104, 155n, 232–3, 242–3
Christian Socialists 84
čitalnice 73, 75
civil society 95–6, 100, 160–2
clericals, Slovene 11–12, 30, 31, 33, 50, 75, 76, 79–80, 83
Committee for the Defense of Human Rights (CDHR) 102–3, 106, 149, 187
Communist
    League of Communists of Slovenia 100, 103, 118, 148, 163, 186
    League of Communists of Yugoslavia 37, 85, 105, 183–4
    Party of Slovenia 18, 81, 84, 115
    United List of Social Democrats 243
confederalism 32, 39, 184, 189
Conference on Security and Co-operation in Europe (CSCE) 191–2, 194, 198

Index

259

Mohar, Lidija 176n
monetary policy 204, 208–9, 217–8

N

Nagode trial 44n, 84
National-Progressive Party (NPP)
    see liberals, Slovene
nationalism 3–4, 6–7, 41–2, 43, 106–7, 148, 159–60, 166–7, 175n, 196
Neue Slowenische Kunst (NSK) 101, 126–7
Nova Revija 41–2, 88, 106, 185–7, 200n
Novice 71, 73

O

Ottoman Empire 4

P

Palacky, František 3
parties, political 189
    competition between 226, 236, 241–4
    see also clericals, liberals, Liberal Democratic Party, Christian Democratic Party,
    Yugoslav Social Democratic Party, Social Democratic Party
Papič, Žarana 143
Pašić, Najdan 164
peace movement 99, 146–7
Perko, Andrej 124
Peter, King 18
Peterle, Lojze 193, 200n, 211, 232
Pirjevec, Dusan 37–8, 86
Pitamic, Leonid 30
Plohl, Rastko 165
Pohlin, Marko 6
Poos, Jacques 192
Popit, France 120, 133
Praxis 164
Preporodovci 14
Prepuluh, Albin 30
Prešeren, Francè 7, 72
privatization
    accomplishments 211–2, 235
    foreign investment and 212
    housing 211–2
    legislation 210–1, 234–5
    politics of 232–6, 245–6
    pre-independence 230–1
Prussia 8–9
publications